sley Clarkson is recognized as one of Britain's most wledgeable writers when it comes to the underworld. first covered the Brink's-Mat robbery as a newspaper rter more than twenty-five years ago and has watched entacles spread out across the underworld ever since. rkson has written numerous true-crime books, including biographies of Brink's-Mat defendant Kenneth Noye, Great Train Robber Charlie Wilson and legendary south don criminal Jimmy Moody. *Kenny Noye: Public Enemy mber 1* was one of the ten bestselling true crime titles the 1990s.

'It's a curse because everyone connected to Brink's-Mat stands to get topped sooner or later.'

> – Legendary south London villain Georgie Francis, shortly before he was shot dead by a hit man.

'People are pointing the finger at one particular character who is virtually a one-man killing machine.'

> – One Brink's-Mat associate, following the latest murder of one of the criminals involved in the heist.

'Like so many of them, Brian knew he had it coming. He crossed the wrong people.'

> – Gangster Gordon McShane, describing the hit-man killing of Brink's-Mat robber Brian Perry.

'He offered me a one-million-pound bribe that I happily turned down.'

> – Scotland Yard detective Brian Boyce, describing Brink's-Mat mastermind Kenneth Noye.

THE CURSE
OF
BRINK'S-MAT

TWENTY-FIVE YEARS OF MURDER AND MAYHEM

THE INSIDE STORY OF THE TWENTIETH CENTURY'S MOST LUCRATIVE ARMED ROBBERY

WENSLEY CLARKSON

Quercus

First published in Great Britain in 2012 by
Quercus
55 Baker Street
Seventh Floor, South Block
London
W1U 8EW

A CIP catalogue record for this book is available
from the British Library

ISBN 978 1 84916 305 7

10 9 8 7 6 5 4

Text designed and typeset by Ellipsis Digital Ltd

Printed and bound in Great Britain by Clays Ltd, St Ives plc

'One by one those involved are being picked off like targets in a funfair shooting gallery. It's bloody terrifying that this sort of thing still goes on in a so-called civilized society.'
– Retired senior Brink's-Mat investigator

What's a jemmy compared with a share certificate?
What's breaking into a bank compared with founding one?
    – Bertolt Brecht, *The Threepenny Opera*

This book is dedicated to ALL the victims of the Curse of Brink's-Mat

CONTENTS

AUTHOR'S NOTE:
THE ROOT OF ALL EVIL

GOLD: Precious yellow non-rusting malleable ductile metallic element of high specific gravity, used as a fundamental monetary medium.

The *Concise Oxford English Dictionary* doesn't quite capture the magic of the word, nor its ability to fascinate and corrupt. For 6,000 years it has been hewn from veins of quartz and pyrites, and panned from the rivers and streams. Today those nations lucky enough to count it as a major resource – South Africa, Russia, Canada, the United States, Brazil and Australia – mine the precious commodity with relentless efficiency. Even in countries where the amounts to be found can't support a highly developed industry, gold fever is just as strong.

Only in the last of the sixty centuries that it has been sought by man have gold's chemical properties been put to uses other than coinage and jewellery. These days it is an essential ingredient in dentistry and the hi-tech industries, providing high electrical conductivity in printed circuits and improving the tonal image of photographic film.

But such is its rarity that even now ninety per cent of all the gold ever produced – estimated to amount to some 2,000 million ounces – can still be confidently accounted for. Forty-five per cent lies in central banks such as the Bank of England and the Bundesbank in Germany, where it is kept as a guarantee of economic stability for the governments in question. The Bank of England (otherwise known as the Old Lady of Threadneedle Street) never lets her reserves drop below 500,000 kilograms. Another twenty-five per cent of the world's gold is in private hands – either those of powerful international conglomerates or hugely wealthy individuals – while the remaining twenty per cent has been used in jewellery, religious artefacts and dentistry.

Even the ten per cent that is missing has not vanished without trace. Much of it is stuck in a time warp, entombed on the ocean's floor in sunken galleons and more modern ships, victims of either the elements or marine warfare, where it waits to be rediscovered.

But the Brink's-Mat robbery changed all that. Nobody in the history of British crime has ever got hold of so much of this precious, incredibly rare metal at once. In one fell swoop £28 million worth of bullion was 'liberated' from a warehouse outside Heathrow airport. Nobody, least of all the robbers themselves, expected to get their hands on this amount of loot. Nor could they have predicted the job's extraordinary consequences.

However I word this note I'm going to upset somebody. One of my main sources for this book put it bluntly: 'There are people who will be fuckin' angry that I've talked to you. They are evil characters and I don't want to upset *any* of them.'

There are few readily available written records covering much of the activities of the Brink's-Mat participants, so I have had to trust the judgment and recollections of numerous people, many of whom would rather not have their names reproduced in this book. It has been dependent on the memories of individuals – fallible, contradictory, touched by pride and capable of omission – but I believe them because these are upfront men, and there are no hidden agendas in this story.

I make no apologies for the strong language, either.

So to all the 'faces' I've met down the years and the 'cozzers' who've given me a helping hand, I say, 'Thank you.'

Without their help, this book would not have been possible.

Much of the book is based on a long series of interviews, conversations and recollections supplied, at times unwittingly, by dozens of individuals over the past fifteen years. I've spent many hours in formal and informal conversations with them. Of course some vital names are missing, and that will frustrate those who were involved in the eras mentioned here. But ultimately I've tried to recreate a story that twists and turns from the mean streets of south London to even harsher prison corridors to Spain's so-called Costa del Crime and across the globe. It's been a fascinating journey which I hope you are going to enjoy and relish as much as I have.

Some of the dialogue presented in this book was constructed from documents, some was drawn from courtroom testimony and some was reconstituted from the recollections of participants.

Wensley Clarkson, 2012

CAST OF CHARACTERS

The Bad Guys

BIG AL – Grassing up a face is never a good idea.

BIG JOHN – Underworld legend who couldn't resist a piece of the action.

BIG PAT – Pumped-up, steroid-addicted psycho who took on the Big Boys and lost.

BRIAN – Being greedy and turning your mates over is never a good idea.

THE BRIEF – Lawman with a crooked angle.

CLIFFY BOY – Found out too late that crime definitely doesn't pay.

THE COLONEL – Ex-squaddie with a real eye for detail who had the inside track on the 'Crime of the Century'.

THE FOX – Mysterious financier who stepped back into the shadows at just the right moment.

GARTH – Back-up man without a plan.

GENTLEMAN GEORGE – A real pro who pushed his luck just a little too far.

GOLDEN MOLE – Inside man who lost his bottle and now has to watch his back.

HIT MAN SCOTT – Chilling *Goodfellas* ice man from across The Pond.

JOEY BOY – Master con man, adept at talking his way into anyone's fortune.

KING OF CATFORD – Suspected 'masterblagger' who got too flash for his own good.

LITTLE LEGS – Old-school East End robber armed with muscle and grit.

MAD MICKEY (aka THE GENERAL) – The brains – with a short fuse and a mission to destroy anyone who got in his way.

MATTY THE GREEK – Old-time fence who thought he knew it all.

THE MILKMAN – Kilburn Irishman who always delivered on time.

KENNETH NOYE – So-called middleman who killed his way to notoriety.

PADDY – 'Active' in every sense of the word, but somehow escaped justice.

THE PENGUIN – Irish mobster with all the right connections.

THE PIMPERNEL – The most artful dodger of them all.

PORKY – Escaped convict with blood on his hands.

SANE MICKEY – Tried to keep everyone happy but ended up with more trouble than he could handle.

SCARFACE – Psycho shooter with a death wish.

SID THE WINK – Double-dealing ex-cop turned merchant of death.

STEVIE THE BUTCHER – 'Carve-up man' who helped hide the bodies.

TERRY THE CHIEF – Head of a modern-day family of criminals who are the most notorious London has ever seen.

The Good Guys

BRIAN BOYCE – Stickler for discipline and completely 'unbendable'.

TONY BRIGHTWELL – Fair-minded but eagle-eyed detective who had a face-off with some of the gang.

STEPHEN CAMERON – Had the dreadful misfortune to encounter a cop killer on the road.

JOHN CHILDS – Undercover man who was first on the scene of the crime that rocked the boys in blue.

PHIL CORBETT – Tenacious officer with a down-to-earth attitude.

TONY CURTIS – The last cop standing.

JOHN FORDHAM – Hard-nosed police surveillance man whose devotion to the cause ended in tragedy.

ALAN 'TAFFY' HOLMES – Sensitive detective constable who allowed the pressure to get to him.

TONY LUNDY – Gritty northerner who *never* took no for an answer.

BOB MCCUNN – Relentless insurance investigator who refused to bow to the hard men of crime.

HENRY MILNER – Hard-working brief who made his name representing some of Britain's most notorious villains.

DANIEL MORGAN – Delved too deeply into the Brink's-Mat aftermath and paid for it with his life.

NEIL MURPHY – Fordham's softly spoken partner who witnessed horror first hand.

ROY RAMM – Astute, old-school copper who relentlessly pursued his prey.

PROLOGUE

BBC TV NEWS BULLETIN, SATURDAY 26 NOVEMBER 1983

'An armed gang has carried out Britain's largest-ever robbery at London's Heathrow airport.

Over £25m worth of gold bullion bound for the Far East was stolen from the Brink's-Mat warehouse, about one mile (1.6km) outside the airport perimeter, between 0630 and 0815 GMT.

Police have said a group of at least six men overcame the guards and successfully disabled a huge array of electronic security devices.

Insurers have offered a reward of £2m for information leading to the recovery of the 6,800 gold bars – which are all identifiable by refiners' stamps.

The members of the gang – who were all armed and wearing balaclavas – also stole £100,000 worth of cut and uncut diamonds.

They dressed in security uniforms to get into the warehouse and then terrorized the guards into giving them the alarm codes.

All the guards were handcuffed, one was hit on the head with a pistol and two had petrol poured over them.

Once inside the safes, the robbers used the warehouse's own forklift trucks to transport the 76 boxes of gold into a waiting van.

The alarm was raised by one of the guards at 0830 GMT after the gang had left.

Scotland Yard Flying Squad chief Commander Frank Cater is leading the hunt for the thieves.

He said: "There is no doubt they had inside information and were a highly professional team."'

The Brink's-Mat gang had expected rich pickings but they'd never imagined the extraordinary level of wealth they stumbled upon that day. Their audacious plot, ruthless in its conception and brilliant in its execution, had just landed them the biggest haul in British criminal history. The Brink's-Mat robbery would go on to make the names and fortunes of many of today's most notorious gangsters. It's become the stuff of legends, and its bloody tentacles provoked a vicious gang war in the underworld that is still raging to this day.

Like the British archaeologists said to have been cursed after they unearthed Tutankhamun's tomb in 1922, the lives of those who were involved in Brink's-Mat would be blighted forever.

But where did it all begin? Why were those robbers drawn to such a high-risk crime? To try and find the answers one must first delve right back into the history of the south London underworld.

PART ONE:
IT'S IN THE BLOOD

'Train up a child in the way he should go,
And when he is old, he will Not depart from it.'

Proverbs 22:6

ONE

Across the Thames from the City of London lies the borough that for centuries was effectively the second-largest city in England: the Borough of the South Works of London Bridge, or Southwark. Borough High Street runs directly from London Bridge.

In 1197 two 'tycoons' swapped a pair of manors from their real estate portfolios. The Archbishop of Canterbury accepted Lambeth, on the Thames bank about a mile west of the Borough, in exchange for Dartford, in Kent. He decided to use it as his town house instead of adding it to his investments, and Southwark innkeeping profited by the increase in travel between Canterbury and London.

Along the bank of the river between east Lambeth and Southwark, the bishops of Rochester and Winchester bought properties which their successors leased out. In Henry VIII's reign, Rochester's cook, Richard Ross, poisoned the soup at a banquet, and became the sole victim of Henry's new penalty for poisoners. He was boiled alive.

Winchester's property soon became notorious for its brothels. The carnival atmosphere of the Bankside was further enhanced by a bear-baiting ring, theatres, and the first of the south bank pleasure gardens. All these attractions encouraged the criminals of the day to head into the crowds to pickpocket and scavenge off the rich visitors. Then they headed back to their homes in the dreadful slum areas around Mint Street ('the Mint') and south of Union Street ('Alsatia').

To the east, numerous leatherworks centred on the district of Bermondsey. But the drawback to the tanning industry was the obnoxious odour that drifted across the entire area. As a result, Bermondsey developed atrocious slums, and by the 1840s Jacob's Island was the worst area of urban deprivation in London. It was from these south-bank slums that the great nineteenth-century cholera epidemics sprang.

With the arrival of the railways, Waterloo station dominated east Lambeth to such a degree that it dragged the residential neighbourhood down even further. The riverside became a dismal region of filthy, rundown warehouses. Squalid Bermondsey became the epicentre of violence and ill-health amongst the poor and deprived, mainly due to dreadful overcrowding.

The nineteenth century's most appalling infanticide took place in the Old King's Head Tavern in Greenbank, Tooley Street, close to where London Bridge station stands today. In 1843, brush salesman Edward Dwyer – whose propensity for violence had already resulted in one heavy jail sentence – was putting in a hard day's drinking at the tavern. By nine in the evening, his wife and mother-in-law had come in and started abusing him in front of his friends for being drunk. They slapped him and left him to look after his three-month-old baby. He left the child on the street outside until his drinking friends persuaded him to fetch it in. Increasingly inebriated, Dwyer began making bizarre drunken remarks to his pals.

'Blood on a brick,' he said 'would look very funny. Blood on the wall would look very queer. If a bullock's head was beat against the wall there would be plenty of blood on it.'

Then before anybody could stop him, Dwyer picked up the baby by its thigh and smashed its head on the bar counter over and over again.

Bermondsey never shook off the stench of real poverty until more than a hundred years later when the combined efforts of Hitler's bombing raids and the economic realities of life in postwar Britain effectively flattened much of the Thameside slums. After the war, the descendants of many of those disease-ridden ghetto victims finally turned their backs on the cobbled streets and were encouraged to start afresh in the suburbs that were gradually sprouting up in the cleaner air and wider fields on the edge of southeast London.

And that is where the Curse of Brink's-Mat begins . . .

Without smog, the concrete jungles of housing developments or shocking extremes of wealth and poverty, these suburbs were supposed to represent the acceptable new face of Middle England, with many appealing features but few of the old inner city's bad habits.

People were desperate to move to these previously nondescript locations between central London and the so-called 'Garden of England' in Kent. And by the time many of the Brink's-Mat gang were born just after the end of the Second World War, these places were starting to assume a comfortable reputation all of their own.

None of the suburbs like Bromley, Bexleyheath and numerous other places that developed around this time were particularly picturesque, but compared with the harsh, dilapidated streets of Bermondsey, Walworth, Rotherhithe and Waterloo they were sheer luxury. In any case, these new suburbs also retained some traditional reminders of London life – a fine range of pubs, chippies and pie and eel shops, and enough memories of the capital and its history to make sure they still felt like home.

Basking in relatively clear air away from the smoky industrial docklands close to the river, the image of these suburbs and their neat gardens as aspiring lower middle class and conservative was very true to a large extent. However many of the new residents found it strange to have swapped those rundown rows of riverside terraced houses in which they'd grown up for the characterless square bungalows that were the essential feature of the south-east London suburbs.

Some of those residents' children would grow up to become the most feared and notorious characters in British criminal history. Yet many had what appeared on the surface to be enviable childhoods in those very same suburbs, even though many of their families still lived on the edge of the underworld, thanks to their connections back in 'the Smoke', as London was known to all and sundry back then.

Most fathers worked hard at 'straight' jobs in the hope they'd provide a more secure livelihood than all the ducking and diving which had become such an integral part of life until and including the years of the Second World War. Despite the vein of dishonesty that seemed to run through so many of these characters, many of them retained a true love for King and Country. They were fierce patriots, yet essentially still imbued with the ethos of thievery, which had been instilled in them by the communities in which they'd grown up. Being totally honest wasn't much of an option when you were growing up in a slum in Bermondsey or some rundown Thameside tenement. It was all about surviving, and many of them took this attitude with them to the suburbs.

As one old south-east London resident put it: 'You can take the boy out of Bermondsey but you can never take Bermondsey out of the boy.'

Villainy was ingrained in many of these families. When their fathers worked in the docks stealing was accepted – virtually encouraged – because it helped impoverished people boost their income to support their families. It was the same in the newspaper print industry, which was booming after the war as circulations sky-rocketed and newspaper owners would do virtually anything to guarantee their publications got out on the streets on time every day. Printers enjoyed a whole raft of 'extras' such as the 'Mickey Mouse syndrome' where at least once a week they'd pick up an extra day's shift money by submitting a fake claim for a day's wages in the name of Mickey Mouse. It was all accepted practice back then, and these same dodgy habits were handed down to their children.

Corner sweetshops were fair game to kids. Many would loiter outside them after school most afternoons. Frequently they'd steal empty bottles of Tizer by slipping through the side gates where all the empties were stored. Then they'd walk brazenly into the front of the shop and claim the penny per bottle they could expect for returning them, and buy sweets with it.

These 'cheeky Charlies' grew up fully alert to everything that was going on around them. They were perceptive and streetwise from a young age. And those remarkably sharp powers of observation would be put to good use in later years.

But in the middle of all this, most families were immensely proud of the way they worked hard and survived, regarding it as a badge of honour. There was rarely any question of scrounging off the state; how you supported your brood was up to you.

Naturally, school was looked on as a chore, and most kids couldn't wait to leave and head off into the real world to try their luck at whatever took their fancy.

Interestingly, many of the boys who grew up to become notorious professional criminals say they were victims of bullies at school, something that, more than anything else, turned them into hard-nosed loners prepared to take enormous risks. It seems that they learned to defend themselves from an early age, and the bigger, older boys at their schools soon left them alone. As with so many things in their lives, these characters would one day exploit those experiences to their own advantage.

Another element to this was that the experience of being bullied at such an early age made many of these youngsters determined to get their own back on society. It was as if they were saying to their peers: 'You didn't look after me when it mattered so I'm going to do what the fuck I want.'

Of course at school that meant regular beatings. In the years after the Second World War, teachers were allowed to hand out corporal punishment with impunity. But all that did was harden the resolve of these youngsters and convince them that they were right to ignore all the usual rules when it came to morals and honesty. In their minds, there was no such thing as being poor and happy. At home, things were little different. They continued to be regularly disciplined by their fathers or whoever happened to be living with their mothers at that time, but this had little effect on curbing their energetic behaviour since it was never accompanied by an explanation of what they'd actually done wrong.

'You just got a good slap and then got on with things. No one talked it through. It was just part of growing up,' one old south London villain explained.

There is no doubt that the violent atmosphere in which so many of these would-be young criminals grew up simply encouraged their aggressive personalities to emerge. Many of them found it difficult to establish a relationship between themselves and the world outside the care they received from their mothers and siblings.

These children who were growing up with an unhealthy urge to steal their way to fame and fortune remained especially close to their mothers. With fathers who worked long hours and spent most evenings at the local pub or at the dogs, not to mention the lengthy periods many had been away during the war, it was hardly surprising. The mums were the ones who slipped their sons a few bob when dad wasn't looking. The mums were the ones who would often come to the rescue of their little boys, *whatever* they were accused of.

Many of these youngsters worked mundane part-time jobs long before they left school, which simply fuelled their obsession with earning big money when they grew up. Nearly all of them cut their teeth on dodgy sidelines such as handling stolen bicycle parts, nicking radios out of cars and even shoplifting. Everything was fair game: cigarettes, spirits and clothing. Often railway containers were raided at night and their contents would end up on local street markets the following day. The docklands were still a breeding ground for criminals, even if some of them had moved with their families out to the suburbs on the border of south-east London and Kent. Many of the husbands and fathers of families in these new suburbs spent much of their time back at their old familiar haunts near the Old Kent Road: stealing remained a way of life.

When talking to some of those involved with the Brink's-Mat job, they agreed that from an early age they'd boast to anyone who would listen about what they wanted to do when they grew up. 'Earn a big fat wedge of cash,' was always their biggest ambition.

But few of these youngsters saw their future in joining the job ladder and climbing their way slowly upwards.

Their ambition was connected to the one thing they believed could help them escape their lives of relative poverty – committing crimes. It was much more lucrative than having a job in Civvy Street.

By vowing to be wealthy they were effectively putting themselves under severe pressure, which meant they would find it virtually impossible to back down if things didn't go their way. As former Kray twins' associate the legendary Freddie Foreman explained years later: 'You went out and you took chances and did all the villainy and put your life on the line, your liberty on the line, but there would be a nucleus of people around you who'd make sure you survived.'

That was the way it was.

Often these youngsters would form a gang and go up to central London to steal wallets and people's belongings from tourist coaches parked in places like Constitution Hill, near Buckingham Palace. Naturally, no one took much notice of kids, often deliberately dressed in shorts and a school cap so as to appear harmless. These scallywags could make as much as five pounds in just one day by selling everything they'd stolen on to a fence. Knowing a fence was the most profitable – and safest – way of making money out of crime. Fences were superbly well organized and considered respectable businessmen in these communities back in in the postwar era. Being a fence was a very profitable and crafty way to make good money out of crime without getting your hands dirty. Everyone – even the youngest children – noticed the aura surrounding them. According to Freddie Foreman: 'They got great respect because of their mannerism and their obvious affluent lifestyle. They always looked smart. They knew how to dress well. They'd have a little business going, they'd drive a decent car and they'd spend their money wisely.'

Mickey McAvoy (who would go on to be the Brink's-Mat robbery leader) and his mates nicked lead off roofs and collected scrap to sell down at the yards which had sprung up where Hitler's bombs had flattened buildings ten years earlier. The youngsters led by McAvoy were soon making ten to fifteen shillings a day from local fences in the Camberwell area where these young scallywags grew up. But McAvoy and many others growing up in south-east London preferred to be out and about on the mean streets, looking for opportunities, not scrabbling around on rooftops. One of McAvoy's oldest friends later explained: 'Even as a kid Mickey had these sharp, beady little eyes that darted around in all directions, scanning the streets on the lookout for trouble or a chance to do a bit of thieving. We looked up to him, even back then. He had an aura about him. You knew he was capable of anything.'

By the mid-1950s, dockworkers on both sides of the Thames – east and south – started losing their jobs as the postwar recession bit even harder. That meant they had to find ways of replacing the high wages (and bungs) they'd been earning over the years. Soon the only really high wages (and bungs) that still existed were as a printer in Fleet Street, where all the national newspapers continued to be produced in their millions. 'The print' was a lucrative trade often passed down through families. But in time even print jobs began to be axed, something that sparked a feeling amongst many that they had to go back to their roots in order to 'make a crust'. The area's new heroes were the 'pavement artists' – robbers – who'd scoop a few thousand pounds on a job and then buy everyone a round of celebratory drinks in their local pub.

True, they'd sometimes get caught by police, stand trial at places like the Old Bailey and go down for a long stretch. But at least they lived in style. Many in these communities frequently got angry about the long sentences handed down to villains, who were in many ways considered latter-day Robin Hoods. No one ever asked whether the crimes being committed were morally wrong; often robbers were seen as simply providing for their families.

Despite this, on the surface the relationship between the police and petty criminals remained a civilized one. Often they'd meet each other in the local pub and exchange pleasantries, even though they might have been 'nicked' the previous week. A lot of coppers and villains had been brought up in the same neighbourhoods and some even went to school together.

In the 1950s and early 1960s bank raids were usually carried out in the dead of night, with a master safecracker pitting his wits against whatever security arrangements happened to be in operation at the time. But as lock design and other security improved, tackling a safe became a much tougher challenge. Even the use of gelignite was no longer a sound bet: a device had been developed that, if triggered by the force of an explosion, simply threw extra bolts across the safe door. Villains introduced oxyacetylene torches to get around this problem, but these proved to be slow and cumbersome and, on occasion, would actually reduce the contents of a safe to charred paper before the door could even be forced open.

In the place of bank raids the armed robbery scene developed into an even more lucrative criminal enterprise. Wages had increased in the post-war boom and firms had to hire companies to transport their cash to factories and offices on pay day – usually Fridays. There were no professional security companies back in those days. More often than not, two or three trusted workers in a company would be given a few extra bob to pick up the cash from a nearby bank. If they were lucky they were armed with a cosh.

Inevitably, some workers began informing their associates about this transportation of relatively large sums of money, giving the villains the sort of essential inside info they needed. As one robber from those days explained: 'It was easy pickings because these "guards" were just ordinary workers and they didn't want to get bashed up or put up a fight to protect the firm's money.'

At that time most wages were carried in canvas cricket bags that could be snatched in seconds, thrown into a waiting car and driven around the corner to a quiet cul-de-sac, usually near a railway path or bridge where a changeover car would be waiting on the other side. Often the takings from such crimes were then quickly 'reinvested' into honest businesses. 'The objective was to get enough money to retire after building up your straight business,' explained one veteran robber. 'Then you could put your kids through good schools, buy your own home and get a decent motor, even maybe manage a holiday abroad.'

Robbers eventually graduated to across-the-counter bank raids. Old-style attacks on bank safes hadn't required any confrontation on the part of the robbers, but going into a bank in broad daylight did. So it was essential for the robbers to be able to guarantee *control* – and that's when firearms began appearing with alarming regularity on the streets of London.

Banks responded by installing reinforced glass screens to protect their cashiers. The risk in such armed raids was obviously higher but the rewards were generally lower. So once again those intent on robbery began looking for new methods. Cash in transit seemed the answer. Because of the increased use of credit and debit cards, Britain has become almost a cashless society, but back in those days consumers still needed ready money and plenty of it.

So it was no surprise that, during the 1960s, specialized security firms began emerging to take on the responsibility of transferring money. Armoured vans replaced vulnerable clerks carrying briefcases. It was these vans and their guards that became the new breed of robbers' primary targets. And it was south-east London 'firms' – gangs of robbers – who soon dominated such crimes throughout the capital. Often wealthy, older criminals financed these jobs but they rarely told the experts how to go about their work. These robbers were thorough professionals.

But as the money in transit industry grew, so did the risks. Post office vans were considered a soft target because they often had just one driver, and he usually didn't even know how much cash he was carrying. The *blaggers* usually had a snitch inside the main post office who'd be able to tell them which days there was a lot of cash on board such vans. A popular target was the pension run to post offices, but that only tended to be if the villains were hard up that week, as the pickings were not usually much more than a few hundred pounds.

The ultimate reward for a career as a robber – besides the cash – was underworld fame. There was nothing like picking up the evening paper, seeing the banner headline POST OFFICE VAN HIJACK and knowing that the local big-time faces would immediately be able to tell who'd carried out the job.

In the middle of this heady environment, prison became the natural breeding ground for even bigger robberies as criminals linked up with new partners inside while serving time. 'Inside clink [prison] was where you met different people and heard different stories and you learned your trade, so to speak. Prison's like a breeding ground. It's like going to university or going to college,' explained one old face. Many of these young south-east London villains would soon be graduating with 'full honours'.

TWO

Some young villains tried to go straight by enrolling in apprenticeships to learn a trade such as carpentry or brick-laying, but the pay was never enough to give them the sort of wealth they craved, many being already obsessed with avoiding the financial struggles of their parents.

Places like the Scala dance hall in Dartford, Kent, were popular with young south-east London tearaways such as Mickey McAvoy and his old mate Tony White. They liked travelling out to the suburbs because there were more young girls around in places like the Scala. No one ever paid the entrance fee. Instead, they'd clamber over the back fence and go through a back door. That's when McAvoy first came across characters like Kenneth Noye, another ducker and diver, but not in the same class as McAvoy because he was 'a softy from the suburbs'. In McAvoy's mind you could only be really hard if you'd grown up in the inner-city areas.

In the early 1960s, a lot of the youngsters from in and around south-east London dressed as Mods with smart, short haircuts, Hush Puppies shoes and black mohair suits, *if* they could afford them. The Mods drove scooters, and their arch-enemies were the Rockers – greasy motorbike fanatics who grew their hair relatively long and wore tatty jeans and leathers.

The Mods and the Rockers were the two main opposing youth social groups who emerged at the time, ahead of the skinhead cult which came a few years later and was fuelled by football crowd violence. There were frequent clashes between Mods and Rockers at weekends when they descended on south coast seaside resorts such as Brighton and Margate.

In the 1960s being a Mod, and many of these aspiring south-east London hoods were, was a serious business. Their favourite bands were The Who and The Spencer Davis Group, and many eventually graduated to The Small Faces. Naturally, the cozzers – as the police were known throughout south-east London and Kent – tried to keep a close eye on the various gangs of the day. But these youths were already well used to the police. Their attitude often manifested itself in a complete and utter disregard for rules and regulations, almost a contempt for society. A few youngsters back then took drugs such as purple hearts (a mixture of amphetamine and barbiturates), but the hard-nosed criminal types like Mickey McAvoy steered well clear of them. Drugs were unknown territory in every sense, and the profits weren't very high because the market was so small.

In their mid-teens many of these characters graduated to the local greyhound track (known as 'going to the dogs'), where they could make themselves a few bob. The dog tracks were usually a hotbed of local villainy, and these ever-observant and perceptive youngsters like McAvoy and others soon worked out which members of the criminal underworld were really on the up. One villain later confided how he'd often slide into a bar at the track and sit in a corner listening to the 'dodgy deals' going down, and then use the information he'd gleaned to make money for himself. McAvoy and his old mate Tony White were fascinated by these tough, edgy older characters in their sheepskin coats who seemed to carry endless bundles of five-pound notes around in their pockets.

The twisted values they learned impacted upon these teenagers' lives with increasing frequency and sent them into something of a moral vacuum. It seems from interviews with countless associates and friends of the Brink's-Mat gang that many of them grew frustrated as youths and developed bad tempers. If they didn't get what they wanted immediately there would be hell to pay.

Often a hair-trigger reaction could be provoked by the smallest incident. But instead of taking a deep breath and walking away from potentially difficult situations, many of these characters would steam straight into their opponents. It was almost a 'shoot now, ask questions later' mentality.

These tough young scallywags went out of their way to develop reputations as hard men. They wanted their contemporaries to know they wouldn't compromise in any way. Part of the fault lay with their parents because they did nothing to teach their children how to control their aggression. They never gave clear guidelines to their sons, and as a result they were allowed to believe they could get away with virtually anything.

And most of the time they did precisely that.

Yet their minds – like those of so many youths brought up in tough, uncompromising environments – were creative instruments which veered off in certain directions depending on their surroundings. These characters would see a situation in a completely different way to others who'd had a more respectable kind of background. People's personalities are said by psychologists to reflect a characteristic set of behaviours, attitudes, interests, motives and feelings about the world. It includes the way people relate to others. Extreme forms of abnormal behaviour are supposed to be easy to recognize but that doesn't mean they can be instantly rectified. The over-generosity to certain people, the need for admiration and complete lack of empathy towards those outside their own exclusive circle displayed by these young hoods are all classic indicators of narcissism. Nearly all of them also had a sprinkling of obsessive-compulsive disorder thrown in for good measure – a preoccupation with orderliness, perfectionism and control.

Some of them – like Mickey McAvoy and Kenneth Noye – were already showing themselves to be what one might call born leaders. With that came a number of other attributes, such as a heavy build, often developed in the local gym, street-wisdom and confidence beyond their years. The message was loud and clear: 'Don't fuck with me.'

Young Mickey McAvoy and his friend Tony White worked weekends as porters at the Covent Garden fruit and veg market where they all humped crates around to 'earn a few extra bob'. As they got older they stopped going to the suburbs and started going to the heavier south London clubs on Friday and Saturday nights where McAvoy in particular sometimes ended up having a 'right tear-up' with rival youths. Another favourite hangout for these young hoods and their chums was at a mobile snack bar on the south side of Albert Bridge, next to Battersea Park. During the hotter summer months, hundreds of south London youths would turn up there, until the police tried to move them along because their presence caused major traffic problems.

The 'hit first, ask later' attitude displayed by teenagers like McAvoy helped them gain confidence and power within their group of peers. One childhood friend explained: 'Mickey was quiet but you knew instinctively he was a powerful character. He had a real work ethic and wanted to earn big money from an early age.'

The other youths who went on to make their names in the south London underworld shared this intense work ethic. They expected to do some graft to earn a crust, but the difference with McAvoy and his pals was that they were after richer pickings than a paltry weekly salary. They wanted the good life and all its trappings.

The desperate poverty that had enveloped his family back in Ireland before they'd moved to Camberwell heavily influenced McAvoy's home environment. London's postwar youths were emerging from their parents' abject poverty as a restless, rebellious generation determined to make a mark for themselves in the world. But while McAvoy and his mates were committing numerous petty crimes, they still retained certain standards and even had codes to abide by. Targeting a man walking along the street and stealing his watch was frowned upon, while raiding a cigarette wholesalers' lock-up or breaking into shops at night was totally legit. 'You don't rob your own – ever,' McAvoy told one south London contemporary when he was a teenager. Not grassing up your mates was taken for granted. As one old south London criminal associate explained: 'If you went on a job and you got nicked and another fella who was on the job with you didn't grass you up, then he'd just done exactly what he was supposed to have done. I'd never look at someone and think: "Oh he didn't grass me up, what a lovely fella." I wouldn't be with him in the first place if I thought he was gonna turn grass on me. Grassing is a terrible, despicable thing. People like myself and my friends would rather fuckin' die than be a grass.'

By his mid-teens, McAvoy and many of his pals had little need for any further education. They were bright, quick-witted youths with an eye for the main chance, and many of them were already earning money by ducking and diving. To adults who employed them in the markets, McAvoy and his mates seemed humorous, happy-go-lucky characters, bursting with energy and deeply proud of their south-east London roots.

According to some of his contemporaries back in the late sixties, McAvoy's aggressive personality really thrived in this semi-criminal environment. McAvoy was fast becoming the kind of person who only saw things from his own perspective. Other family members noticed how fearless McAvoy became in his teens, as well as the way he'd try to manipulate situations to suit himself at others' expense. He also often seemed incapable of realizing when he'd hurt other people's feelings. He felt little remorse and certainly no sympathy for the victims of his early scams and crimes.

Yet beneath this rock-hard exterior lay an inner sadness. McAvoy found it difficult to take part in the normal activities like team sports that his peers were involved in. Being a teenager is supposed to be a time in which the developing individual learns how to be happy and derive happiness from as many situations as possible. This wasn't the case for McAvoy.

Out on the streets of south-east London as a teenager, McAvoy carefully hid his true feelings. One old pal explained: 'Mickey didn't like to give anything away about himself. He seemed a bit tense a lot of the time but his mind was always turning over, thinking about what he could get away with. He was incredibly observant. He'd spot things in the street before anyone else and that made him someone you always wanted on your side.'

An example of his sharp entrepreneurial eye were the road races to coastal resorts like Ramsgate and Whitstable organized by McAvoy and his crew. Like all kids back then, the characters who would eventually grow up to pull off the most lucrative crime of the twentieth century were obsessed with cars, often because their fathers couldn't afford one. With war rationing and low wages, they were still considered a luxury. That naturally made cars an object of great curiosity – and envy – to kids. As they grew older their fascination would turn many of them into juvenile car thieves. These trips went a bit further. They featured young 'drivers' who were already experts behind the wheel, even though they were under the legal driving age of seventeen. McAvoy and his mates all put heavy bets on who would win before the vehicles – always stolen – set off through London and into the countryside of south-east England. McAvoy, in his mid-teens at the time, was the 'ringmaster' of these trips and handled all the bets when they came in.

Many of McAvoy's contemporaries may have been petty thieves, but to become a real outlaw you had to do everything *your* way. Nobody and nothing else mattered, apart from your loved ones of course, and that ruthlessness made you more feared and respected. No one could get away with pulling a fast one on Mickey McAvoy because beneath that suspicious expression lurked a cold, calculating individual capable of making split-second decisions that could mean the difference between life or death to certain individuals.

Naturally the young Mickey McAvoy played up to his growing reputation. When he walked into certain taverns the place really did go quiet like it does in the movies. But McAvoy wanted to be more than just a bit of local muscle; he saw himself as a leader of men, a skilful criminal capable of taking on and beating anyone, especially the arch-enemy, the cozzers. McAvoy, who had boxed at a local club where he'd gained a reputation as a ferocious fighter, remained, according to his childhood friends, 'very handy with his fists, so no one dared take him on'. Those who knew him back then say McAvoy was 'solid, not particularly tall, not a bully by any means, not even frightening. He would never take any liberties but he was a right fuckin' hard bastard.'

While Mickey McAvoy was undoubtedly a hard-as-nails character, he also showed great loyalty to those he liked. He knew when to help rather than hinder. He was shrewd yet arrogant, and wanted wealth so badly that he was happy to take advantage of his own popularity. McAvoy was highly charismatic – even as a teenager he was capable of ordering his contemporaries to carry out minor crimes such as stealing milk off doorsteps and bottles of pop from shops. It was a sign of what was to come. He was, in the words of one of his contemporaries, 'a strange combination of hard heart and soft mind. Capable of beating a man, but also just as likely to help an old lady cross the street.'

McAvoy was a genuine creature of circumstance, a product of his tough upbringing and a complex, contradictory man who was utterly dangerous because he did not recognize the traditional boundaries in life. And he'd undoubtedly become addicted to crime from a very early age.

By the time they'd left school McAvoy and his pals were already burgling and carrying out raids on the nearby docks, so it was inevitable they'd graduate to bank robberies. These were the jobs that cemented a south London villain's reputation more than anything else. Once word got round that McAvoy was 'going across the pavement' then he really would be a 'made man' as far as the rules of the underworld were concerned.

This move into more organized crime represented a real step up for a young hoodlum. As one of his childhood friends recalled: 'When you're on a blag, it's like being part of a football team. Each person has their role and you count on the rest of them to pull their weight. It's a fantastic feeling when it works out. We'd get tip-offs about likely targets and the normal percentage for that kind of information was ten per cent of whatever you get. It was all a game but a fuckin' lucrative game when it worked.'

Once McAvoy and his gang had picked a day to commit a blagging, they'd work on getting all their tools together and steal a car to ensure a fast getaway. A classic blagging for McAvoy and his young pals would be a man collecting takings from betting shops. McAvoy's crew would usually be armed with at least a cosh, and just the mere threat of it would be enough to 'persuade' their victims to hand over the cash.

As one veteran robber who worked with McAvoy back then explained: 'Mickey was well known as being a good man to go to "work" with because he was very sound, game, and if you went across the pavement, Mickey would be the first one out of the car and the first one in to grab the dosh.'

As a young hood with a few bob in his pocket, McAvoy and others such as his close friend Tony White began frequenting the clubs, dives, spielers (illegal gambling clubs), pubs and hotels 'up West'. The two youths sometimes worked as enforcers for the violent and unscrupulous characters who ran protection rackets in the West End. Though they were nothing more than hired hands trying to earn some extra cash between robberies, they started to meet older, more experienced villains, including a quiet but impressive character called Brian Robinson, who had a reputation as a 'real pro' and also came from the same south-east London manor as McAvoy.

The older, more conservative Brian Robinson had spent a few years in the army, where it seems he honed his skills before getting out and developing into a very smart, supposedly independent 'entrepreneur' of crime.

All these young villains also quickly learned the importance of 'greasing palms', especially when it came to the local cozzers. That type of bribery and corruption undoubtedly coloured their attitude towards the police in later life. Their argument was simple: 'How can you trust a copper if most of them want a backhander? They're all the enemy, and most of them are less honest than we are.'

Characters like McAvoy, Robinson and White didn't recognize *anyone* in authority – apart from perhaps the occasional criminal name – as they developed into fearsome villains on the streets of south-east London. As far as they were concerned, policemen, judges and Home Office officials were nobodies. This new generation of villains were on their way up the ladder and nothing was going to stop them.

When Mickey McAvoy had a violent clash with a much older south-east London criminal, it looked like he was going to get his comeuppance. But even as a youngster, McAvoy didn't hide from anyone. He said later that taking on this particular face and 'giving him a right hiding' had been a good bit of 'PR'. In other words he'd sent out a message to other criminals that he was already a top dog.

A number of south-east London pubs became hotbeds for local criminals, and these younger hoods – observant and perceptive as ever – watched closely. Just like they'd done years earlier at the dogs, they'd often slide into a bar and sit in a corner listening to the dodgy deals going down.

As Mickey McAvoy's circle of acquaintances grew, so did his criminal habits. One friend from his school days got himself a job in a meat warehouse and immediately became involved with McAvoy in smuggling out carcasses of beef on lorries. McAvoy had numerous such 'little earn-ers' on the go, and was constantly on the lookout for new targets.

The criminal ascendancy of men like McAvoy, Robin-son, White and many others besides owed much to the period of transition that Britain was going through during the sixties and early seventies. There weren't so many spivs on the streets to talk to if you wanted a decent piece of meat for tea because the Arthur Daley-type characters had faded out when wartime rationing ended in the mid-1950s. Now people – especially the poor – had to fend for them-selves. That forced characters like Mickey McAvoy and his pals to go out on the streets and look for new challenges – and banks were obviously the most lucrative targets.

THREE

By the time they were in their late teens, streetwise, muscular hoods like Mickey McAvoy and Tony White looked a lot older than their age. They'd long since infiltrated the legendary clubs and bars in and around the Old Kent Road in the heart of south-east London, and now they were constantly on the lookout for 'work'.

It was no surprise that, as their circle of acquaintances grew, so did their criminal activities. Crime was endemic. It was part of the fabric of the society they came from. South-east London had always been a law unto itself. Why should things change just because a lot of the families had moved out to the suburbs?

It was little wonder that by this time the area had developed into London's acknowledged epicentre of armed robbery, especially since these youths often stayed at home with their families because they didn't want to end up in crummy bedsits. They'd wait and buy their first property once they had stolen themselves enough cash. The criminal influence could be traced back to a subculture which, in many ways, still exists to this day.

The Great Train Robbery of 1963 played a part in this

process because most of the robbers came from south-east London. The heroic status those criminals achieved in the eyes of many was nowhere more evident than on the streets where young hoods like McAvoy and White grew up. Armed robbery had taken on a romantic hue all of its own, and by the early seventies it was positively glamorous. People still saw these local villains as budding Robin Hoods striking blows against the traditional enemy: the police, the filth, the cozzers and all the other derogatory names they were called. Criminals were celebrated and talked about in the youth clubs and pubs because they were seen to be getting one back on the Establishment. When, in 1978, an armed police officer shot two gun-toting robbers dead in Peckham, south-east London, and wounded a third as they tried to snatch £50,000 from a security van, extra police had to be drafted into the area to prevent a riot. Women shouted abuse at police officers from the balconies of their flats; children taunted them in the street; and seven people at a pub frequented by the robbers were arrested on charges ranging from threatening behaviour to assault. South-east London pubs like the Frog and Night-gown, the Connoisseur, the Prince of Wales and the Beehive in Peckham all became notorious haunts for young hoods like McAvoy and White, and a number of pubs were places where guns could be obtained almost over the counter. Many of those very same taverns were now considered virtual no-go areas by the police.

Back in those early days only a brave and foolish man would try and muscle in on legendary criminals such as south-east London's most feared family, the Richardsons, who were treated like royalty south of the Thames. During the sixties, the Richardsons ran a hugely profitable empire stretching from south London scrapyards and West End drinking clubs to gold mines in South Africa. Their leader Charlie Richardson was known as the hardest man in south London. Even the Krays were wary about venturing onto his turf.

But when, in the late 1960s, Richardson was eventually brought to court and found guilty of fraud, extortion, assault and grievous bodily harm, a trial during which a judge called him 'a disgrace to society', some of the up-and-coming younger hoods noticed gaps appearing inside the south-east London underworld. As one senior Flying Squad officer from that era explained: 'The whole place opened up. People with strong personalities decided to move in.'

As these new 'faces' began feeling their way through what had once been considered Richardson 'territory', all sorts of new criminal enterprises began springing up. Billy Hayward, one of the most feared gangsters in south-east London, had already secured a place in gangland folklore by engaging in a nightclub battle with the Richardson gang over who should control local protection rackets. One of Hayward's men – Dickie Hart – was shot dead in the 1966 clash, which became known as 'the Battle of Mr Smith's Club'. This event effectively led to the gradual destruction of the Richardsons' criminal empire, since it prompted a public outcry about gangsters on the streets of London, something the Metropolitan Police were forced to crack down on heavily. Despite this extra police pressure, 'Mr Smith's' turned Billy Hayward into an underworld legend.

Hayward encouraged aspiring villains like Mickey McAvoy, Tony White, Brian Robinson and others to commit crimes on behalf of himself and other older criminals who would then invest the stolen goods and money in small businesses such as minicab companies, launderettes and sometimes even the stock market.

Inevitably the police began taking a closer look at these emerging villains. Many younger criminals reacted by having running feuds with certain local cozzers, who were forever trying to arrest them for a variety of petty offences. In some cases the police got so desperate to lock them up they would resort to illicit 'fit-ups' to ensure they took some of these faces off the streets.

The old-school villains warned the up-and-coming youngsters that they needed to keep certain policemen on their side. Eventually, they started winning over a few 'friendly coppers' by tipping them off on certain stolen shipments they'd heard about, so they'd then be left to their own devices on other, bigger jobs. It was a classic case of back-scratching. But Mickey McAvoy was no grass, and swore he would never play that game.

Nevertheless, characters like Mickey McAvoy, Brian Robinson and Tony White had encountered enough 'big names' by this stage to know that if they were going to infiltrate the upper echelons of the south-east London underworld, they'd have to share warm pints of bitter with some hard characters. As legendary former Krays associate Freddie Foreman later explained: 'You'll meet a certain person and you'll get a rapport with them, you'll like them and the best way to know that they're okay is through the belly of that man.

You get drunk with them. You have a night out and then you see the way they perform and handle themselves. If he doesn't get soppy and start running off at the mouth and get insulting to women and he can conduct himself with or without a drink, then you know he's a good guy.

'Once you've formed a relationship with another criminal he would have your unquestioned loyalty. You got involved with them because they were, in a twisted way, completely trustworthy. You knew they wouldn't turn you over. You had their trust and they had yours.' These were the kind of values that appealed to people like Mickey McAvoy.

It is now clear that control of what the popular newspapers liked to call London's 'underworld' switched to a new kind of villain in the late 1960s. The older underworld heroes who emerged immediately after the Second World War were larger-than-life characters that Fleet Street crime reporters dubbed with names such as the 'King of the Underworld' and the 'King of the Dog Dopers'. But eventually these so-called big names were replaced by professional robbers, organized in carefully selected teams constantly on the lookout for lucrative targets. These characters didn't run clubs in Soho and protection rackets or pimp women. They were real pros who saw the less glamorous but more lucrative robbing of banks and security vans as their chosen career.

Crime in the late sixties was heading for epidemic proportions, especially in London. Tens of millions of pounds' worth of stolen property changed hands every week. Violent offences were up by more than ten per cent each year from 1965, and the number of drug convictions was slowly beginning to rise, although it was not yet the profitable business it would eventually become.

Many believed that the jailing of London's two most notorious criminal families – the Krays and the Richardsons – in the late sixties would destroy the menace of organized crime. They couldn't have been more wrong. New, better organized crime networks quickly emerged which were often run by outsiders, rather than blood relatives. They were prepared to finance everything from bank robberies to drug deals. Hijacked goods lorries were another particularly popular source of income at the time, with the driver usually being bunged a few bob in advance to ensure a successful raid.

It seemed as if no amount of police activity could stem the tide of crime that was sweeping the nation at this time. The older crime bosses had been happy to hide behind hard-core do-or-die young villains for too long. Now those so-called 'kids' were vowing to run their own operations without any interference from the 'old boys'. These characters resented all authority, even in the shape of older, supposedly wiser villains.

Mickey McAvoy and many of his contemporaries effortlessly crossed the line from being cheeky Charlies into cold-blooded out-and-out criminals, prepared to end a man's life if they had to. They'd long since lost touch with the law-abiding world and so-called normal behaviour, choosing a life of crime from which nothing was going to deter them.

There was also another side to criminals like McAvoy

that made them virtually fearless. They were not afraid of going to prison. In fact they accepted that it would happen sooner or later and if it did, they'd take their 'bird' (sentence) and deal with it. After all, it was part and parcel of their chosen profession.

The late sixties was a time of great unrest in prisons across Britain. In Parkhurst, on the Isle of Wight, a huge riot erupted after inmates began protesting about conditions. For forty terrifying minutes on 24 October 1969, seven members of staff were in fear of their lives as riot-crazed inmates held them captive. One prisoner came within a whisker of slitting the throat of an officer. Nine prisoners – including some legendary south-east London faces – eventually surrendered. Accounts of their daring behaviour spread like wildfire through the pubs and drinking clubs south of the Thames.

Villains believed the authorities were trying to break their spirit and stop them planning new crimes with other inmates whenever they were banged up. Most criminals' other main preoccupation inside prison was keeping fit. They exercised furiously, narcissistically pumping up their already vast physiques with punishing regimes that many of them would maintain for the rest of their lives. Every time they did a press-up they saw it as a mark of defiance against the system. They'd never be beaten. Ever.

By the time the early 1970s hit south-east London, it was also filled with sharp-eyed detectives determined to win back the streets after all those gangster-filled years of the sixties, dominated by the Krays and the Richardsons. In 1973 Scotland Yard's Detective Chief Superintendent

Albert Wickstead, aka 'The Grey Fox', head of the Yard's Serious Crimes Squad, sanctioned raid after raid, which resulted in 235 officers taking 93 men and one woman into custody. One senior detective told the *Daily Express* at the time: 'The other side have never been hit so hard.'

The operation had been carried out by Scotland Yard's much-feared Flying Squad, based at Limehouse police station in the middle of the East End. They were single-mindedly trying to take on the south London robbers. It would lead to cat-and-mouse games that would last for at least two decades and be peppered with accusations ranging from bribery to the alleged participation of certain officers in actual robberies.

The Flying Squad had been in existence for so long that the Squad's nickname in rhyming slang, The Sweeney (from Flying Squad/Sweeney Todd, the notorious Fleet Street barber who turned his customers into meat pies), was already regarded as a cliché. The Squad was set up at the end of the First World War, when London experienced a crime wave as large numbers of men recently released from the armed forces emerged onto the streets of the capital, many of them hardened to violence after the carnage on the Western Front.

The Sweeney enjoyed rapid crime-busting success, and in 1920 was provided with two motor tenders, capable of a top speed of 35mph. (The speed limit at the time was just 20mph.) Then a *Daily Mail* journalist referred to them as 'a flying squad of picked detectives' and the name stuck. Their exploits went on to figure in a number of British films, and in the mid-1970s the squad would be immortalized in a TV series, *The Sweeney*, starring John Thaw and Dennis Waterman.

But the glamorous, hard-nosed image of the Flying Squad left detectives wide open to accusations of corruption, either through turning a blind eye to what was going on in return for a cut of the action or – if the information led to the recovery of stolen property – pocketing some of the reward money that the detective claimed on the informant's behalf.

A strategically placed officer could also, for a fee, ensure bail was granted, hold back evidence and details about past convictions from a court, or pass on to a person under investigation details of a case being made against him or warnings about police operations in which he could become compromised.

In the mid-1970s – just as villains like McAvoy, Robinson and White were making a name for themselves – the newly appointed Deputy Assistant Commissioner David Powis ordered a crackdown to stop corrupt policemen from creaming off reward money meant for informants. He insisted on meeting all the informants as part of a vetting process and that, in the future, all payments amounting to more than £500 would be handed over by the DAC himself.

The Flying Squad itself had already come under close scrutiny. In November 1971, the *Sunday People* revealed that Commander Kenneth Drury, then head of the Flying Squad, had been on holiday in Cyprus where an infamous Soho pornographer – a man with nine convictions to his name, including a spell in Dartmoor prison – had been his host. Drury was served with disciplinary papers and suspended. He immediately resigned rather than face a full disciplinary hearing. But before doing so he wrote an article for the *News of the World* claiming that a criminal called Jimmy Humphreys had been one of his informants.

The furious pornographer – aware of the effect that such a claim could have on his many contacts – responded a week later through the columns of the same newspaper, saying he had never received any money from Drury and had in fact wined and dined the police chief on a total of fifty-eight occasions during which Humphreys always picked up the bill. At his eventual trial, Flying Squad chief Drury said it was 'absolutely essential' for Flying Squad officers to mix socially with people connected with the criminal fraternity.

Drury claimed: 'During my career, I made a point of mixing with criminals. It is essential that you do so. You cannot expect them to give information about crimes if you ostracize them except when you want information from them.' The problem with the Drury philosophy was that it left detectives wide open to accusations of corruption. Drury himself was convicted on five counts of corruption and jailed for eight years. Not surprisingly, the Flying Squad was then completely overhauled. Instead of dealing with serious crimes in general, they would in future tackle armed robberies only, with the squad's officers forming a central robbery squad run from a co-ordinating unit at Scotland Yard and four smaller groups strategically placed around London. The message was loud and clear to blaggers: 'We are out to get you.'

But the biggest problem – as far as the villains were

concerned – were the so-called 'supergrasses', who'd become the key to police success. These characters were a cut above the usual 'grasses' and 'snouts' who helped the police with their inquiries in exchange for a free pint or a fiver. The stakes were much higher, and often that meant immunity from prosecution in exchange for the inside track on major robberies. It was a breakthrough for the police but, inevitably, it came at a cost.

Hard-hitting detectives from the Flying Squad were actively persuading some members of close-knit gangs to inform on robberies in advance. Perhaps the most notorious of all supergrass cases was the controversial 'chit-to-freedom' that bank robber Bertie Smalls negotiated from Britain's law-keepers. Characters like Smalls played their cards close to their chest. His chips were times, places, hauls and Christian names. Smalls and other grasses believed that what they had to offer would be enough to win the most important gamble of their lives – freedom. Smalls became one of the most hated men in the London underworld as a result of 'joining the other side'. Many villains shared the opinion of one of their own number who said he'd 'gladly kill that bastard for nothing. He's vermin and should be wiped off the face of this earth.'

In May 1974, Smalls helped convict seven men at the Old Bailey of robbing the Barclays Bank at Ilford of £237,736 and Barclays' Wembley branch of £138,111. After that, he was guarded by twelve armed detectives at a secret hideout twenty-four hours a day, knowing full well that a £60,000 contract had been put on his head. Back in south-east London, Mickey McAvoy and others were outraged. 'This ain't about money. It's about respect and not grassin' up people. It's the ultimate sin, ain't it?' he told one associate.

The Flying Squad regularly hauled in up–and-coming young villains like McAvoy, suspecting that they were connected to particular crimes, but with no way of actually proving it. McAvoy and some of his contemporaries were even approached by crime bosses to help frame high-ranking police officers, just before the police were due to give evidence in major trials. The aim was to smear their names to such an extent that their evidence would be seriously questioned in court. But McAvoy didn't fancy that sort of work. He still much preferred robberies to framing 'the filth'. He knew that was asking for trouble.McAvoy had big plans to turn himself into a major-league criminal carrying out only the biggest, most lucrative robberies. He already had a reputation to maintain, and he certainly wasn't prepared to start grassing up other villains to the cozzers. But some of his criminal contemporaries had other ideas. They believed that swapping certain information with the enemy might actually give them more space to develop their own criminal enterprises.

And in the middle of this virtual war between the cops and the robbers, security van hold-ups and bank robberies were getting a lot harder to pull off. Guards equipped with batons and truncheons were now being used much more regularly to escort large quantities of cash, which meant the robbers were going to have to step up the levels of threats and maybe resort more frequently to violence if they were to continue robbing with abandon on the streets of London.

FOUR

The seventies saw the ethnic make-up of the old London criminal manors completely transformed by the arrival of hundreds of thousands of immigrants, particularly from Asia. Mickey McAvoy didn't really like what he saw. He believed in the good old-fashioned ethos that England was for the English, conveniently forgetting that his family were originally from Ireland. The Mister Patels running the street-corner stores in his home manor of Camberwell and the West Indian bus conductors were a source of constant irritation to McAvoy and his mates. Overt racism was rife, and there were few who would refrain from openly slagging off other races.

There had also been other, even bigger changes afoot in south and east London. Much of the capital was gradually being gentrified. Some areas were even being colonized by office blocks. The old faces really had faded away; the Krays and the Richardsons had been inside prison for a while and many of their old associates had fled to Spain's Costa del Sol, safe in the knowledge that they couldn't be extradited back to the UK. The shadowy, secretive figures who'd taken over the underworld were not interested in flashy cars or hobnobbing with the rich and famous. They were ambitious, greedy and extremely cold-blooded, and they believed that keeping a low profile would guarantee them a much longer reign in the underworld than the loud-mouthed crime families of old. Many of these deadly characters were even building property empires on a bed of 'black' money by financing major crimes and then pouring their cash into major London building developments. These would eventually include the Docklands area near Wapping, later to be turned into the financial centre of the capital.

By this time Mickey McAvoy and his mates Brian Robinson and Tony White had pulled together a classy team of robbers more than capable of stealing from the supposedly robber-proof security vans that were being built to withstand armed raiders. These vehicles were factory-tested with pick axes and cutters. Even shots were fired at them. The idea was to turn the vans into fortresses on wheels, complete with a supposedly sophisticated alarm system. A whole industry had developed around finding the means to stop robbers getting their hands on the money while it was on the move. Security firms even copied the military by having their staff wear uniforms.

So it was no surprise that by the mid-seventies blaggers began shooting at guards much more frequently. Most villains would swear blind that they never intended to injure anyone but simply used the 'fear factor' of firing a gun to scare their victims into surrendering their money.

However the police – especially the Flying Squad – saw this as the villains openly stepping up the war on the streets of London. They became obsessed with catching robbers preying on security vans, which meant they spent much of their time chasing their tails. On payday – which at this time was on Thursdays – many Flying Squad detectives were simply sent onto the streets of London to look out for robbers. The reality was that the police simply weren't prepared or equipped for the latest surge in the crime of robbery. It was a perfect time for young robbers like McAvoy and his associates to thrive. The police were stretched at the best of times and had always relied on solving crimes after they were committed rather than preventing them. It was an uphill struggle that inevitably led to a closer relationship between criminals and the police, something which in itself would lead to even bigger problems later with police corruption and bribery.

In the summer of 1976, McAvoy, Tony White and Brian Robinson met up with a couple of well-respected, older armed robbers in a pub in south-east London. 'That's when Mickey hit the big time,' explained one old south London face. 'It's all about a man who knows a man who knows a man.' The three hard men were asked outright if they were interested in being part of a team of robbers looking to expand beyond London and hit the lucrative south-east England market. It sounded more like a sales job than a recruitment pitch for a gang of armed blaggers.

McAvoy, Robinson and White saw this as a definite step up the criminal ladder. The two old-timer financiers in the pub were offering to back McAvoy and his associates with cash in exchange for a percentage of the takings from every robbery. The gang's total haul would eventually exceed £2m, making them at that time one of the most successful teams of robbers ever seen in the UK.

The robbers were soon operating nationwide: from London to Essex, across to the Midlands and as far north as Dundee in Scotland. McAvoy wasn't the main brains behind the gang, but he was a highly influential team member. In fact there was no overall 'Mr Big' in charge as such, because a hard-core committee of criminal faces financed and selected the jobs to be done, checked details of layout and security, and then suggested the right men for the job. Brian Robinson – older than McAvoy and White – eventually became the self-proclaimed 'Colonel' – the man who'd pull each job together. Robinson was well built, with a round, deadpan face that gave little away. He'd served in the army before returning to the mean streets of south London. The former painter and decorator was so proficient at organization that police later said he could have become a millionaire businessman if he'd used his talents more honestly. One detective recalled: 'Brian was a modest, unpretentious fellow who kept a really low profile. There was no flash car or flash house. God knows what he did with his money but we never found any of it.'

Other robbers came in and out of the gang as it sparked terror and stole fortunes up and down the country, but McAvoy, Robinson and White were at the core of most raids. McAvoy and the other two often suggested new targets they'd seen on their travels. The team initially had one golden rule: try to pick the most isolated spot for the actual robbery, whether it was a moving target – a van – or at a factory. 'The quieter the better because then we knew the cozzers would take a lot longer getting there,' one team member later explained.

Fast and efficient getaway vehicles were a vital tool for any big robbery. The gang would go on to steal literally hundreds of them during their reign. A well-stocked arsenal of weapons was also essential. There was a jester-like range of disguises, including ginger wigs, coloured spectacles, false beards and large moustaches. Some robbers were even prepared to dress up as women to confuse potential witnesses.

McAvoy and the gang's other strong-arm men were expected not to hesitate to fire their weapons – usually revolvers and shotguns – although the intention was to warn people off rather than actually do them harm. They used sledge-hammers and iron bars to shatter windscreens. The gang's weapons were initially obtained by breaking into gun shops. But there were a number of shady criminal gun dealers emerging in the underworld at this time, including one notorious character who, even though he had once been a policeman, would eventually become their favourite 'merchant of death'.

The gang often relied on bent security guards, who'd tip them the nod when a van was carrying a particularly large amount of money. If security guards didn't respond well to approaches from the gang then sometimes one of them would pay a little visit to the guard's family as a 'friendly reminder' that they were not to be crossed.

Meanwhile the Flying Squad's message to the robbers of

south London was clear: You'll be shot dead if you carry arms. To some criminals at that time, the police had become judge and executioner all rolled into one. But all it really did was stiffen their resolve to beat the police *by whatever means*.

In the late 1970s, a number of south-east London professional villains known to McAvoy and Robinson joined a Freemasons' lodge in west London following an introduction from a well-known Kent criminal who had big 'connections' inside the Freemasons. According to one police source inside this shadowy organization, one villain's membership was actually proposed and seconded by a serving police officer.

The Masons' lodge they joined included members who were police and dealers in gold bullion and other precious metals. The criminals saw it as a perfect opportunity to ease their way into an important group of new contacts. They began smoothing their passage in by making some substantial donations to several charities.

Membership of a Freemasons' lodge was a natural step for any ambitious south-east London criminal keen to infiltrate a circle of acquaintances that crossed all social divides and included several judges and magistrates. The Freemasons are a controversial society, not least because of the vast number of policemen who are members. Though many look upon the Masons as a mysterious and secretive organization, others claim they are nothing more than a very discreet gentlemen's club with tens of thousands of members across Britain. How much power and influence they wield amongst this country's politicians and lawmakers will probably never be known.

But there was absolutely no doubt that it was the presence of senior policemen in the Masons that fuelled the villains' interest in joining. As one police officer later explained: 'These criminals cynically manoeuvred themselves into the Masons as if it was the right pub for them to be seen at.' Some police officer members of the west London lodge were outraged by the presence of known criminals in their ranks. But others saw it as an ideal opportunity to pick up new informants.

McAvoy and others encouraged their criminal associates to be Masons because they saw membership as further evidence of their status within the London underworld. It could also have more practical benefits. On a number of occasions, criminals wriggled out of an arrest for handling stolen goods thanks to their membership of the Masons. One police source recalled the day he arrested one notorious south-east London villain who later played a big role in laundering the Brink's-Mat gold.

'He's on the square,' a Mason detective told the arresting officer at a Kent police station.

'So?'

'Can't you help out?'

'Where are you coming from on this?'

'Oh, it's like that is it?'

'Too bloody right it is.'

A number of Freemason police officers began happily lying and vouching for the villains who were members because they genuinely believed that to a certain degree membership put these characters above the law.

And of course all of the villains in the Masons swiftly mastered the art of the Freemasons' handshake. This involved putting the thumb between the first and second finger and pressing the knuckle on the middle finger, which would indicate that the person in question was on the third degree – Mason-speak for being a member.

Whenever these criminals met a policeman they thought was a Mason they'd make a point of speaking to him very carefully to ascertain his membership. The conversation would have bizarre overtones:

'You ever been taught to be cautious?'

'Yeah, well my mother always taught me to look left and right before I cross the road.'

If the person they were speaking to said yes then that would be followed up with passwords.

'Are you a regular attender?'

'Yeah.'

The moment someone said that back they knew they'd connected with a fellow Mason.

FIVE

Mickey McAvoy, Brian Robinson and Tony White – not to mention dozens of other south-east London blaggers – clearly considered themselves highly professional criminals. Robberies on banks and armoured vans carrying wages were still booming during the late seventies, despite the latest technology, which was supposed to make it harder for the villains to strike. The criminals even started using new secret weapons all of their own. Take the argon arc gun, a high-powered electric torch that could cut its way through metal. The guns weren't available in shops, and could only be ordered, which should have made it easier for the police to trace them back to their owners. But McAvoy and his associates eventually found a factory in west London that stored the argon guns and broke in and stole six of them.

One typical job was the audacious 1977 hijacking of an armoured van on the streets of Croydon after inside information was provided to the gang, making them aware that at least £100,000 in cash was up for grabs. The gang pulled in front of the armoured van before turning around to ram it head-on. The terrified guards flung open the doors and were immediately hauled out of the van and coshed by the group of masked men, although one of the gang later insisted they were 'only glancing blows, designed to mark, not injure them'.

One robber jumped in the back of the van and ripped open the wages compartment before the blaggers formed a chain and began slinging boxes from hand to hand into the boot of their getaway car. Within a few minutes they'd quit the scene and swapped their first car for another one half a mile away. It was the sort of job that got the south London underworld sitting up and taking notice of McAvoy, Robinson and their brash young band of robbers.

There were at least two or three substantial robberies every week in London and south-east England at this time. One of the most legendary was a classic blagging in the Blackwall Tunnel on 29 September 1977. It caught the eye of just about every south London villain at that time.

This particular job was a huge boost to a legendary south-east London hard man called Jimmy Moody, who even went so far as to dress as a policeman to hold back the traffic, which brought this reaction from a lawyer who later defended him in court: 'Those were the days when an awful lot of policemen came from the same background as the villains they were chasing. It was hard to tell the Flying Squad guy and the armed robber apart, and Jim made a very plausible copper!' There were even rumours a detective had provided the police uniforms for the job. Other officers were later said to have been given 'pay-offs' from the takings of the Blackwall Tunnel job to ensure the robbers weren't apprehended.

In the Blackwall Tunnel raid 'PC' Moody created a gap in the traffic and forced a security van to stop just past the bend about two-thirds of the way into the tunnel. At the same time, two of the robbers staged a crash behind them to block the tunnel just before the bend. The gang used three stolen cars and a stolen van to surround the security wagon. The team had done their homework because once inside the tunnel, the security van's radio was useless.

'PC' Moody then leapt out of his car and 'confiscated' the keys of several motorists behind them in the tunnel at gunpoint so they couldn't drive off and raise the alarm.

In the pubs and clubs of south-east London, the Blackwall Tunnel hijack went down as a brilliantly executed job. It helped popularize a new four-letter word, which summed it all up – the *buzz*. As Moody's co-robber Bernie Khan later explained: 'The buzz on that job was better than any drugs. All that adrenalin pumping through you was fuckin' incredible and the feelin' of elation once you'd snatched that cash was out of this world.' Moody was eventually arrested for his part in the crime as well as his involvement in other raids. In 1979 he was sent on remand to Brixton prison to await trial for armed robbery. He escaped before the trial was heard, only to be murdered by a hit man while he was on the run.

Nevertheless, McAvoy, Robinson, White and others had great admiration for jobs like the Blackwall Tunnel robbery. All three actively sought bigger and more lucrative targets. Groups of heavy-looking men regularly called round for meetings with McAvoy at the house his family had moved to in Dulwich, south-east London. He told his family the visitors were just part of a betting syndicate. McAvoy's loyalty to his 'associates' was almost as strong as his devotion to his wife and children.

When keep-fit fanatic McAvoy turned his garden shed into a mini-gym complete with weights, chest expanders and a punch bag so he could be in prime condition for jobs, his wife would only jokingly ask him: 'Going in for the next Olympics?'

'No, just keeping fit for my job,' would come the response. But it was a different job from the one his family no doubt wished he had. McAvoy's obsession with keeping fit had started in his teens thanks to a genuine belief that a healthy body led to a healthy, clear mind. He believed his fitness meant he was much less likely to make any costly mistakes when he was out robbing and thieving.

The two sides of Mickey McAvoy's character were already clearly defined. If you saw him out with his young wife Kathy and two young children on a sunny Sunday afternoon in south-east London, you'd never guess he was a ruthless criminal already responsible for many robberies across the capital. Often when he got home after a job Kathy would be watching a TV news item about a robbery. But if she carefully asked McAvoy about it, his reply would always be the same: 'Good luck to 'em.'

There were rules in south London and one of the most important ones was to never directly admit your crimes to anyone, not even your own wife and family. Wives were often infuriated when their husbands so blatantly ignored their attempts to find out more about their husbands' activities. That's when villains like Mickey McAvoy would usually take a deep breath and reply along the lines of: 'Darlin', don't worry. I won't let you down. Just don't ask questions.'

Like so many other south London villains before him, McAvoy seemed to thrive on his 'two lives'. As one old friend later explained: 'Mickey was essentially a loner. He rarely got too close to people. It's a funny thing to say but he was also a very good family man.' McAvoy thoroughly enjoyed the security of a stable home to return to after days and nights of partying and thieving. He knew he couldn't survive in the real, 'bad' world if he didn't have a bit of the 'good' world as well.

Mickey McAvoy managed to be an even-tempered character *most* of the time. But when he did lose his temper the sparks would really fly and that was why he was known as 'Mad Mickey' to so many criminal associates by this time. McAvoy revelled in this nickname because it was like a warning sign to other criminals not to cross him under any circumstances. Wherever McAvoy went, there was always a hint of the 'other side' in his expression. Said one south London villain: 'McAvoy had this scowl which was permanently etched across his face. He already had a lot of enemies so he never fully switched off.'

Nonetheless, many south London villains were already impressed by McAvoy: 'He'd always have money in his pocket but he wasn't flash. Mickey didn't trust no one, and that's the best way to be in this business. I think the only person he ever truly trusted was himself. You see, Mickey was already well-known but he wasn't really *known* by anyone, if you see what I mean.'

Brian Robinson's reputation was as one of those classic villains renowned as 'a man with a plan'. One of his oldest south London friends explained: 'Brian loved the planning stages of any job. He mapped things out very carefully and often came up with something a bit different that would catch people off guard.'

Robinson was respected by all who came into contact with him. He was a professional villain but he also – like McAvoy – had a normal home life with a wife and children whom he clearly valued more than anything, apart from his work. One old associate explained: 'Brian kept things low-key but he was tenacious and hard-working. He saw blagging as his profession and he was quietly proud of his skills, although he never ever blew his own trumpet.'

It was during the early planning stages of yet another new job that McAvoy met a man known as 'The Fox' at a West End nightclub. The Fox – who would eventually play a pivotal role in the life of so many of the Brink's-Mat robbers – had a resonant, gravelly voice with a very slight cockney accent. He told McAvoy he'd easily be able to find some extra financial backing for any 'special' jobs, which might potentially net them a fortune.

The Fox had once been a top blagger himself, as well as being a renowned fixer for criminals as far back as the late 1940s. There were even rumours that The Fox had been involved in helping finance the Great Train Robbery nearly twenty years earlier. He said he was in close touch with a bunch of other big-time villains, all of whom were keen to invest some cash in the right type of job.

McAvoy and his older associate Brian Robinson knew perfectly well that in order to move up the ladder of southeast London villainy they needed to hit a really big target, one that would cement their criminal infamy and maybe even assure them the sort of riches that might mean an early and happy retirement.

McAvoy's obsessive quest for cash even led to him getting involved in a sideline that many other villains back then would have frowned upon: he was arrested after his brother and another man were found with a quarter of a million pounds' worth of cocaine at Heathrow airport. McAvoy had allegedly wanted to sell on the cocaine to help finance bigger and more lucrative robberies, or at least that's what he later claimed to associates.

A search of various premises by detectives following the Heathrow arrest also uncovered a large number of shotguns and pistols, as well as two chainsaws. McAvoy was not just an armed robber, police suspected, but possibly even an underworld armourer as well. McAvoy naturally later claimed he was 'fitted up' by the cozzers, but whatever the truth of the matter, he'd now marked himself out as a player in the first division of robbers, which meant he would be given constant attention by his sworn enemy – The Sweeney.

By a strange twist of fate, McAvoy's alleged involvement with the drugs haul at Heathrow brought him into contact with a couple of characters who had extensive knowledge of London's premier airport and the industrial estates that surrounded it. McAvoy was told in no uncertain terms that they represented lucrative targets since many of the warehouses were used to store valuable goods between flights in and out of Heathrow.

McAvoy mentioned this to his old mate Brian Robinson. This information reminded Robinson that his irritating brother-in-law Tony Black worked at the Brink's-Mat warehouse near Heathrow. Brink's-Mat were one of the best-known security companies in the world at the time so it was a safe bet that some very interesting cargoes were stored on their premises. Robinson approached Tony Black very casually, and his sister's husband immediately began talking openly about the vast amounts of gold and cash and travellers' cheques that were frequently stored in the warehouse overnight between flights in and out of the United States.

Robinson knew that Black was hard up because he was a gambling addict, and there was no way his relatively low security guard's salary would cover his debts. That made Black vulnerable, or in the words of one detective, 'a sitting fuckin' duck'.

The Brink's-Mat warehouse looked as if it had the potential to be the biggest target of Robinson and McAvoy's criminal careers. So for many weeks the team used an empty building near the warehouse to allow them to watch the movements of vans in and out of the Brink's-Mat building. They hadn't yet told Black of their robbery plans because they didn't want him to know they were serious until it was too late for him to change his mind about being involved in the heist.

Day after day McAvoy and his associates built up a second-by-second work schedule for the Brink's-Mat guards as they peered through the windows of the abandoned warehouse. It was crucial to know the exact movements of the Brink's-Mat staff so the robbers could work out the point in the day when the warehouse, stuffed with cash and gold, was most vulnerable.

McAvoy, Robinson and their main other partner in crime, Tony White, even tried to finance this complex, risky job themselves by carrying out the robbery of a security van which they believed would be carrying a quarter of a million pounds in cash. They didn't want to share the spoils from this new 'Big Job' with people like The Fox and his band of armchair villains.

But after the relatively simple hold-up, McAvoy and the gang were bitterly disappointed to discovery they'd only managed to steal about £30,000 in total. Each member of the team was given a few thousand pounds to tide him over until the next big job, while the remaining money was kept in reserve to put towards the raid on the Brink's-Mat warehouse.

McAvoy, Robinson and his other fellow robbers were just as addicted to the 'buzz' of committing robberies as their underworld heroes from the Chainsaw Gang, who caused havoc by robbing several security vans during the 1970s and early 1980s. They earned their nickname because they used a chainsaw to open the back of security vans, almost as easily as if they'd used a tin opener on a can of baked beans. They'd long since proved beyond doubt they had the bottle to carry out spectacular jobs. The only disappointment was the money, which often fell hundreds of thousands of pounds short of expectation.

Nevertheless their reputations in south London remained intact, since it was acknowledged that they had no control over how much money was on offer. It was simply a question of bad luck.

McAvoy's underworld associates even seemed to believe the rumour that he only got involved in the earlier cocaine deal with his brother because he was planning to use the profits to finance more robberies. But no one on the fringe of the south London underworld knew precisely where or when the Big Job was going to be carried out.

Meanwhile the police stepped up the pressure by knocking on McAvoy's front door in south-east London, inquiring about his movements on the day of certain robberies. McAvoy was always so confident they had no evidence that he'd agree to go down to police stations to 'try and clear up any misunderstandings'. A few times he was even asked to appear in identity parades but he was never once picked out as a serious suspect. McAvoy later recalled that many ID parades were comical. 'They [the police] were just testin' the water and they'd try and make me wear something different from the others in the line-up just so they knew I'd be more likely to be picked out. Talk about fuckin' bent.'

Hardened south London villains like McAvoy and his gang never made any statements to the police, even after they were charged. They'd later insist that 'once a few bob had been thrown in the right direction', they'd usually get bail, despite the serious nature of their alleged crimes.

In the middle of all this police 'harassment' as they liked to call it, McAvoy and Robinson were carefully and expertly planning the Big Job – the raid on the Brink's-Mat ware-house near Heathrow airport.

In the aftermath of any raid that didn't go completely according to plan McAvoy would become obsessed by the idea that someone inside his gang must have been a police informant – a grass. McAvoy told another gang member that if he ever found out one of his team members was a grass there was only one way to deal with him. 'I'd have him fuckin' done.' And Mad Mickey meant it. Like so many of his fellow south London villains, he remained convinced informants were 'Judases who should have been drowned at birth'.

Aside from the chance to make money and glory, another reason why McAvoy became so desperate to pull off the Big Job at the Brink's-Mat warehouse at Heathrow was that he and his criminal associates knew that van hijacks and going across the pavement (bank robberies) were going to get too dangerous one day. Drugs looked like the safer option when it came to earning fortunes from crime.

Eventually the time came for Brian Robinson to fully reveal to his brother-in-law Tony Black their intention to rob Black's employers at Brink's-Mat. Black, still desper-ately in debt, jumped at the chance to help the gang in exchange for a share of the proceeds.

The gang had thoroughly established the movements of the Brink's-Mat staff through Black, as well as their care-ful surveillance operation. Initially McAvoy had found it hard to believe that such a small, relatively lightly guarded warehouse could hold such extraordinary amounts of cash and gold overnight. Back in those days, most robbers still presumed banks were the places really worth raiding. Now the Big Job looked like a dead cert.

However McAvoy and Robinson had little option but to accept that they needed some serious financial backing after the disastrously low amount of cash obtained from the previous robbery. McAvoy got in contact with the same character he'd met earlier – The Fox – who'd pledged upfront cash to the gang if they ever went after any really big targets. There would have to be some serious investment of cash in certain items before they would be fully ready to pull off the Brink's-Mat raid.

The Fox introduced McAvoy and Robinson to a family of north London criminals called the Adamses (known in the underworld as 'the A-Team'). They had been quietly but firmly asserting themselves as the capital's most powerful clan of villains since the Krays and the Richardsons. The Fox insisted that the A-Team were London's most proficient money launderers and as such they would be a vital cog in the team's machinery when it came to dispersing all the cash immediately after the robbery.

The A-Team were headed by Terry Adams and his brothers Sean (known as Tommy) and Patrick (Patsy). They were the three eldest of eleven children who'd been brought up as Irish Catholics in a north London council flat. They'd first broken through in the underworld by using their fists to extort money from market stallholders. This had been followed by a meteoric rise to power in the late 1970s and early 1980s thanks to drug trafficking, extortion, hijackings, security fraud and large-scale blaggings. Based in

Clerkenwell, north London, the Adams family managed to evade prosecution for years by running their syndicate at arm's length. Their reputation for violence meant that detectives had long since labelled them as being 'far worse than the Krays'.

Meanwhile other 'professionals' in south London made themselves available to McAvoy and Robinson as word of the Big Job spread through the upper echelons of the underworld. Amongst others 'circling' were three members of the legendary 1963 Great Train Robbery gang, who were keen to invest some of their money in this new opportunity. Two of them even pressed to be on the actual robbery team because of their previous 'unique' experience.

One of them was Charlie Wilson, who had long been credited with being one of the leaders of the GTR. He contacted McAvoy but was snubbed; McAvoy, to ensure that no one tipped off the police about the job in advance, told him that the job had been cancelled. Too many of McAvoy's criminal associates had been grassed up in recent times, and McAvoy believed that the fewer people who knew that the job was still going ahead the better. He could just about live with the rumours of a Big Job, but if the date of it ever leaked out, the job would be doomed.

McAvoy and Robinson both believed that if they let any big names like the GTR duo join the raid then they would lose control of the job, and the money would end up in the hands of villains who weren't even a proper part of his gang.

In the middle of all this, a legendary face called George 'Georgie Boy' Francis was forging a close relationship with McAvoy and Robinson. Embedded deep within the underworld, with a string of convictions for theft and violence, Francis had risen to criminal prominence in the late 1970s when he became part of a group of armed robbers who decided to move into drug trafficking.

Specially converted containers were sent to a shoe factory in Pakistan, where millions of pounds' worth of cannabis were hidden by legitimate goods and shipped back to the UK. The first four runs went like clockwork. Francis and other members of the gang began living the good life – buying cars, jewellery and making a show of lighting their cigars with £20 notes in south London pubs.

But when the fifth drug consignment arrived, customs officers were watching. Lennie 'Teddy Bear' Watkins, driving a lorry filled with £2.5m of cannabis, spotted the surveillance team, and as soon as he realized they'd been seen, customs investigator Peter Bennett moved in to make the arrest. Watkins shot Bennett dead. Watkins was sentenced to life, and the rest of the gang were put on trial. Underworld sources claim that Francis talked to associates about nobbling the jury to ensure he was not convicted. As it happened, the first jury failed to reach a verdict. This resulted in a retrial that led to his acquittal. While Francis walked free, several other members of the gang, faced with the same evidence, had pleaded guilty.

When McAvoy heard about the A-Team's role in helping Francis escape justice, it was another impressive 'calling card' on behalf of the north London crime family, even if he still viewed them with great suspicion because they were from the wrong side of the Thames. Francis was not only up for the Big Job but he also reiterated what McAvoy had already been told – that the Adams family from north London would be the ideal people to launder the proceeds.

Another character who came on the scene at this stage was one of Mickey McAvoy's oldest mates, south-east London robber Brian Perry. Perry had been recruited to be part of the Brink's-Mat robbery team itself alongside Robinson, McAvoy and Tony White. Perry would also eventually play a pivotal role in organizing the distribution of the proceeds afterwards. Perry, in his late thirties, was a classic south-east London villain with a successful minicab business, which was actually a money-laundering siphon for the proceeds of numerous crimes.

The robbery team would also be joined by John 'Little Legs' Lloyd. He was an old-school villain from across the river in the East End but he'd moved to Kent with his wife Jeanie and had long been accepted by the south-east London criminal fraternity as one of their own. Lloyd was renowned as a hard-nosed blagger and a successful one at that. His name had been linked by the police to many of the most outrageous robberies of the 1970s. He was just the sort of pro that McAvoy and Robinson needed on their team for the Brink's-Mat job.

The A-Team, led by the debonair Terry Adams, introduced main players McAvoy and Robinson to a character called Brian 'The Milkman' Wright. He wasn't going to get his hands dirty with any actual robbery, but he was a renowned fixer with superb contacts. Wright and the Adams had known each other since childhood as their parents were Irish immigrants from north London.

His background presented a major problem for McAvoy

and Robinson. They didn't fully trust anyone from outside their own manor, but they had to get over their prejudices after being read the riot act by old-time financier The Fox, who believed the job could turn out to be bigger than anyone expected. He wanted the sort of expertise that would ensure no last-minute hitches, and if this meant calling in help from north of the river, then so be it.

The A-Team brought along one very extrovert character to the Big Job who seemed to flit effortlessly back and forth across the Thames without even raising an eyebrow. Mickey Green was nicknamed 'The Pimpernel' because of his extraordinary ability to avoid arrest. Green had first cut his criminal teeth as a robber in a notorious gang from Wembley, north-west London, in the late 1960s. But by the early 1980s he'd spread his wings far and wide and was well known to the underworlds of both London and southern Spain, as well as southern Ireland. He was an expert at laundering large amounts of stolen cash and knew all the tricks of the trade. Over the coming years he'd have a significant part to play in the Brink's-Mat story.

The Big Job that McAvoy and Robinson had dreamed of carrying out since they began thieving as teenagers was in danger of being taken over by a bunch of other faces from the London underworld before the planning for it had even been completed. McAvoy was struggling to retain control and leadership, and it made him short-tempered at just the time when he knew it was crucial to remain patient and wait for the perfect moment to raid the Brink's-Mat warehouse. Inside man Tony Black nervously told his brother-in-law Brian Robinson and Mickey McAvoy that he'd overheard mention of a 'fuckin' huge' quantity of money *and* gold that was imminently going to be stored overnight between flights to and from the United States.

Black revealed that Brink's-Mat had stepped up security at the warehouse in recent weeks, presumably because of the larger than usual quantities of cash and gold that were coming in. He told Robinson about all the latest alarm and security systems in place in the building, and even drew a diagram of the entrances, corridors and connecting doors. Robinson pressurized Black into making sure that he would inform them when an extra-large consignment was on its way to the warehouse.

Early on the evening of Friday, 25 November 1983, Tony Black rang Robinson from a phone box on his way home from work to say that a big shipment had just been delivered but it was only going to be in the warehouse until the following lunchtime.

At last the Big Job was on.

SIX

HOUNSLOW, WEST LONDON, 6.25 a.m., 26 NOVEMBER 1983

If it wasn't for the CCTV cameras and spotlights mounted on the walls of Unit 7, a steel-and-brick-built box on a scruffy trading estate near Heathrow airport, it's unlikely the building would have caught the attention of even the most curious of onlookers. But when the huge orange-and-white armoured shutter doors rolled open, its real purpose was revealed. Chunky dark-blue Brink's-Mat vans with barred and tinted black windows came and went from the well-protected loading-bay day and night. Unit 7 wasn't Fort Knox or the Bank of England, but it did hold one of Britain's biggest safes, used to store currency, precious metals and other high-value consignments en route for Heathrow airport.

It was still pitch black and icy cold that Saturday morning as the early shift of workers waited outside kicking their heels and blowing clouds of condensation while waiting for the 6.30 a.m. 'opening time'. This was when the automatic timer would neutralize the sophisticated alarm system, allowing the keys to be inserted without triggering the flashing lights, bells and alarms that were linked to the local police station and other security companies.

Security guard Richard Holliday had been the first to arrive in his beige Ford Consul. He was quickly followed by another guard, Ron Clarke, on his moped. Guards Peter Bentley and Robin Riseley pulled up moments later, and the four men mumbled greetings to one another. The fifth guard rostered for duty was Brian Robinson's brother-in-law, Tony Black. Typically, he was late, and still hadn't arrived when supervisor Michael Scouse, 37, drove up. Scouse, a former special constable, was the longest-serving member of staff on duty that day, with twelve years on the Brink's-Mat payroll. His seniority singled him out that morning as the 'keyman'.

Scouse entered the unit alone and locked the door behind him, leaving the crew outside while he went to a downstairs office and collected the key from the safe. This switched off the alarm system covering the perimeter walls and windows. He then went back to the main door to allow the rest of the crew in. The outside door was relocked from the inside before Scouse reactivated the alarm system, climbed the stairs and walked through to the radio-control room to look through the paperwork for the day's duties. Meanwhile, the other four guards went into the rest room to take off their coats. Holliday paused briefly to switch on the radio-room aerials and the surveillance cameras before joining his mates. Just then the doorbell rang. The guards heard Scouse go downstairs to let in guard Tony Black, who was ten minutes late.

'You look a bit rough,' quipped guard Bentley as Black walked into the rest room. The 31-year-old Black did indeed look pale, unkempt and apprehensive, as if he had just clambered out of bed and raced to work. He confirmed Bentley's suspicion that he had overslept, then, mumbling something about having to use the toilet, he disappeared downstairs again.

Riseley glanced at his watch. It was 6.40 a.m.

Robbers Brian Robinson, Mickey McAvoy, Tony White, Brian Perry and two other men were sitting in a stolen blue Transit van on the Heathrow trading estate, waiting for their inside man Black to give them the signal. Black would then let them into the Brink's-Mat warehouse where, the gang had been told, there were goods – gold, cash and jewellery – worth up to £3m. Thanks to Tony Black, the robbers even knew which of the two security guards had the combination numbers to allow access to the safes located in the vaults.

Black hadn't gone to the toilet. He had gone to the front door to let McAvoy and his gang in.

Brink's-Mat's so-called state-of-the-art vault in their warehouse was protected by nothing more than a single, fixed surveillance camera inside the building which was on the opposite side to the main door to the vault. There was an alarm on the door, which sounded when the gang pushed their way in, but no one could possibly hear it upstairs, nor was it connected to anything outside the trading estate.

*

'Get on the floor or you're fuckin' dead.'

The masked figure filling the doorway of the rest room upstairs spat out the words in a harsh cockney accent, motioning urgently to the stunned guards with a 9 mm Browning automatic. Robin Riseley dived from his chair to the floor, quickly followed by Clarke and Holliday.

'The first thing I knew,' recalled Riseley, the guard who, along with Scouse, had the combination numbers, 'was a man pointing a semi-automatic pistol at my face and telling us all to hit the floor.'

From the ground, Riseley caught a brief glimpse of a white man, about 5 feet 8 inches tall and wearing a trilby hat and a dark car coat or anorak over a black blazer, black trousers and a black tie. He might have been dressed for a funeral but for the yellow balaclava that covered all but his eyes.

For a tense beat or two nothing happened. Someone later called it a hesitant silence. Then the gunman with the Browning automatic made a move that was to earn him the nickname 'The Bully' among the guards. Without a word, he jerked his weapon arm upwards and – a silver blazer button glinting in the neon light – smashed the weapon down on the back of guard Peter Bentley's neck.

The guard had angered him by being too slow to react when the door first crashed open. Believing it to be a colleague playing one of their regular practical jokes, he'd stood by the sink continuing to make the tea. As he slumped to the ground, Bentley's head hit the table and then the floor, dazing him momentarily and opening up two deep, bloody gashes in his scalp. The attacker's gun arm then calmly beckoned through the open door to someone waiting outside, and three more robbers rushed into the room.

'Lie still and be fuckin' quiet,' ordered The Bully, as his henchmen began to immobilize the terrified guards, yanking their arms behind their backs and handcuffing them, before binding their legs together at the shins with heavy-duty tape. Cloth bags with strings were then pulled down over the guards' heads and fastened around their necks.

One of the guards was close enough to the gunman to distinguish the herringbone pattern of the tweed hat and the crispness of his starched white shirt. He even saw a lock of fair hair protruding from the balaclava as the bag was placed over his head.

Bentley felt hands roughly pulling at the house and car keys on his belt. Then his watch was snatched off and thrown across the room. Blood from his throbbing head trickled down his face and neck. A moment later a voice – sounding almost sympathetic – asked if he was okay. Bentley nodded and the drawstring was loosened a little.

Meanwhile Holliday was finding it difficult to breathe. Thrashing about on the floor, he attracted the attention of one of the robbers who bent down and untied the drawstring, pulling the bag back to clear his upper lip. To ease the discomfort further he was turned on his back. Ron Clarke was similarly treated, first roughly bound, then casually asked if he was in any distress.

Moments later another robber spoke – this time with no discernible accent – and barked out orders. 'Get that radio tuned in. If you hear anything, tell us,' he ordered one of the other robbers. The guards immediately realized that this man was the 'commanding officer'.

Seconds later several of the robbers left the room. Then a radio crackled through frequencies as it tuned in to a Metropolitan Police wavelength. There was precious little happening outside the Brink's-Mat warehouse: two police officers could be heard discussing a spot-check on a vehicle, but there was nothing else. Two members of the gang then returned and hauled Holliday to his feet before dragging him down the corridor into the locker room.

He was then lowered to the floor and pushed back against a girder. They tried to handcuff him to the steel strut but failed because it was too large for his arms to encircle. He was handcuffed to a radiator instead. Fellow guard Ron Clarke was then hauled in and handcuffed to the same radiator. They were left alone to listen to the noises echoing in the vault directly below them.

Senior guard Scouse was pulled to his feet in the rest room and dragged outside into the corridor, where he was thrown against a wall.

'Breathe in,' ordered one of the robbers.

Scouse felt his shirt being pulled up to his chin and then a hand tugged violently at his waistband.

'Breathe in deeply or you'll get fuckin' cut.' Just then the knife sliced through his belted jeans from the buckle to the crutch. As Scouse filled his lungs he became aware of an overpowering smell. Had a rag been waved under his nose?

Scouse and Riseley had been identified earlier by Tony

Black as the men who held the combinations. Now their ordeal was about to begin in earnest.

Risely recalled: 'They slipped a hood on my head and then there was a knife in the crotch of my trousers and before I could say anything they were down round my ankles and there was a liquid being poured on me.'

Scouse recalled: 'I heard this voice say, "If we don't get what we want, if the police turn up or the alarms go off I'll . . ."'

Then the voice stopped momentarily.

'D'you recognize that smell?'

One robber – later identified as Mickey McAvoy – then poured petrol into Scouse's lap. The next instant Scouse felt the fuel seeping into his genitals.

'You'd better do as I fuckin' say, or I'll put a match to the petrol and a bullet through your fuckin' head,' said McAvoy. 'I know you live in a flat in Ruislip High Street above a TV rental shop. We've been watching you for nine months and setting this up for twelve. Now, let's get on with it. You have two numbers.'

The two guards were taken down to the vault, which they believed held a million pounds in used banknotes. Scouse punched in his half of the combination, but when Riseley was pushed forward to complete the sequence there was a problem. Riseley later recalled: 'The company had just changed the combinations and I hadn't memorized the new one, so the safe wouldn't open. They felt I was messing about. I heard someone say: "It looks like we got a hero," and he started rattling a matchbox in front of my face and then pulled out a diver's knife and said he was going to castrate me if I didn't give him the numbers. He was furious. Well, I was doing my best.'

After twenty minutes of trying and failing to break into the safe the robbers turned their attention to the drums and boxes scattered around the floor. As they opened the various lids and discovered scrap silver, degraded platinum and highly traceable travellers' cheques, it seemed the job was going to end in disappointment.

With a gun in his back, Risely finally coughed up the half of the numbers that he knew after bravely refusing to reveal them at first. After they had been punched in, he looked over his shoulder and declared that the alarms were now neutralised. The robbers were finally inside Unit 7's vault.

It was shortly before 7 a.m. and the fluorescent lighting revealed a carpet of drab grey containers, no bigger than shoeboxes, bound with metal straps and bearing handwritten identification codes. One of the robbers marched up to one of the unprepossessing cartons in the corner and snapped off its lid.

Inside were twelve perfectly formed bars of pure gold. As if to check they weren't dreaming, the robbers prised off a few more lids to reveal the same awesome sight.

It was an enormous amount to be held in one place at a one time, more than the gang could ever have imagined. There was a total of 60 boxes containing 6,800 gold bars, weighing a total of 3½ tons and worth £26,369,778.

They also found several hundred thousand pounds in used banknotes locked in three safes. One pouch contained travellers' cheques worth £200,000. In the other were polished and rough diamonds valued at £113,000.

As box after box was opened and the veritable Aladdin's cave of treasure was revealed, the atmosphere became increasingly electrified as – with scarcely concealed excitement – the gang hurriedly began passing bars to their battered Transit. Soon this unexpected windfall was starting to make the vehicle's axles bend under the weight. More than one eyewitness later reported seeing an old van with a wheezing engine riding very low on its suspension through the streets of nearby Hounslow.

No one within the robbers' immediate circle had any experience of dealing with this amount of gold – the gang had been expecting to find only cash – so the call for help in dealing with this incredible haul would have to be put out far and wide.

The robbers gathered up everything they could cram into the van as the time ticked away. The atmosphere was buzzing as the team moved the last of the gold out of the side of the loading bay and into the vehicle. Virtually no words were exchanged, as one of them said later: 'You could have cut the silence in half. It was that tense.' As that rusting old transit van eventually scraped its way out of the warehouse, none of the robbers could have known that they were in possession of something so dangerous that it would eventually cost many of them and their associates their lives. Inside the van, Mickey McAvoy and the rest of his team sat in complete, stunned silence as the enormity of what they had just done began to sink in. 'We just couldn't believe we had just pulled it off and we kept looking in the back of the van where the gold was, as if it might just disappear and we'd wake up from a dream,' Brian Perry told one criminal associate many years later.

Back in the warehouse, the alarm was raised when a local mechanic who was servicing one of the Brink's-Mat vans had a problem with the vehicle's alarm system and called the warehouse only to be told by a terrified security guard: 'Phone the fuckin' police. We've been turned over.' He immediately slammed the phone down and rang 999.

The lives of a lot of people – both innocent and not so innocent – were about to be blighted forever.

SEVEN

McAvoy and Robinson and the rest of the gang split up after a quick meeting at a south London 'flop house' following the raid. They were all under strict instructions not to communicate with each other for at least a month. Usually at flop houses the proceeds are split between the robbers, but on this occasion the team all agreed that they would have to sit on all the gold for some time before starting to turn it into hard cash.

Not all the robbers were happy about this arrangement, but McAvoy and Robinson made it clear that there was no choice in the matter. However the sheer size of the gold bullion haul was only the start of their problems. McAvoy later told one associate that all the gang members knew only too well that the police would be put under enormous pressure to solve the robbery because of the vast amount of gold that had been stolen. In one fell swoop, the gang had single-handedly humiliated the long arm of the law.

Scotland Yard commander Frank Cater needed the Brink's-Mat job like he needed the proverbial hole in the head. Months before the raid, another firm of London robbers had coolly taken £6m in used banknotes during an Easter 1983 robbery on a Security Express depot in London's East End. On that occasion a guard had also been doused in petrol.

That job had been dubbed the 'Crime of the Decade' by the tabloids. Cater wondered if the same gang was now also responsible for the Brink's-Mat raid. Before these two heists the previous holder of the title had been the Great Train Robbery, which took place near Leighton Buzzard, in Bedfordshire, in 1963, and that had netted a relatively paltry £2m.

One senior detective described the Brink's-Mat raid to one reporter as a 'typical Old Kent Road armed robbery, executed with customary efficiency and ruthlessness'. The police knew perfectly well which corner of London to concentrate their inquiries in. But breaking down the barriers that existed between the law and the gangsters was another thing altogether.

Less than a day after the Brink's-Mat robbery, Lloyds of London announced a reward of £2m for information leading to the return of the stolen gold, which had already leapt in value by more than twenty pounds an ounce since the robbery had taken place.

Rather than disappear in the days following the robbery, McAvoy and Robinson told the other gang members to make sure they were seen around their usual haunts, because if they went to ground it would be sure to alert the police to their involvement. Not surprisingly – as word spread across the underworld about the magnitude of the job and the vast amount of gold that had been stolen –

various top London faces let it be known that they would be pitching for the 'rights' to turn all that gold into ready cash. 'The robbery was the simple bit. Now the real fun would begin,' said one of those criminals who knew the raid would end up as an excuse for other villains to muscle in on McAvoy and Robinson's Big Job.

Initially McAvoy and Robinson steadfastly refused to see any of these villains because they didn't want to give the law any excuse to pull them in. They believed they'd get away with their audacious crime if they kept cool and low-key, but there was one obvious fly in the ointment – Robinson's brother-in-law Tony Black. He wasn't a villain and was, in the words of one robber, 'bricking himself'. Robinson got a message to Black telling him not to worry, and although the police would probably pull him in as an obvious inside man, as long as he said nothing they would never be able to get proof of his involvement.

Of the six Brink's-Mat guards on duty that morning, Tony Black stuck out to the police like Ronnie Kray at a boy scouts' meeting. The fact that Black had been out of sight of the others in the minutes before the raid was significant, and within hours of the raid being carried out the police began to put together some damning intelligence on Black. Not least of which was that he had a brother-in-law called Brian Robinson.

The police knew all about Robinson. Over the previous two years, he'd escaped prosecution on two armed robbery charges. One was thrown out by a magistrate because of insufficient evidence; the other, for handling money taken in an armed raid, was dropped when the Director of Public Prosecutions (DPP) also decided there was not enough evidence to bring a conviction.

But the police decided to bide their time when it came to Tony Black, so they held off arresting him and instead put a shadow on him in the hope he might lead detectives to the actual robbers. It looked as if McAvoy and Robinson's strict instruction to the whole team that none of the blaggers should even see each other was a good plan. The same applied to any further contact with the 'wobbly' Tony Black, who they all knew was the weakest link of the entire Brink's-Mat job. For almost a week, Black was shadowed by police and seen making numerous, nervy-looking calls from phone boxes. However, it seemed that he never actually got to talk to whoever it was he was calling, because he'd end up slamming the phone down and cursing as he left phone box after phone box.

Black and the other guards were eventually called back to the warehouse to help police make a video reconstruction of exactly what had happened. Afterwards, police were struck by how nervous Black looked throughout the reconstruction, although they knew that wasn't enough evidence in itself to arrest him. They needed a confession, and they were sure that would come with time. The 'let him stew' philosophy was a tried-and-trusted police technique and it looked sure to work this time as well. The police just needed to bide their time and Tony Black would eventually crumble.

At 8 a.m. on Sunday, 4 December – just eight days after

the Brink's-Mat robbery – all six guards on duty the day of the robbery were taken to Hounslow police station for questioning. In fact it was all a charade, because only Tony Black was properly interrogated. For six hours he was questioned and re-questioned about his movements on the day of the robbery and subsequently. Eventually, Scotland Yard investigator Detective Inspector Tony Brightwell rose to his feet and told Black: 'There are certain points which have arisen as a result of the original statement which you made, the video reconstruction of events and during this interview . . . to put it bluntly, we are not happy with your story. We will leave you to have a rethink.'

The detective and his colleague then left the interview room and – using yet another tried-and-trusted police tactic – let him sweat for more than an hour while they discussed his story over coffee in the canteen. Brightwell and his colleague returned to the interview room at 4.52 p.m. They were certain of their ground, and the investigators planned to deliver what they hoped would be their *coup de grâce*.

They deliberately took their time taking down Black's statement all over again – going through every detail with him – in order to rack up the tension. It wasn't until the early hours of the following day – 5 December 1983 – that a detective sergeant accompanied by two colleagues completed Black's twenty-one-page statement after more than eight hours of questioning. Put simply, they wore Tony Black down until he told them about his involvement.

Afterwards, Black admitted to investigators: 'I'm feeling much better now. It's like a weight off my mind. It was just too big. I couldn't handle it. There's one thing though.

I'm worried about these people, what they're going to do to me . . .'

Minutes later Commander Frank Cater entered the room and waved his three detectives out. They believed they already knew the identity of one of Robinson's accomplices. Black said that he thought the surname of the big man known as 'Tony' was a notorious south London blagger called Tony White. Criminal intelligence had already confirmed that a Tony White and another criminal, Mickey McAvoy, were known acquaintances of Robinson. It was also known that White owned a vehicle similar to a car seen circling the trading estate a few days before the robbery.

The three detectives who'd left the interview room went straight downstairs to collect the mugshots they'd already put to one side from police files. There were two folders, each containing twelve photographs of various individuals. In each batch they placed mugshots of McAvoy and White.

Shortly before midnight, after Commander Cater had finished with Black, DS Branch pushed the carefully collated folders under Black's nose. The first file was opened, and the pictures spread across the table. Black immediately pointed to a photo of Mickey McAvoy.

'That's Mick,' he said. He had confirmed the detectives' suspicions. The photograph he pointed to was of the man the other guards had dubbed The Bully, aka Mad Mickey McAvoy.

They pushed the second folder over the table and Black again picked out another photo almost immediately.

'That's Tony,' he declared. It was a photograph of Tony White.

In the early hours of Tuesday, 6 December, Tony Black was led back to his cell, understandably wondering if he had just sentenced himself to death. The gang might be still out and about enjoying their liberty but detectives knew that it was only a matter of time before they'd have them under lock and key, thanks to Black.

'It was obvious from the start there had to be an inside man,' Detective Tony Brightwell later explained. When Brightwell decided to take all the guards back to the warehouse and film them, *in situ*, talking about the robbery, Black had quickly emerged as the only viable candidate. 'He was extremely nervous and, in my opinion, obviously lying. When the film was shown to the rest of the Flying Squad officers it was rather like watching a B-movie whodunnit where everyone sort of jeered when he came on.'

Black was not a professional criminal. Having made a full, detailed, confession, he then agreed with detectives to turn Queen's evidence. Out of the original six-man gang, he'd fingered three of them: Robinson, McAvoy and Tony White.

But detectives had decided to continue playing a waiting game for the time being. They suspected that once the trio knew that Black had grassed on them they'd probably try and make a run for it. The detectives were hoping the villains might first lead them to the gold. It was a risky strategy but the sheer magnitude of the raid meant that none of the usual rules applied.

PART TWO: THE AFTERMATH

London. December 1983.
Margaret Thatcher is in full swing.
Life's all about money, money, money.
And a team of professional villains have just nicked
  twenty-eight million quid.
It's the Crime of the Fuckin' Century

EIGHT

The Brink's-Mat gang knew that Tony Black had been picked up and was singing like the proverbial canary but now they faced a dilemma. If they stashed the gold and disappeared, it would be seen as clear confirmation that they'd been on the raid. They decided, instead, to stay put. In doing so they pinned their hopes on two factors; the first was strength of the alibis that they'd all created as a precaution to cover their tracks. The second was the belief that Black might still not actually crack to the point where he actually identified them, although they feared that that was highly unlikely.

Unsurprisingly, police surveillance experts at Scotland Yard's specialist C11 unit focused on Brian Robinson and Mickey McAvoy. Initially McAvoy proved to be cautious about his movements to the point of near-paranoia. But he then made a classic error by suddenly quitting his council house in Dulwich and moving into a mansion on the borders with Kent. He also bought two Rottweilers and named them Brink's and Mat. He'd clearly got his hands on some of the cash from the raid. Some of the other gang members were irritated by his 'clumsiness'. Keeping a low profile was paramount, but he just didn't seem to appreciate that and gave the impression of being more interested in making sure that the underworld knew he was 'the money'. But it wasn't just other criminals he was looking to send a message to. 'He couldn't resist it,' explained one old south London associate. 'Mickey hated the cozzers and he liked the idea of them "suffering" a bit. It was obvious all it would do was wind them up and make them even more determined to nick him. He should have just sat tight.'

Nevertheless, police continued to 'sit' on McAvoy, Robinson and White following Black's confession, watching and waiting in the hope at least one of them might lead the cops to the gold. It turned into a stand-off. The villains didn't want to arouse the cops' suspicions and the cops didn't want to show their cards in case they hadn't got enough to make any charges stick. It was a typical game of cat and mouse.

In the end the police decided they had to swoop, just in case the suspected robbers disappeared.

In the early hours of a cold December morning, eleven days after the bullion robbery, Tony White, Mickey McAvoy and Brian Robinson were taken to separate police stations. By making sure they couldn't communicate with each other, the cops were looking to prevent them working out that they'd been grassed up by Black. It was imperative that the men were kept separate so they did not communicate with each other. Another three people were also detained in relation to the handling of the proceeds from the raid. They were White's wife Margaret, McAvoy's first wife Jacqueline and Mrs Patricia Dalligan, who lived at the house in south-east London where Black claimed the robbery had been planned.

In the interrogation room at Heathrow police station, Tony White was surly and uncommunicative and denied all knowledge of the robbery. Police wanted to know why there were groceries in the boot of his car and packed suitcases in his bedroom. They also wanted to know why White's young son was not at home. Officers believed White had been expecting a visit when the police raid occurred and had sent his son away. They also reckoned he'd cleaned the house to remove any forensic evidence that might have linked him to the raid.

'If I sit here with my mouth shut, you haven't got fuck-all. I know that,' White told one officer.

At West Drayton police station, near Heathrow, Brian Robinson was also cautioned. He gave them what appeared to be a cast-iron alibi. The detectives rolled their eyes and took it down, knowing full well that professionals like Robinson always cooked up an alibi before any job. Over at Chiswick police station, Mickey McAvoy was proving just as frustrating for police officers.

By the end of the following day, all the detectives involved in interrogating the three men compared notes. Robinson had politely denied any wrongdoing; White had been aggressively blunt; and McAvoy had maintained a stony silence. Robinson had a detailed alibi backed up by his wife, his sick mother and a brother, who would all have to be interviewed by detectives. White could bank only on the word of his wife to confirm a Saturday morning lie-in. McAvoy would not divulge his alibi unless his solicitor was there to hear it.

The police had Black's detailed confession, but so far the only evidence against the three men was circumstantial, and there was not much of that. Naturally, all three men had refused to sign the contemporaneous notes of the interviews because they feared this might incriminate them. They knew that the veracity of the unsigned records could therefore be questioned in court. Any mistakes the three robbers might have made, any slips that opened up a chink in their armour, could be dismissed as fabrication. Without signatures at the bottom of each page, any such documents could be labelled so-called 'verbals', a well-known practice of corrupt officers at that time, in which prisoners' statements were completely fabricated in order to guarantee their guilt.

Within a few days, legal wrangles in the high court looked set to release all those who'd been pulled in by the police in relation to the Brink's-Mat robbery. The starring role went to a lawyer whose legal skills would be called upon by a number of other people involved in turning the Brink's-Mat gold into cash.

Tony White's brief, Henry Milner, was an engaging public-school-educated character who specialized in representing people accused of serious crimes such as armed robbery. He issued a writ of habeas corpus (essentially a demand that the detained individuals had the chance to go before a judge rather than be held indefinitely without a trial) on behalf of all six people held by police in connection with the raid.

'Mr Milner' – as all his clients called him – had already earned himself the respect of some of the most powerful criminals in London. He had no fears about the twilight world of gangland crime and he was not even shy about saying how he'd helped turn cases around, especially if his clients had been 'verballed up'. He once explained: 'It's a lot of fun defending criminal cases.'

Henry Milner's north London upbringing, Jewish boarding school education in Oxfordshire and degree at the London School of Economics couldn't be further removed from the backgrounds of the Brink's-Mat robbery gang. At weekends, Mr Milner retreated even further from the London underworld by pursuing his three hobbies: Tottenham Hotspur, bridge and traditional American music. But to his clients he remained the man they could trust to try and get them out of the tightest spots imaginable.

Legal eagle Mr Milner's one-man operation offered an exclusive service to ten or twelve rich clients a year. Mr Milner offered an entirely personal service, and all his clients came through word of mouth. His modest office was squeezed between two jewellery shops in London's Hatton Garden. His only employee, secretary Eileen, had worked for him for many years. Though Mr Milner's tiny waiting room had nothing but a handful of glossy mags to flick through, the lawyer's own office was panelled with dark oak and constantly filled with clouds of smoke from his ever-present fat Cuban cigars. They sat on his desk in a walnut veneer box crafted in a prison workshop and sent to him by a former client.

Mr Milner's first big professional breakthrough as a brief

had come back in 1978 when he represented one of London's best-known faces who, as Mr Milner later admitted, 'appeared at the Old Bailey as regularly as Frank Sinatra at the Albert Hall'. Mr Milner's 'lovable rogue' was eventually acquitted of criminal charges in six successive court cases. That was when word went out that Henry Milner was a brief to be trusted.

Mr Milner was once asked if there were any cases he wouldn't handle. He responded: 'That's a difficult question because I do a lot of cases the public finds distasteful, like drugs. But I have never handled cases involving sexual offences on elderly people or young children.'

Luckily, Mr Milner was a born optimist. 'You've got to look confident even if you don't feel it,' he explained. 'If you show a weakness or fear they will jump on it. Defendants are as shrewd as anything. They know whether you are on the ball.'

Mr Milner didn't have a close relationship with any of his heavyweight clients, especially the so-called superstar gangsters. He said he'd never been out socializing with them apart from having the occasional sandwich at lunchtime. One retired blagger explained: 'Mr Milner's a real pro. A complete gent. He doesn't have to hang around with the likes of us to understand the criminal mind. The guy's bloody brilliant. If you've got him on side you're about fifty per cent more likely to walk out of court a free man. He's a tasty operator.'

Mr Milner prided himself on always having complete control of a case. That meant deciding which witnesses to call, influencing a counsel's closing speech and occasionally putting his foot down. He was also renowned for picking top barristers with a knack of winning.

Unsurprisingly, Mr Milner was well accustomed to the age-old question from many of his clients. 'What are my chances?' To his credit, he always gave them the straightest possible answer. Although he did once admit to a journalist: 'You start with "hopeless", "very, very poor", "fifty per cent", "evens" or "quite good". If you put it above "good", you're in trouble if they're found guilty.'

So when Brink's-Mat came around in 1983, Mr Milner was sitting pretty to receive a windfall of clients. First through the door was Tony White, followed by McAvoy. Others would soon pay a visit.

Back in court that day, less than a month after the robbery, Victor Durand QC read a sworn statement by Henry Milner that, in effect, challenged the police to charge all six prisoners or release them. At that time the law clearly stipulated how long police were allowed to hold suspects in custody without a charge, unless it was under the Prevention of Terrorism Act. Durand informed the judge, Mr Justice Taylor, that all the prisoners had been denied their right to legal advice, and Milner's statement said he had repeatedly asked for access to the prisoners but had been stopped from seeing them by Flying Squad officers.

When counsel representing Scotland Yard replied that the habeas corpus action would be defended, the case was adjourned until the next morning, but it never reopened. At 9.30 that night White was charged, followed by Robinson and McAvoy. The other three were released. The next morning the three robbery suspects were brought to Feltham magistrates' court and remanded in custody on the charge of stealing gold and other valuables worth £28m from the Brink's-Mat warehouse, near Heathrow airport.

Back in west London, detectives investigating the Brink's-Mat robbery suspected that John 'Little Legs' Lloyd was one of the original six members of the gang who robbed the warehouse. Lloyd had disappeared after being tipped off that the police were onto him. Indeed he didn't resurface again until nine years later when he insisted that he hadn't been one of the robbers and the Crown Prosecution Service announced that there was insufficient evidence to proceed against him. Despite claims that he was thousands of miles from London, for much of the time Lloyd was actually in the capital and Kent. Yet such was Lloyd's status in his old haunts that he could drink and live openly without the police ever being informed. That was a measure of the criminal respect for Little Legs.

Amongst the criminal fraternity, the Brink's-Mat robbery had already become the stuff of legends. The tabloids quickly dubbed it 'The Robbery of the Century' while others referred to it as a 'brilliantly executed raid'. To stumble upon so much gold and then get away with enough to set dozens of people up financially for life was the sort of dream scenario that few villains could ever hope for, even if three of the robbers had already been arrested.

But the sheer size of the Brink's-Mat haul of gold bullion continued to create a huge problem because the gang needed a mechanism, a conduit through which the gold could travel. It had to be smelted and sold back into the gold industry before it could be turned into cash.

In the south London underworld there was a great fear that Robinson, McAvoy and White would turn supergrasses in exchange for lighter sentences. McAvoy and Robinson were particularly outraged by such rumours because informing on their criminal associates was something they would *never* even vaguely consider.

The gang had to look outside their close circle of associates to find people to handle the gold. Though the three members behind bars were still pulling the strings, they inevitably had to allow others to get involved, something that made the whole laundering operation even more risky. After using a wobbly character like Tony Black as their 'inside man', this turned out to be the second big mistake they made. Here were villains who'd known each other for years, and now they were having to put their trust in people such as Kenneth Noye, introduced to the gang by John 'Little Legs' Lloyd. McAvoy and Robinson had heard many whispers about Noye. Some even said he was a police grass. Those sorts of accusations are thrown around in all heavy criminal circles, and they are usually taken with a pinch of salt. But the amount of gold involved was so large that everyone felt as if they were treading on thin ice. One false move and they would either be dead or in prison.

Kenneth Noye and his associate Brian Reader had taught themselves everything there was to know about gold over the previous few years. The precious metal had become a favourite commodity with which to swindle the British government out of value-added tax (VAT), a fifteen per cent premium levied on a variety of goods, including items made from gold, when they were sold. Paid at the time by the buyer to the person selling the gold, it should then have been returned to HM Customs and Excise.

In his initial discussions with them, Noye had convinced McAvoy and Robinson that not only was he the best man to help them turn the gold into cash, but that there were a variety of scams that could easily be operated in order to deprive the taxman of his share. One was to smuggle gold into the country, then sell it to a reputable dealer. The fifteen per cent VAT would then be pocketed by the smugglers.

Another scam was to draw up documents showing that the gold had been exported immediately after its arrival in Britain, which meant it was not liable for VAT. The honest trader, meanwhile, would still have to pay the fifteen per cent VAT to the 'company' selling him the metal. That 'company', usually based in short-let office accommodation, would fold within a matter of months without making any VAT returns.

Although similar scams could have been worked on other goods that were subject to VAT, gold was particularly suitable because its high value meant large returns with a minimum of delay. It also had an official price, fixed twice daily by the London gold market, so the smugglers did not have to worry about commercial competitors undercutting their prices, and it was compact and easy to transport.

In the early 1980s, VAT frauds in general had one further major attraction – the maximum penalty for indulging in the racket was just two years' imprisonment. Small wonder then that VAT fraud involving gold had grown increasingly popular among well-organized, professional criminals in the London underworld. Kenneth Noye was one of the top operators in that field.

It was around this time that residents in Jenton Avenue, Bexleyheath, on the suburban edges of south London and Kent, began noticing some strange activity at a house occupied by Kenneth Noye's elderly parents. Almost every Saturday for years Noye and his wife Brenda had visited his mother and father with their sons Kevin and Brett.

But in the weeks following the Brink's-Mat robbery, Brenda began turning up at the bungalow at least an hour before Noye arrived in his Ford pick-up. Noye was then seen by neighbours carrying what looked like very heavy batteries from his pick-up through to the garage next to his father's house.

An hour or so later, Noye would emerge from the bungalow with more 'batteries' which he carefully laid on the flatbed of the pick-up truck before driving off. Brenda Noye and the children followed shortly afterwards in the family Range Rover or Ford Granada. Noye went through exactly the same routine every Saturday morning for months following the Brink's-Mat robbery. It was only a long time later that the neighbours put two and two together. Lugging those heavy bars across the forecourt to his parent's house wasn't easy, and other residents in the classically suburban street must have wondered what he was doing. However, typically, they were afraid to 'interfere'.

But there were other problems with handling gold. The

true origin of ingots of gold had to be disguised, and that meant removing identification numbers and assay marks. Many ingots carried their own individually designed hallmarks to signify their purity and, in some cases, a serial number. Absolutely pure gold does not exist – some contamination is always present, however expertly the metal has been refined. But bars with the number 9999 meant they were 99.99 per cent pure, the highest level to which the metal can be refined, while 999 bars, known in the trade as ten-tola bars (a tola being an ancient Indian unit of weight) were only marginally less pure.

To pull off any scam involving gold, any villains – or receivers to whom it was sold – as well as removing the identifying marks, had to disguise the purity of the bars. Failure to do so would create a risk that legitimate traders would quickly become suspicious that the quantities they were being asked to buy were either smuggled gold or stolen bullion.

That meant specialized smelting equipment was needed, the sort sold by only a handful of shops in Britain, most of them in the Hatton Garden area of central London, internationally renowned as a centre for the jewellery trade. Such shops were on their guard against suspicious customers ordering smelters, so the gang would have to tread very carefully.

A month after the robbery, Flying Squad officer Bill Miller got a tip-off that a man had been seen in London's Hatton Garden jewellery district trying to buy an industrial gold smelter. A week later Miller was undercover in Worcestershire, watching a smelter being loaded into the back of a gold Rolls-Royce. 'He was easy to follow because the smelter was too big for the Rolls and the boot wouldn't close,' explained Miller. 'So we followed him all the way back to Kent.' The car was parked up outside a cottage while the driver went inside.

Miller stayed with the vehicle all night and was relieved by a specialist surveillance team in the morning. When the driver returned to the car, the team followed on behind. 'Within five minutes they lost him,' Miller later recalled. When they returned to the cottage later in the day the smelter had gone.

The driver of that Rolls-Royce was a man called Mickey Lawson, who happened to be best friends with Kenneth Noye. Lawson's and Noye's children knew each other, and their wives played squash together. Lawson had actually purchased the smelter from William Allday and Company in Stourport-on-Severn. The Rolls-Royce would soon be regularly seen at Noye's house in Kent. One of Lawson's fingerprints would eventually be found inside that same house. The operating instructions for the smelter they had seen in the back of the Rolls-Royce were later found in Kenneth Noye's shed.

Lawson later insisted to police that the furnace had been bought by him on behalf of a mystery Arab who had taken it from him shortly after he'd purchased it. Lawson claimed he'd bought the furnace under a false name for VAT purposes. But in the weeks and months following the robbery, Lawson was one of the villains who found themselves under the watchful eyes of detectives.

Besides increasing their knowledge of the gold business,

the Brink's-Mat gang also had to constantly keep improving their contacts. Successful fences would always be looking for new ways of cultivating police contacts, but with a haul like Brink's-Mat, making new contacts to help turn the gold into cash became an urgent need. The gang members already in custody had their own 'favourite' detectives to whom they'd be constantly suggesting ways in which they could 'help each other' over certain matters. But the gang also began to speak to more and more members of the criminal fraternity. Something that made them increasingly uncomfortable

Meanwhile new members of the gang's outer circle were starting to get more deeply involved following the arrest of McAvoy, Robinson and White. Take Kenneth Noye. He took on a senior role, much to the annoyance of the actual robbers, who nonetheless had little choice in the matter. Noye was a master manipulator who prided himself on having his finger in dozens of pies, from bent coppers to crooked judges. He boasted of 'owning' an MP in south-east London.

Noye befriended a blonde woman who was working as a civilian at a Kent police station, not far from his home in West Kingsdown. Noye persuaded the woman to meet for a drink after work one night. They began a passionate affair and she provided him with information about the progress of the Brink's-Mat investigation. When Noye discovered he was sharing the woman's affections with a senior detective it only made the affair even more exciting and 'productive'.

Once the police began to watch Noye more regularly

over the coming months, its surveillance teams soon established that besides gold, Kenneth Noye had another obsession – women. He was even finding time to have an affair with Jenny Bishop, the wife of one of his oldest friends, and had bought her a £50,000 townhouse in Dartford which he'd furnished from upmarket Harrods at a cost of more than £20,000 (costing £250,000 and £60,000 respectively at today's prices). Noye considered the property a good investment. It was also much cheaper and safer than a hotel.

The Brink's-Mat gang had befriended many detectives in both the Kent force and the Met long before the actual robbery took place. Some of them had even been asked to CID functions and parties held inside police stations. Naturally many of those officers who knew the gang members were now stepping back from the investigation, fearful that they might be 'smeared' by the robbers and their associates.

Out and about in their favourite pubs in south-east London and Kent, the remainder of the Brink's-Mat gang tried to gauge the intensity of the police investigation by speaking to certain second-division criminals, many of whom had their own contacts in the police.

Kenneth Noye and his criminal associates got close to the remaining three members of the Brink's-Mat robbery team during this period, although they were careful to ensure that the Brink's-Mat investigators did not observe them doing anything in connection with the stolen bullion.

On one occasion during the early stages of the investigation, Kenneth Noye and a number of other criminal faces attended the marriage of the daughter of one of south-east

London's best-known villains. A wedding photographer innocently started snapping away at Noye and some others. Noye immediately lost his temper, pushed the photographer up against a wall and removed the film from his camera. He had a particular aversion to having his photo taken, even at a public function such as a wedding. In this instance, Noye suspected the photographer might have been a policeman in disguise.

As his cousin Michael later told this author: 'Kenny didn't like any photos of himself to be floating around. He knew that if people outside his own circle didn't know what he looked like then he'd be able to move around much more easily.'

Despite the care he was taking, Noye was considered a 'bit of a bumpkin' by certain members of the actual Brink's-Mat robbery gang. After all, he'd never got his hands dirty carrying out the actual raid. He was simply there to turn the gold into cash.

As Kathy McAvoy – Mickey McAvoy's second wife – later explained: 'Noye wasn't from south-east London. He was from the Kent suburbs and that just isn't the same. Bexley-heath ain't south-east London in the true sense. Noye wasn't the real thing and he knew that others thought that, too.' There was also a feeling amongst some of the Brink's-Mat faces that 'outsiders' like Noye might not keep to the code of honour that existed between the team involved in the actual robbery.

At that same wedding where Noye threatened the photographer, he was seen alongside his old mate Brian Reader, one of south-east London's most notorious burglars. The two men had done some gold business together in 1981 that ended up earning them at least £200,000 each. No wonder they both believed they could clean up once they had their hands on all the Brink's-Mat gold.

The remaining members of the Brink's-Mat gang and its backers sat tight for the moment, believing that nothing was going to prevent them from eventually coming into a fortune. They began looking around for safe, 'straight' investments for the cash they believed would be raised from the gold. Some of them even began selling off their own legitimate businesses so that it gave them a perfect alibi for having so much cash swimming around. As one ex-robber explained: 'The cozzers were watching everyone closely and so selling businesses provided a legitimate reason to be in the money, so to speak. It was a wise move and it frustrated the police no end because they knew who was connected to the job, but they had fuck-all proof.'

Friends and family of the remaining robbers were kept in the dark about the sudden surge in transactions, although inevitably word started to get around that some of the robbers who'd escaped prosecution were falling into the classic trap of being too flash for their own good.

NINE

In the Scotland Yard archives there is an unsigned statement allegedly made by suspected robber Tony White in which he not only admits to being on the robbery, but wonders whether he can take the £2m reward if he returns his share of the gold. In this statement White is also said to have read Black's confession and told the police: 'I agree with the fucking thing, but I can't remember who done what, or where. Can't we leave it at that?' This was before the police were required to tape-record interviews, and at his later trial White would claim the statement was a police fiction. When Scotland Yard were asked to produce the relevant copy of Black's confession to see if White had left his fingerprints on it, they first claimed to have mislaid it, before eventually confirming that they had had the copy destroyed for security reasons.

Whilst this was going on, Kenneth Noye and his associates had formed an offshoot of the Brink's-Mat gang that was busily working out how to turn all the gold into cash. Soon Noye and his mob would be generating a virtual torrent of money. In the four months following the robbery, one bank handled transactions of more than

£10m, mainly in grubby plastic bags, no questions asked. To make it safe for use, it had to be carefully laundered to avoid being traced back to the raid.

And in the middle of all this, The Sweeney just couldn't fathom out how the gold was being turned into cash. The villains were taking the mickey out of Scotland Yard, and it was really riling various high-powered officers.

Two-timing Brink's-Mat guard Tony Black was quickly sentenced to six years' imprisonment. With remission for good behaviour he wouldn't serve more than four years, and was likely to get parole after just two. The sentence was accompanied by a grim warning from Judge David Tudor-Price: 'Never again will your life be safe. In custody you will be segregated at all times, and you and your family will forever be fugitives from those you so stupidly and so wickedly helped.'

Commander Frank Cater told the court that for the prisoner's own safety, he wanted Black to spend the time leading up to the trial of the three alleged robbers in police custody, rather than prison. The chief of detectives was utterly determined that nothing should stop Black from giving evidence when the time came. The application, which had been sanctioned at a senior level after talks between Deputy Assistant Commissioner Kelland and the Home Office, was readily granted.

On Monday, 25 October 1984, White, Robinson and McAvoy were brought before Judge Tudor-Price at the Old Bailey, the Central Criminal Court, to answer two counts each: those of conspiring to commit robbery and of robbery itself. All three pleaded not guilty.

Then Tony Black – nicknamed 'The Golden Mole' by the tabloids – stepped into the witness box and spent the following two and a half days giving evidence. He gave the court a full account of how Robinson 'persuaded' him to help the gang, and the subsequent meetings and phone calls that took place both before and after the robbery. Black admitted he was scared for his life. By the time he'd finished there was no doubt that both Robinson and McAvoy had been the two criminals Black had dealt with.

But Black's testimony provided little or no evidence against White, and none of the other guards had managed to identify him. White's extremely skilful counsel John Mathew QC also strongly challenged the accuracy of a statement White allegedly gave police after his arrest. When it was discovered that the log book from Heathrow police station containing the alleged statement had 'gone missing' it also seriously undermined the prosecution's attempt to prove a case against White.

The trial itself garnered enormous nationwide publicity which fuelled the legendary status of the Brink's-Mat robbery. It was portrayed in many papers as a cops-versus-robbers struggle. Behind the scenes the police knew their investigation had been far from successful, and they continued to knock doors down, trying to follow up any lead, any source they had in a bid to trace the gold and the rest of the criminals. When the media dubbed it the 'Crime of the Century' it rankled with many detectives who felt that they were far from finishing their inquiries.

After a month-long trial, Judge Tudor-Price explained to the jury that he would be summing up the case under five headings. The first would be the robbery itself and the 'uncontroversial' evidence of the 'five honest guards'. That would be followed by his consideration of Anthony Black's confessed involvement. Parts three, four and five would deal with the case against each of the accused.

At 10.42 on Thursday, 29 November 1984, Tudor-Price brought his careful and thoughtful summing-up to an end.

'Members of the jury,' said the judge, 'in this case allegations have flowed thick and fast, and it is for you to decide which ones have substance.'

It wasn't until 3.19 p.m. the following Sunday that the jury finally returned with a verdict. White was found not guilty. McAvoy and Robinson, however, were found guilty of robbery. All verdicts were delivered with a majority of ten to two.

Next morning the two robbers were each sentenced to twenty-five years' imprisonment. Without parole, Robinson, aged forty-one, would be sixty-six when due for release and McAvoy, thirty-three, would be fifty-eight. Yet both men replied to the sentences with a simple and polite 'Thank you.'

Back at his home in south-east London, Tony White broke his silence to a waiting horde of reporters. 'If I'm innocent, then the other two are innocent. The evidence was the same for all of us. None of the three of us were involved. The reason the police pulled us in was because they've wanted us for a long time, and were waiting for something like this to get us.'

For Black, Robinson, McAvoy and White the Brink's-Mat job was over. But as far as the police and many of the others connected to the Crime of the Century were concerned it was only just beginning.

Two days after Robinson and McAvoy were jailed at the Old Bailey, one of their criminal associates, Garth Chappell, withdrew £348,000 from the account of a company called Scadlynn, at Barclays Bank in Bedminster, Bristol. Over the next three weeks he took out another £1.1m from the same account. The withdrawals had actually been going on throughout the trial.

In total about £13m had been sitting in the account of Scadlynn. The money was laid out by respectable gold merchants such as Johnson Matthey and Engelhard as payment for large amounts of gold. Unbeknownst to the buyers, this had been smelted from the high-grade Brink's-Mat gold – using the smelter purchased from the foundry in Worcestershire and driven to Kent in the gold Rolls-Royce – mixed with copper to disguise its origins. The Assay Office in Sheffield, which was responsible for handing out hallmarks to jewellers and gold merchants, had been an unwitting accomplice in the laundering of the gold, even awarding Scadlynn a seal of approval which effectively gave the 'dirty gold' a clean bill of health.

The main player behind the smelting of the gold, besides Kenneth Noye, was a 31-year-old 'businessman' from Bath called John Palmer, later dubbed 'Goldfinger' for his alleged involvement in the handling of the Brink's-Mat gold. Amazingly, he would at one stage be ranked alongside the

Queen in 105th position on the *Sunday Times* Rich List.

But it wasn't just Noye who was active. The three other members of the actual Brink's-Mat robbery gang who had not been apprehended began coming out of the shadows in order to make sure they got a share of what they believed was rightfully theirs. But their way of asserting their position risked drawing the wrong kind of attention upon themselves. Suspected robber Brian Perry and his associate Gordon Parry began taking flights to Jersey, the Isle of Man, Switzerland, Spain and the United States.

Other members of the gang and their associates began purchasing big houses in Britain, which naturally alerted the so far powerless authorities to their financial affairs. As one investigator later explained: 'They should have just sat on it and invested it discreetly but in the end they couldn't resist chucking their cash around.'

Back on the mean streets of south-east London, various other firms continued to carry out armed robberies. Sources inside the underworld have confirmed to this author that members of the Brink's-Mat team helped finance some of these smaller blaggings. The Brink's-Mat robbery was already influencing everything from crime to property prices. In places such as the London Docklands, warehouses were suddenly at a premium because a number of them had already been bought with the proceeds of the robbery. And at this point the dramatic aftermath of the so-called Crime of the Century was only just beginning to reveal itself.

*

In November 1984 – a year after the robbery – south London villain Brian Reader met up with his old friend Kenneth Noye at Noye's wife Brenda's squash club, in Dartford, Kent, where they discussed how to convert yet more of the Brink's-Mat gold into cash. This time they agreed the price would be three per cent above the fix price (the price at which gold is sold on the bullion markets) and that deliveries of the gold would start after Christmas. Because of the number of forgeries flooding the market at that time, payment would be made in new £50 notes that could be easily verified.

With the middleman Reader happy to pay for the gold on these terms it was clear that a VAT fraud was being committed. Kenneth Noye was also well aware that such a complex operation, which needed dozens of people to run it, required high levels of organization. Noye should have been perfectly happy making over a million pounds a year out of his own lucrative role in handling the gold. After all, it had the potential to go on for years without any hindrance. But then he got greedy, and that's when the word started going out that Noye was *the man*. In other words, Noye was Handler Number One – the man who was now responsible for turning most of the gold into hard cash

By early January 1985 Brian Reader alone was reckoned to have handled Brink's-Mat gold that had come through Noye worth £3.66m. It was being smuggled to Britain from Holland – where it had been taken after the raid as part of a complex additional 'earner' involving VAT fraud on the gold itself – in the Tupperware lunchboxes of various lorry drivers who worked for a haulage company with close links to one of Noye's oldest Kent friends. The drivers took their vehicles to the quayside and left them to be shipped over to Britain unaccompanied – with the Tupperware boxes still on board. British drivers then picked up the lorries when they arrived and took them to their destination. Next Reader would collect the gold and take it back to his home in south-east London, from where Noye would pick it up a few days later.

It seemed like the perfect system to the two men, and they'd convinced themselves that they were on the verge of making more money than most people could even dream of. But when it comes to crime there is always a problem lurking around each corner.

TEN

To maintain an effective surveillance operation against Brink's-Mat handlers Noye and Reader, Scotland Yard needed to carefully reinforce their Brink's-Mat inquiry team. Following the successful convictions of Robinson and McAvoy it had been reduced to just twenty officers.

A new senior detective was drafted in to take charge of the investigation and build up the squad to full strength once more. That man was Acting Detective Chief Superintendent Brian Boyce, a former member of the anti-terrorist squad, who'd actually assumed that promotion opportunities had long since passed him by.

Boyce – the son of a West End barrow-boy – had one ambition on entering the police service: to become a top detective at Scotland Yard. Having achieved that aim (he was with Commander Frank Cater when the Kray twins were arrested) he had no desire to swap the gritty life of a detective out on the streets for the cosier confines of high office, complete with never-ending bureaucracy and Whitehall constantly breathing down his neck.

Brian Boyce had an air of determined independence about him. He was an accomplished jazz musician, a mountaineer of considerable prowess and a man with a strong interest in comparative religion. His was a professionalism born of sheer love for the job. He was also an officer who inspired great loyalty among Scotland Yard's elite detective force.

During his National Service twenty-six years earlier in Cyprus, where he helped track down EOKA guerrillas, Boyce had picked up some vital experience of surveillance and intelligence-gathering – knowledge he was able to use on the Brink's-Mat case. Boyce insisted that both Noye and Reader were put under even more rigorous surveillance in an operation that initially was to only involve C8 officers (C8 was the new title for the Flying Squad, though few people used it).

On Tuesday, 8 January 1985, detectives moved into position in a row of bushes by the public road in West Kingsdown, near the entrance of the long driveway to Kenneth Noye's home, Hollywood Cottage. Within minutes, at 9.05 a.m., they watched as Brian Reader's green Vauxhall Cavalier left Noye's home and drove back to his own house.

Twenty minutes after arriving, Reader left his house in Grove Park, shadowed by four unmarked Flying Squad cars. He drove to Cowcross Street in central London, close to Hatton Garden. He then parked up outside Farringdon Underground and mainline railway station and went to a telephone booth in the ticket hall to make a call.

One detective managed to walk close enough to Reader to see the phone number he was dialling. It turned out to belong to a nearby shop. Reader then walked out to the street, looked up and down, returned to the phone and dialled the number again. The same thing happened once more before Reader left the station and went into a café on the opposite side of the road.

Two detectives watched from a distance as Reader sat at a table in a booth with two other men. One of them was 24-year-old Tommy Adams, an asphalter by trade, but one who also happened to be a member of the notorious Adams family from north London. They'd been brought in as 'decent handlers' who would help provide a route for the gold to be turned into cash. The other man was a well-known figure around Hatton Garden, a gold dealer called Christopher Weyman who ran a business called Lustretone Ltd, in Greville Street.

Reader wrote something down on a piece of paper, which he showed to the two men. Next the three of them left the café and walked across the road to Reader's car. Adams leaned in and brought out what looked to be an unusually heavy, oblong parcel about one foot long. Adams then placed the parcel carefully in the boot of a nearby white Mercedes sports car, which Adams and Weyman drove away in.

Meanwhile back at Hollywood Cottage other detectives saw a Ford Granada belonging to Kenneth Noye's friend Michael Lawson drive up to the house. The Granada was being driven by a man aged about twenty. The same car left soon afterwards and was later spotted outside Noye's former home in Heaver Avenue, West Kingsdown, less than a mile away. That house was now owned by John 'Little Legs' Lloyd, one of the members of the Brink's-Mat gang who had never been apprehended by police.

That Tuesday afternoon Kenneth Noye was seen leaving Hollywood Cottage with another man in a blue Range Rover. Once again, C8 officers followed from a discreet distance.

After twelve miles they watched the Range Rover turn off the A20 Sidcup bypass into the secluded car park of the Beaverwood Club, a Spanish hacienda-style nightclub set back from the road behind a screen of trees. Noye stayed for five minutes before driving off again. Although the police did not realize it at the time, this was a special secret rendezvous spot used by Noye to meet Reader away from any prying eyes.

Police were in no doubt that Noye was the key to the distribution of the Brink's-Mat gold, but they knew that they had to move in closer to observe Noye if they wanted to gather concrete evidence. That would require a highly specialized team of undercover officers who could remain outside for long periods of time, no matter what the conditions.

As a result, C11 officers from the Met's Specialist Surveillance Unit took up position near Noye's house in West Kingsdown. They were a handpicked group, no more than eight in total, who had been trained in reconnaissance and close-target surveillance by specialists from the SAS. The C11 team training course included hiding beneath floorboards for three days at a time, in a gap just 18 inches high, and spending a similar length of time dug into a hole in the ground in open countryside.

Because Kenneth Noye lived in Kent, approval had to be obtained from the Kent police force since the operation was on their 'territory'. And that threw up a different set of problems.

When the Met had arrested Kenneth Noye back in 1977 for receiving stolen goods, they'd done so without the knowledge of the local force because they were well aware that Noye had 'friends' there. His relationships with certain Kent officers had long been of great concern to the Met. So it was decided that only the highest-ranking Kent officers should be put fully in the picture.

The C11 surveillance team working near Noye's house in West Kingsdown established a command centre in a ground-floor room in the Stacklands Retreat House, a convalescent home for Anglican clergymen opposite the entrance to Noye's home, which was situated on the quiet, wooded School Lane. A hideout made from branches and leaves was carefully constructed in bushes under an oak tree near the gates to the Retreat so that round-the-clock observation could be carried out on Hollywood Cottage.

Just above the huge cast-iron gates that formed the entrance to the driveway to Noye's home, a video camera disguised as a bird box was placed in an overhanging tree. Meanwhile on the road outside Reader's house over in Grove Park, a variety of vehicles were used to keep watch.

At midday on the day after C11 had first moved into position, Brian Reader drove from his home in Grove Park to the Crest hotel, in Bexley, where Kenneth Noye was already waiting in his Range Rover. As Reader's Cavalier approached, Noye did a U-turn and drove off towards London. Reader immediately followed. Not long afterwards the two vehicles turned into a side road and parked. C11

Detective Constable Myrna Yates, thirty-six, shadowed the pair on foot and – remaining hidden from view – watched as Noye handed Reader a black briefcase.

The following day Noye and Reader again met at lunchtime in the car park of the Beaverwood Club. Fifteen minutes later Reader departed and police shadow WDC Yates followed him to the Royal National hotel, in Bedford Way, Bloomsbury, in central London. WDC Yates followed him into the hotel lobby to find Reader sitting at a table talking to Christopher Weyman and Tommy Adams – the same men he'd met a few days earlier at Farringdon station. Ten minutes later they drove off in the same white Mercedes.

C11 officers tailed the Mercedes through north London to Paddington railway station. Adams was carrying what appeared to be a very heavy brown briefcase, and both he and Weyman seemed agitated. They made two telephone calls, then bought two first-class rail tickets and boarded a train for Swindon, eighty miles west of London. On board the train with them were three surveillance officers.

On arrival at Swindon station, Weyman made several phone calls. Then the two men sat and waited. Eventually they got up, shook hands and waved to each other as though they were about to part company. One moved off, only to be followed at a distance by the other – a deliberate ploy to try and establish if someone was following them. Further down the road the two men met up again and headed for a fish-and-chip bar in a street opposite the station.

Eventually a black Jaguar XJS pulled up. Inside it was Garth Chappell – the 42-year-old managing director of

Scadlynn, the bullion company to which so much of the gold had already been delivered. Chappell was with Terence Patch, a Bristol businessman who occasionally worked for the company.

Adams and Weyman immediately placed the heavy briefcase in the boot of the Jaguar. It sped off – with detectives following – back to Scadlynn, which was based in North Street, Bedminister, a rundown area of Bristol. At about 6.30 p.m. Adams and Weyman returned by train to Paddington station. They were clutching another briefcase. This time C11 shadows followed the two men as they got into the same white Mercedes from earlier and drove to Russell Square in central London, where Weyman handed the briefcase to Colin Reader.

The following day Reader made yet another visit to the car park of the Beaverwood Club, near Kenneth Noye's house in Kent. Reader made a phone call from a public call box and stayed in the car park for just eight minutes this time. Then the trail went cold for almost a week as none of the suspects did anything to alert the attention of the police surveillance operation.

Six days later, Brian Reader made an evening visit to Kenneth Noye's home at Hollywood Cottage. Next he drove to Cowcross Street, where once again he was met by the white Mercedes. This time a man got out of the Merc and leaned into Reader's car while he examined some papers. But their C11 shadows couldn't make out what was being said. Eventually the man returned to the Mercedes and drove off. Police almost immediately lost the car in thick London traffic.

Five days after this Reader paid yet another visit to Cowcross Street, where he met Tommy Adams in the café they'd used before. Twenty-five minutes later a London black cab pulled up. Weyman and a man wearing a brown sheepskin jacket got out, both carrying boxes. Tommy Adams emerged from the café and opened the boot of his sports car where the boxes were then placed. The group adjourned to the café for thirty minutes, then the boxes were transferred to the boot of Reader's car. Reader, followed by C11, then headed out of London to Noye's home at Hollywood Cottage in West Kingsdown.

The following day Reader returned once again to that same café in Cowcross Street. This time he was seen talking to an acquaintance who was a jeweller, and who'd long been suspected by police of being a fence for stolen goods. While the two men were talking, the white Mercedes drew up and Weyman entered the café where Reader got something quite small wrapped in a green Marks and Spencer's carrier bag from his pocket and placed it on the table between them, keeping his hands resting carefully on the package.

Weyman then handed an envelope to Reader, who immediately let go of the package. As he'd already done several times, Reader went back to Noye's house, where he stayed briefly before heading home.

But within fifteen minutes of arriving back at his own house in Grove Park, Reader drove back to the Royal National hotel again. He rejoined the jeweller from earlier that day and they sat looking out of the window until the white Mercedes arrived again.

As soon as it pulled up, Reader and the jeweller left the hotel and joined Weyman. The three of them walked across to Reader's Cavalier. Adams – who had left his sports car to join them – was handed a large package wrapped in brown paper, which he dropped into his own car before moving off.

Adams then headed for the M4 motorway. An hour and a half later he took Junction 15, the Swindon turn-off, and 200 yards further on pulled into the car park of the Plough, a small country pub. Adams parked directly behind the Jaguar previously seen by C11 outside Scad-lynn Ltd.

The boots of both cars were opened and a group of men clustered around the Mercedes. Two men lifted a heavy object out of the boot and transferred it to the Jaguar. Surveillance officers knew it had to be gold.

The Jaguar then left the pub car park and headed westwards with C11 in discreet pursuit. The car went off at the Bath exit of the motorway but was soon lost in a maze of twisting country lanes close to where one of the suspects lived. The next morning detectives saw it parked outside Scadlynn.

On the following Thursday evening, Brian Reader once again visited the Royal National hotel. This time Weyman appeared with a large brown leather briefcase with fold-over flaps. Reader took the case to Kenneth Noye's house later that same night.

The police surveillance team had no doubt that huge amounts of the Brink's-Mat gold were on the move.

*

After almost three weeks of surveillance, operational commander Brian Boyce gave a briefing in a south London police station to the twenty or so officers who'd been involved in the operation so far. On the basis of the data collected, warrants were obtained from a London magistrate for raids on thirty-six addresses in Kent, London and the Bristol area. But that didn't necessarily mean the raids would happen instantly.

Boyce believed that all or part of the £26m worth of Brink's-Mat gold was at Noye's home, Hollywood Cottage, but he couldn't be absolutely certain because a number of the transactions involving Reader had been somewhat confusing. Reader had been seen handing over heavy packages but he had also received some, which he'd then taken to Noye's home. Was it possible that Reader was also acting as a conduit to Noye from some other source, delivering the gold to Hollywood Cottage for some kind of processing before handing it on further down the chain?

There was also another dilemma for Brian Boyce and his senior detectives. If the Flying Squad postponed some of the raids, would those people who hadn't been arrested think that they had escaped detection and unwittingly lead police to more of the Brink's-Mat bullion at a later date?

Brian Boyce had three options: he could pounce on Noye's house at West Kingsdown and then decide what to do about London and Bristol. Or he could intercept the gold at Scadlynn and follow up with further raids in Kent and London. His final choice was simply to move in while the gold was actually in transit and then decide which raids to carry out.

Boyce concluded that the movements of Reader and Noye would determine which of these three options he chose. Meanwhile the special surveillance unit would continue their observation of Hollywood Cottage to provide the most detailed information possible on movements. C8 officers were on constant standby at the Retreat House to remain in contact with the C11 post.

A second C8 team was posted close to Reader's home in Grove Park, with a third team placed in central London and a fourth taking up positions in the M4 area, west of London. A smaller fifth unit was to be kept mobile, ready to give back-up when and where it was required.

Boyce set a time limit of seventy-two hours for the operation. That meant they had to move in at some point within that time span, otherwise it would have to be aborted. Frustratingly, it was primarily the cost of police overtime that made this a necessity. Another factor was that seventy-two hours was the maximum time that a surveillance officer could be expected to remain hidden and continue to be competent.

Although Boyce and his senior officers had just been informed by their Kent colleagues that Noye kept firearms at Hollywood Cottage, Boyce decided that none of his men would be armed. Boyce saw no actual evidence that his officers' lives would be in danger. Noye's shotguns, he felt, were not kept for criminal purposes but were part of the Kent country-squire image he had been trying to build for himself in West Kingsdown.

Furthermore, Brian Boyce believed that in this instance they were dealing with the middlemen, not the robbers themselves. Boyce's decision was also influenced by the outcry two years earlier when Stephen Waldorf, a film editor, was shot five times and seriously wounded in a London street after having been mistaken for a violent criminal. Brian Boyce had been working at C11 at the time, and was one of the officers responsible for authorizing the arming of the officer who'd pulled the trigger.

One last factor behind Brian Boyce's decision was that if an armed officer of one force entered the jurisdiction of another, the chief constable of the second force had to be informed immediately and to provide armed officers from among their own men as back-up. There remained a real fear that someone inside Kent police might tip off Noye about the surveillance operation, so Boyce wanted to confine knowledge of it to as few people as possible.

Brian Boyce couldn't know for certain if the gold was hidden in Noye's house itself, or somewhere in the grounds. He was aware that there were a number of concrete bunkers in the garden where the gold might be stored. Another problem was that the gates to Noye's mansion were always kept locked and could only be opened by remote control after callers had been identified over a closed-circuit television system.

Boyce did not want to give the occupants warning of a raid. He feared that they would flee or hide incriminating evidence in the grounds while police were still trying to get in. Boyce's observations to his C11 specialists struck them as nothing out of the ordinary – this was the kind of work they had been trained for – but even the best-laid plans are always at the mercy of unforeseen circumstances.

ELEVEN

Until daytime surveillance team DC Russell Sinton and DC Stephen Matthews witnessed an innocent-looking domestic drama there hadn't been any activity at Hollywood Cottage on the morning of 26 January 1985. Kenneth Noye's wife Brenda was about to take their two sons Kevin and Brett to stay with her mother when the Ford Granada she intended to use failed to start. Believing that one of the battery terminals needed cleaning, Noye took a knife from the kitchen and tried to sort it out. When that failed, he started the car with jump leads from the Range Rover parked alongside. Brenda Noye and the two boys eventually drove off in the Range Rover and Noye left moments later in the Granada, having tossed the knife into the footwell of the passenger side of the car.

Over at Brian Reader's home that same day there was no movement until 1.10 p.m. when Reader was seen driving off in his Vauxhall Cavalier in the direction of Noye's house. Two Flying Squad officers – DS Anthony Yeoman and DC Bruce Finlayson – were close behind in a covert surveillance vehicle.

Four miles down the A20, Reader turned into the car

park of the Beaverwood Club. But this time Kenneth Noye was nowhere to be seen. Four minutes later Reader left the car park with DS Yeoman and his partner following at a discreet distance. What those officers did not realize was that Reader thought he'd arrived too early at the car park. Reader then drove up the A20 to the Ruxley Corner roundabout two miles away, where he turned and doubled back on his tracks. The officers following feared they would be easily spotted by Reader and pulled back to such an extent that they lost him.

In fact, Reader had turned up at the Beaverwood Club too late for his meeting with Noye, which had been arranged for 1.00 p.m. Noye, despite the problems with his car, had been there on time. He had waited some twenty minutes, even joining the AA at a nearby kiosk, before deciding that Reader wasn't going to show up.

It wasn't until 2.25 p.m. that afternoon that Reader was next spotted outside the imposing gates to Hollywood Cottage. C11 officers Sinton and Matthews watched as Reader, finding that the gates were locked and no one was in, drove away.

A few miles away Kenneth Noye was enjoying a secret liaison with his mistress Jenny Bishop. They were seen drinking together in a pub, then visiting a mutual acquaintance before stopping for a couple of hours at the love nest he'd bought for her in Dartford. Later that afternoon Noye and his wife Brenda arrived back at Hollywood Cottage separately.

At 6.12 p.m. Brian Reader turned up at the house once again, and this time was able to enter the gate. Nearby a new surveillance team had moved into position. The watching police were convinced that Reader and Noye had missed an important rendezvous earlier that day.

Acting DI Robert Suckling was parked two miles away in a C8 vehicle near the Brands Hatch motor-racing track. He immediately ordered the two-man surveillance team into the grounds of Hollywood cottage. Even by 6.15 p.m. the January evening was bitterly cold. The only vague sound was the hum of traffic from the motorway a mile away across the fields.

'Move in.'

Deep surveillance officer DC John Fordham, forty-three, signalled to his partner DC Neil Murphy, thirty-seven, and they headed silently towards the perimeter wall of Noye's grounds.

Fordham, a dedicated family man with three children from Romford, in Essex, was the more senior of the two. Called 'Gentleman John' by friends and colleagues because of his old-fashioned good manners, Fordham had been in C11 for nine years. He'd even turned down promotion to remain at the sharp end of police work. Fordham had been a late entrant into the police force, joining in his late twenties after a variety of jobs, including work as a merchant seaman and a prison officer in New Zealand. He had also travelled extensively throughout Europe and Asia.

But once in the force, Fordham's professionalism, sense of responsibility and quiet self-confidence singled him out as an above-average officer. Unusually for the Metropolitan Police, Fordham became a detective without having to sit the customary formal examination. He won four commendations for bravery, and by the time he was assigned to the Brink's-Mat inquiry he had a reputation for being, in the words of one senior Scotland Yard officer, 'one of the most experienced and best-trained surveillance officers in the country'.

His partner and back-up man, bachelor Neil Murphy, came from a close-knit mining family in a County Durham pit village. He'd joined the Met nine years earlier in 1975 following a short career as a regular soldier. Murphy loved solitary sports like skiing and windsurfing. He had the right degree of fitness and self-sufficiency for the job and something else too – an actor's eye. Even when off-duty he would constantly study the mannerisms of people in an effort to improve his powers of disguise. In 1980 Murphy was recommended for a posting to C11.

Murphy's dedication to the job had so impressed John Fordham that after his apprenticeship they'd continued working together, and the teacher-pupil relationship developed over the years into one of real friendship, although it was always clear that Fordham was the senior partner.

Back outside Hollywood Cottage, Fordham and Murphy had emerged from behind their makeshift observation post hidden behind some bushes and were creeping across the quiet country lane until they reached the low wall at the front of the grounds. Both were dressed in rubber wetsuits, camouflage clothing and balaclavas. Fordham and Murphy were also carrying yeast tablets to pacify Noye's Rottweilers if required, though they knew that they did not always work. Fordham's kit included a pair of light-intensifying night-sight binoculars, a webbing scarf, gloves, two balaclavas, a woollen helmet, a camouflage hood, a peaked, camouflage-coloured forage cap and a green webbing harness to keep the larger radio set in position while crawling through the undergrowth.

Beyond the wall the two officers could see more than a hundred yards of sweeping driveway by the light of a string of mock-Victorian lamps. There were small copses and shrubbery to one side and an open lawn to the other, dotted with newly planted saplings.

At the top of the driveway were the lights of Hollywood Cottage. Seconds later – without a word being spoken between them – the two officers went over the wall, crouched low and waited to see if they'd been spotted.

A minute later, satisfied that all was clear, they moved towards the house, leapfrogging forward, one of them advancing while the other held back as a lookout to warn if they had been seen. Keeping close to the perimeter fence, they made for the copse and shrubbery in front of the large barn, known as the apple store. That would give them enough cover to watch events at the house undetected.

Both undercover officers communicated with police through two radios that each of them carried. Their experience had taught them that the tiny body-set radios (these were radio devices that were integrated into the officer's clothing, however they were easily affected by movement, so were of limited use) usually worn by surveillance officers were often inadequate for good reception in rural areas. The proximity of the aerial to the ground tended to interfere with transmissions, particularly when they were sending messages. So they were each equipped with a larger set for sending messages, while using the smaller set for receiving. Fordham and Murphy's contact man outside the grounds was DS Robert Gurr, a crusty C11 veteran. But the rule for such operations was that once they had to take up their close surveillance positions, they were effectively on their own.

Fordham and Murphy got to the cover of the shrubbery and copse surrounding the garage some 60 yards in front of the house. Fordham was in front on one knee beside a tree waiting for Murphy to move forward when one of Noye's Rottweilers appeared out of the darkness.

Murphy was startled. His hand flew to his pocket and he tried to feed the yeast tablets to the dogs but they weren't interested. They continued barking louder and louder. Fordham grabbed his radio set.

He whispered: 'Dogs – Hostile.' It was picked up by the other officers in the Retreat across School Lane.

Inside the house, Noye led Reader into the kitchen to admire some photographs of the house, taken earlier that month, showing the cottage covered in snow. A cup of tea was made, then Noye took Reader into his study to discuss business.

'What the fuck happened to you today, Brian? Why didn't you show?' started Noye angrily.

Just then he heard the dogs making a commotion outside.

Noye opened the study door and shouted to Brenda.

'Brenda what's happening with those dogs?'

Moments later Brenda Noye appeared in the room.

'They're down by the barn. I'm not going down there. It's too dark.'

Brenda Noye was one of the three to head off down into the darkness towards the dogs. Noye grabbed his leather jacket from behind a chair and headed for the front door.

Outside – after gesturing to Fordham – Murphy began to withdraw. He presumed Fordham would follow him. The first maxim of a C11 officer is: 'Blow out rather than show out.' In other words, if his presence is discovered he should withdraw. Failing that he should identify himself as a police officer. But with such hostile dogs there was only one option.

At 6.25 p.m. Murphy radioed to his colleagues: 'Neil out toward fence.'

He walked through the shrubbery and made for the end of a wooden fence that separated Noye's land from another house in School Lane. Outside Hollywood Cottage, Kenneth Noye found a torch in the Granada parked in the garage. He also grabbed the knife he'd been using earlier to clean the battery tops.

Holding both items in his left hand, Noye walked down the drive calling to the older of the dogs, Sam, and one of the puppies, Cleo. The other dog, Cassie, was still in the kitchen. Reaching the apple store area, Noye saw the dogs on a pile of sand barking into the shrubbery. He swung the torch in the same direction. Noye then moved into the wooded area, letting the beam pan the ground in front of him.

At 6.27 p.m. Fordham came on the radio.

'Somebody out, halfway down drive, calling dogs.'

At the boundary fence, Murphy walked up to the end furthest from Hollywood Cottage and, using a tree for support, climbed up to balance on top to take stock of the situation. Looking down to where he had last seen the Rottweilers, Murphy spotted a figure with a torch obviously searching in the shrubbery.

The light suddenly moved towards Murphy, prompting the police officer to drop into the garden on the other side of the fence. Murphy then tried to attract the attention of the dogs to help his partner.

Hoping that perhaps Noye would think he was an irate neighbour and call off the dogs, or that Noye would come down to the fence to see who was behind it, allowing Fordham to escape, Murphy shouted through the fence: 'Keep those dogs quiet!'

Just then a noise to his left attracted Kenneth Noye's attention. He swung the beam of light in that direction. The light instantly fell on a hooded figure just four or five feet away. Noye froze with horror. All he could see of the man was two eyeholes and a mask.

Noye later said that the figure struck him a blow across his face. Immediately after being hit, Noye claimed he dropped the torch, grabbed the knife from his pocket and put his left hand up to the other man's face and grabbed him.

'Brenda. Help!' he screamed in the direction of the house.

Then Noye used all his brute strength to smash his fists into the man over and over again. But still the man kept coming. Dressed in black, and with that mask on, he seemed huge to Noye.

Noye began to plunge his knife into John Fordham's body, and in the tussle that followed both men fell to the ground. Fordham came down on top of Noye, who struck him again and again. Noye then broke free and began running up the drive. He looked back momentarily and saw the figure staggering to his feet and starting to move towards the garden wall.

In Hollywood Cottage, Brenda Noye rushed upstairs to their bedroom cupboard and took out a shotgun – one of at least half a dozen that the couple kept there. She also grabbed four cartridges from the same cabinet.

Loading the gun as she ran, Brenda Noye – in tracksuit and slippers – and Brian Reader headed down the drive in the direction of where they'd heard Noye shouting.

Halfway down, Noye ran towards them.

'There's a masked man down there,' shouted a breathless Noye.

He grabbed the gun, which was by now in Reader's hands.

Running back to the copse with Brenda and Reader close behind, Noye picked the torch up off the ground and made towards the gate. Then Noye spotted the dogs surrounding the masked figure lying slumped on the ground. He went straight to the man.

Just a few yards away, Fordham's partner Neil Murphy was walking back along the lane towards the wall at the front of the cottage grounds when he heard a woman screaming. Moving into some bushes beside the entrance to the Retreat, Murphy looked into the grounds and saw two men and a woman. Both of the men were shouting and looking down at the ground, one of them pointing something.

Murphy immediately radioed in: 'Man compromising John. Stick/shotgun.'

Murphy later claimed that at one stage he saw one of the men step forward and kick the figure on the ground. He remained in his hiding place, transmitting back to the Retreat everything he could see and hear. He was following classic C11 training. He was there in a surveillance role, not an operational one.

'Who are you?' shouted Noye angrily. 'Who are you?'

Fordham was still wearing his balaclava hood.

Noye noticed the policeman's night-sight binoculars. After the event he said that he thought he'd been dealing with a rapist or a peeping Tom.

'Who are you? Take that mask off!' shouted Noye.

No response from the masked figure.

'Who are you? Take that mask off!'

Noye pointed the shotgun at the man. There was no reaction.

'If you don't take that mask off and tell me who you are, I'll blow your head off,' threatened Noye.

Then, according to Noye's later testimony, Fordham groaned and started to take off his hood.

'SAS.'

A beat of silence followed.

'On manoeuvres.'

'Show us your ID, then,' ordered Noye.

There was no reply. Even by torchlight John Fordham looked deathly pale.

Next Kenneth Noye proved just how adept he was at thinking on his feet.

On leaving the shrubbery, he found he was bleeding from a cut near his eye and nose, injuries caused during his struggle with Fordham.

Kenneth Noye believed he needed photographic evidence of the struggle.

'Get a camera, Brenda, quick,' ordered Noye.

And, as an afterthought:

'You'd better call an ambulance for 'im.'

Noye stood by John Fordham for a few moments, looking down at the policeman.

He knelt down and opened Fordham's jacket to get a closer look at the wounds he had inflicted just moments earlier.

In a much quieter voice he asked Fordham: 'What on earth are you doing here?'

Fordham didn't answer. His head fell back awkwardly, so Noye put his arm under him to get him into a better position. Then a police car burst through the gates to Hollywood Cottage.

The first men into the grounds were Flying Squad detective constables David Manning and John Childs. They had been in an unmarked police car in the Retreat's drive, moving slowly forward, when the order came.

'All units AM [a C11 code],' came over the radio.

Childs and Manning tore into School Lane. The gates to Hollywood Cottage had been left partly open after

Reader's arrival, and they swept through them into the driveway.

Within seconds the car's headlights illuminated a body collapsed on the ground with a figure armed with a shotgun next to him. The dogs were still pulling and tugging at Fordham.

'Stand by, all units!' screamed John Childs into the car radio set. That meant they were not to enter the grounds at that point.

'I am a police officer,' shouted Manning at Noye, holding up his warrant card.

Noye moved towards him, pointing the shotgun and shouting, 'Fuck off, or I will do you as well.'

'Put the gun down and get those dogs away from the officer,' said Manning.

Moments later the Rottweilers turned on Manning, snapping at his feet. One of them jumped up at him.

As he tried to knock the dogs away, Manning took off his jacket and wrapped it around his arm. Ignoring the shotgun pointed in his direction, Manning then walked over to where Fordham was lying.

'He's done me. He's stabbed me,' muttered the wounded officer.

The Rottweilers jumped up and tore at Childs's clothing but he managed to struggle past them back to the car, from where he called an ambulance and ordered all police units in.

Meanwhile Kenneth Noye began walking back towards his house, still levelling the shotgun at Manning before he disappeared into the darkness. Looking down at John

Fordham, Manning could see blood on his chest and stomach, and he immediately began giving first aid, but Fordham quickly lost consciousness. In the confusion that followed, Brian Reader fled from the scene by foot. He scrambled over garden fences and through private properties.

It was the start of the longest night in all those people's lives.

TWELVE

Back at John Fordham's side Noye reappeared and found himself face to face with DC Manning.

'He's a police officer,' Manning told Noye.

'The SAS man?' replied Noye. 'What are you on about? He's a police officer? Look at him! He's masked up!'

The dogs were getting in the way again. The third Rottweiler, Cassie, had also joined them.

'Get those dogs out of the way,' said Manning.

'I can't get the dogs out of the way. They haven't got their collars on and they don't pay any attention to me anyway.'

'Go and get the leads.'

Noye moved off towards the house and bumped into his wife Brenda coming down the drive. She had the camera, flash gun and mobile phone. Noye took the camera from her as well as the flash, which he put in his pocket.

'I couldn't get through for the ambulance,' said Brenda.

Noye grabbed the mobile phone off her.

'Go and get the dogs' leads,' he repeated.

Noye then returned to the three police officers.

'My wife couldn't get through for an ambulance.'

'I've already got them,' said DC Childs.

The dogs were still barking and jumping up.

'Where's the dog leads?' asked Manning, growing increasingly agitated.

'I've sent my wife.'

Noye later claimed that he was ordered by Manning to take the shotgun and leave it in a broken position up against the wall besides the front door to the house. Just after that, another car pulled up and two men jumped out, armed with what looked like baseball bats.

Those two men were DS Yeoman and DC Finlayson, who had earlier that day followed Reader from his home to the Beaverwood Club and later trailed him to Noye's home at Hollywood Cottage. They'd been stationed outside the Portobello Inn just half a mile from Noye's house.

Yoeman noticed Noye was carrying a camera over his shoulder.

'Come here, you,' he yelled.

Noye ignored them all and disappeared between the garage and the swimming pool building.

When he reappeared some moments later, Finlayson grabbed Noye's left arm and said: 'Police.'

'I know' replied Noye, as cool as ice.

'What's been happening?'

'I took the knife and did him. Old Bill or not, he had no fuckin' business being here.'

Noye was then cautioned by Finlayson. He did not reply. They started walking back towards the front door of Holly-wood Cottage.

First on the scene, DI Suckling noticed Brenda Noye standing by the front of the house.

'You're being arrested,' he told her.

'Why?' she asked.

'A policeman has been very badly hurt here tonight. You're being arrested in connection with that.'

'He shouldn't have come here.'

Brenda Noye was put in the back of a police car.

Meanwhile other policemen were pouring into the grounds of Hollywood Cottage.

It was only then that officers noticed Brian Reader had disappeared.

'Where is he?' one officer asked Noye.

'Mind your own fuckin' business,' replied Noye.

'D'you realize that the police officer you stabbed is dying?' asked the officer.

'He shouldn't have been on my property. I hope he fuckin' dies.'

The officer lunged at Noye and pushed him hard against the wall.

'What sort of animal are you that could wish anybody dead?'

At that moment another police officer appeared alongside his colleague.

While Noye and Brenda were kept under arrest at the house, police officers continued trying to save the life of John Fordham.

'Let me go,' Fordham moaned as he drifted in and out of consciousness.

He was given cardiac massage and mouth-to-mouth

before, shortly after 7 p.m., the ambulance arrived. Neil Murphy accompanied Fordham on the journey to Queen Mary's hospital in Sidcup.

As the ambulance set off, Murphy helped paramedic Bryan Moore by holding the oxygen mask over Fordham's face. Murphy thought he saw signs of life in his colleague until Moore pointed out that this was just the oxygen going in and out of Fordham's body. His pulse had already stopped.

Twelve minutes later they arrived at the hospital where Fordham was seen by duty surgeon Graham Ponting. He could detect no sign of a pulse, although tests showed there was still some electrical activity in the heart. He found at least ten stab wounds on the body.

A blood transfusion into Fordham's ankle was set up and an operation carried out. Several more attempts were made to get the heart going again, using direct injections of drugs and electrical shocks, but at 8.20 p.m., Fordham was pronounced dead.

Pathologist Dr Rufus Crompton, who examined the body the following morning, found the stab wounds consistent with blows from a single-edged blade about one centimetre wide and seven centimetres long. Five of the wounds were on the front of the body; three were on the back; one was in the armpit and one was on the head.

The two wounds that were fatal both penetrated Fordham's heart. One was delivered with the force of a punch and severed the fifth rib to enter the left ventricle. The other, two centimetres below, had just nicked the right ventricle. In both cases the knife had been plunged in to a depth of seven centimetres, and a small bruise beside the entry point of each wound suggested that the knife had been pushed in to the hilt.

The close proximity of the five wounds at the front of the body suggested that after the first one, all the rest had been inflicted while Fordham was immobile. They were consistent with a right-handed assailant, face to face with the policeman, who had delivered the blows to the front and had then reached behind to stab Fordham in the back.

Police always suspected that Reader was involved, but charges against him in connection with the actual killing were dropped, although he would be jailed for nine years for his part in handling the gold.

Three other wounds to Fordham's back looked to have been inflicted by a knife held like a dagger. Indicating that he had been trying to get away from his attacker, these wounds proved Fordham was still on his feet when he sustained them. Noye always insisted he never held a knife in that way. The torso also had a bruise to the chest. It was consistent with a blow from a light object, a fall, a punch or a kick.

Half a mile away, Brian Reader had scrambled through bushes and across fields before eventually reaching the main A20 road which leads back to London. But for a man who had just witnessed a killing connected to a notorious gold bullion robbery, he chose an extraordinary way to make good his escape – Reader tried to hitch a lift.

At 7.40 p.m., Kent Police Detective Sergeant Barry McAllister was at the wheel of his squad car when he spotted Reader standing by the side of the road on the outskirts of West Kingsdown just past a pub called the Gamecock. McAllister was fully aware of the description of the man missing from Hollywood Cottage.

Also travelling into West Kingsdown from the London direction as Reader stood thumbing a lift were Flying Squad detectives Alan Branch and John Redgrave, who were in an unmarked car. Redgrave immediately recognized Reader from surveillance duties he'd carried out on 8 January outside Farringdon Street station, while Branch knew him from the station and Russell Square two days earlier. Both detectives leapt from their vehicle to detain Reader, but by that time Reader was already running up to the Kent police car.

DC Paul Gladstone, in the passenger seat, wound down his window as Reader approached.

'Any chance of a lift to London?' asked Reader.

'Yes, get in,' replied Gladstone.

As the car pulled off, Gladstone revealed that he and McAllister were policemen and asked Reader where he had come from.

'The pub,' replied Reader, indicating the Gamecock.

'Where were you before that?'

'What's all this about?' asked an increasingly anxious Reader.

'We're looking for a man in connection with a serious incident tonight. Where did you come from before the Gamecock?'

Reader did not reply but shoved his right hand into his pocket. Fearing that he might be armed, Gladstone asked to see what he was holding. Reader showed him a few coins. He was then ordered to put his hands on top of the front passenger seat. Reader was handcuffed and driven back to the car park at the Portobello Inn, where other Kent CID men were waiting.

Told that he was being arrested on suspicion of assaulting a police officer earlier that night, Reader replied:

'What?'

The charges were then repeated.

'You must be joking!' he said.

That night Kenneth Noye, his wife Brenda and Brian Reader were all taken to Swanley police station. Noye was convinced that evidence against him would be invented and statements concocted. As a result, he immediately demanded his legal rights. He wanted the case to be dealt with by Kent police, amongst whom he considered he had some good 'contacts'.

For more than twenty-four hours following his arrest, Noye continually asked for Kent to be involved. He was very wary of Scotland Yard, particularly the Flying Squad. He also insisted on pointing out his facial injuries, knowing that they would be crucial in paving the way for a plea of self-defence.

One of the first policemen to see Noye in custody was station sergeant David Columbine. He asked Noye if he knew why he was being held.

'Haven't a clue,' responded Noye.

'You're here for the attempted murder or murder of a police officer,' said Columbine.

'Is that all?' Noye allegedly replied. He was searched and

nearly £850 in cash was found on him. When Noye was asked to sign a form listing what had been taken he at first refused, then appeared to cooperate but instead wrote down the name and address of a firm of solicitors.

At 11.30 p.m. that evening PC Fred Bird went to Noye's cell (the small women's cell at the station) to ask for his clothing for forensic examination. The officer knew little else about Noye's alleged crime because he was in such a truculent mood at this stage that he would not even admit his own name.

'You're not having my clothing until I have seen my brief,' Noye replied, using the London slang word for his solicitor.

'I want this photographed,' he added, pointing to his bruised eye and bloodied nose and the mud on his clothing.

'If I do, will you allow me to take your clothing?' asked Bird.

'Yes.'

Noye was escorted to a first-floor room where the photographs were taken. One of these, clearly showing Noye with a black eye, was later released by the police.

On returning to his cell, Noye said: 'All right, you can have my clothes.'

As they were being taken from him he asked: 'Will I be moved to London?'

'No. The offence happened in Kent. You will be dealt with here,' he was told.

At that stage the killing remained a Kent police inquiry.

Then Noye blurted out: 'I didn't know he was a police

officer. All I saw was a chap in camouflage gear and a balaclava mask. I wouldn't have stabbed him if I knew he was a police officer.'

'I can't discuss this with you. Can I have your name?' asked Bird.

Noye wouldn't say.

Bird told him he was being silly and told him he could well be facing a murder charge. The stark warning seemed to work, for the next moment Noye stuck out his hand and said: 'My name is Kenny Noye.' He repeated that he hadn't known Fordham was a police officer.

Later that same night Noye was transferred from Swanley to Dartford police station. In the early hours of that Sunday morning, Noye was examined by police surgeon Dr Eugene Ganz. His attitude by then had become 'commanding'. Ganz noted that Noye virtually ordered him to make a note of the injuries to his eye and nose. Both wounds were relatively trivial but the doctor also recorded that Noye's face was smeared with blood.

Noye also complained about a pain in the abdominal area and the back, saying he had been kicked, but there was no sign of bruising. There was swelling on the back of his right hand. When the doctor noticed the scratches on his left hand Noye refused to allow it to be examined saying: 'That's nothing.'

Noye's first formal interview took place at lunchtime on the day after the killing of John Fordham – Sunday, 27 January 1985. He was seen by DCI Peter Humphrey, a Kent policeman, and – as was the case at a number of the interviews involving Noye, his wife and Reader – another detective made a note of all the questions and answers throughout.

That first interview lasted just seven minutes. Noye refused to answer questions unless his solicitor was present.

'I was promised my solicitor when I got to Swanley last night. Now it's Sunday, one o'clock, and I still haven't seen him,' he grumbled.

DCI Humphrey was unmoved. 'Has anyone told you that the man you stabbed last night has died?' he asked.

'No reply unless my solicitor is present,' responded Noye.

Noye then named Scotland Yard Detective Chief Superintendent Ray Adams – who had investigated Noye a decade earlier – as someone who would vouch for the fact he 'was not a violent man, or a killer'. It seems that Noye had friends in high places, and they didn't all work for the Kent Constabulary, either.

Adams has always refused to talk about his relationship with Noye. But other officers who worked with Adams described Noye as follows: 'Half of us thought he was a terrific asset and the other half thought he was bent as arseholes and taking us to the cleaners.'

Following that first interview at Dartford police station a short statement was drawn up of what Noye had said. Noye even requested that the letters 'p.m.' be inserted after the time 'one o'clock'. He then asked that a line be drawn from the end of the last word on each line to the edge of the page to prevent anything being inserted later.

That afternoon Noye's request for a solicitor was granted. Raymond Burrough – his legal representative for twelve years – was ushered into the cell to see Noye. Burrough had earlier reacted with amazement when told about the incident at Hollywood Cottage. The Kenneth Noye he knew was a 'jovial sort of fellow – gregarious'.

But the Kenneth Noye who greeted his brief that afternoon was very agitated and distressed. Noye insisted he'd been defending himself and said that he was extremely worried about Brenda. He briefly began outlining what had happened to Burrough but the solicitor cut him short. The cell door had been kept open a foot or two by officers guarding Noye, and two of them remained outside within hearing distance.

Burrough didn't think it was a suitable environment to listen to his client's instructions. He later described it thus: 'One could almost cut the atmosphere with a knife.'

Noye didn't realize that Brian Reader had also been transferred from Swanley to Dartford police station and was actually in an adjacent cell.

At 3.15 that Sunday afternoon, Reader was seen by Detective Superintendent David Tully of the Kent police force. Reader immediately expressed concern about his wife, who was a diabetic and due to go into hospital the next day for treatment to her pancreas.

'Where's my wife?' demanded Reader.

He was told that she'd been arrested and was at Gravesend police station.

'I want you to know, Mr Tully, that she is a very sick woman and needs medical attention,' said Reader.

Tully assured Reader he'd personally go to Gravesend to make certain she was all right.

'Thank you,' said Reader. 'She needs special food, like boiled fish, otherwise she gets ill.'

Tully got back to the subject at hand.

'At some stage you will be interviewed about the incident at Mr Noye's home on Saturday evening. You understand that you have been detained in connection with that incident?' asked Tully.

Reader tried to look concerned. 'It's a very serious matter,' he told the detective. 'I know a police officer has been murdered, and I was told I was responsible. I want you to know, Mr Tully, that I do not know anything about it and I did not have anything to do with it,' added Reader.

Reader then said he would not answer any questions without his solicitor being present. His brief's name was Stanley Beller, of Beller Jarvis, based in Oxford Street, central London.

'You must understand,' said Tully. 'A large amount of money was found at your house when your wife was arrested, and she, as you well know, will be asked to account for the possession of that money.'

'That money is mine. It's nothing to do with my wife,' said Reader.

That Sunday afternoon at Hollywood Cottage the most significant piece of evidence linking Noye and Reader to the Brink's-Mat bullion case was discovered. Lying in a shallow gully beside the garage wall, and hidden from view by a tin of paint covered by a rubber mat, was a red-and-white piece of material. Wrapped in the cloth were eleven gold bars, amounting to some 13 kilograms, at that time worth at least £100,000.

The roughly cast bars were all of a similar size: 3 inches long, 1 inch high and 1 inch wide. Some of the same red-and-white material was later discovered in Noye's Ford Granada, and operating instructions for the model of the furnace bought by Michael Lawson thirteen months earlier were also found in Noye's apple store.

THIRTEEN

At Kenneth Noye's Hollywood Cottage, police began an even more thorough inch-by-inch search, including an aerial reconnaissance by a helicopter equipped with infra-red devices capable of pin-pointing metal buried underground or hidden in buildings. The grounds were checked by a line of policemen moving slowly forward, shoulder to shoulder.

Very rapidly there were some significant discoveries:

1. Numerous copper coins of the kind used in the re-smelting of gold found in several rooms.
2. A child's drawing pad containing a picture of a gold bar found in a kitchen drawer.
3. A 1985 edition of the *Guinness Book of Records* with a circle drawn around the entry naming Brink's-Mat as the largest British robbery.

A police dog searching the area of woods behind Hollywood Cottage discovered a flick knife as well as a similar weapon inside Noye's Ford Granada. At the back of the house, close to the corner of the swimming pool, another knife was found that appeared to be the one used to stab John Fordham. The white-handled knife had its blade thrust into the ground at the foot of a tree.

A camouflage hat worn by Fordham was found close to the shrubbery where he had hidden it. In the lounge, officers were astonished to discover that 'Goldfinger' by Shirley Bassey was primed to go off on the stereo system whenever anyone walked in.

Close examination and forensic tests revealed globular fragments of gold – which would have been produced in a smelting process – on the boot mat of Noye's Ford Granada. Traces were also found on the boot mat of Brian Reader's Cavalier as well as the rear mat and rear floor area of Noye's pick-up truck parked near the apple store. Inside the store similar gold traces were found on a leather apron and two gloves, as well as the front mat of a Cadillac parked nearby and on a pair of gloves found in Noye's Range Rover.

The wood panelling in all the rooms was removed and secret compartments were discovered. One was hidden at the back of a built-in bedroom cupboard and contained antique Meissen porcelain worth about £3,000, which had been stolen two years earlier from the home of local aristocrat Lord Darnley (more china would be found at one of the houses in Hever Avenue, West Kingsdown).

Secret compartments were also found under a corridor leading to the swimming pool and in an alcove above the pool. Paving stones from the patio were torn up and tiles removed from the swimming pool, but no more gold bars were found.

Next to the houses in nearby Hever Road, West Kingsdown, where Noye's parents and his sister and her husband lived, neighbour Rosemary Ford discovered a bundle poking from beneath her back-garden fence in a green Marks and Spencer's carrier bag. It was crammed with £50,000 in £50 notes with the prefix A24.

At first Mrs Ford thought it was a practical joke, so she took it to another neighbour to inspect it. Realizing it was the real thing, she handed it over to the police at Hollywood Cottage.

Following the discovery of the gold bars in the grounds of Hollywood Cottage, the Metropolitan Police – now in charge of the investigation – steamed further into Reader and Noye. Noye was interviewed virtually immediately by DI Tony Brightwell, acting DCI Suckling and DC Michael Charman. For much of the time Noye stood close to the cell door, shouting intermittently that he did not want to be interviewed by Flying Squad detectives and that he wanted his solicitor present.

The truth of what was said during that interview is disputed by both sides. But one moment, when Noye tried to take the conversation away from the gold by asking the officers if they knew the dead officer, summed up the differing accounts. He was told that John Fordham was known to all of them, that he was married with three children – a girl aged twelve, and two older boys.

According to the officers present, Noye then said: 'You must hate me. I have killed one of your mates and there is no way out for me. All you want to do is make sure I go to prison for the rest of my life.'

Noye later emphatically denied most of the remarks he

was alleged to have made during his early interviews with the Met. He insisted that his replies to most questions had been: 'No reply unless my solicitor is present.'

Later that night the three Flying Squad officers returned to Noye's cell for another interview. According to their statements, Noye tried to convince them that his only concern was the death of the policeman.

'You could ask me a thousand questions, and I could give you a thousand answers. The gold is nothing to what I have done. I am not interested in telling you about the gold. My only worry is the murder. If I tell you about the gold now, I'm only adding to it. It won't make any difference to what you charge me with, will it?'

When the interview ended, Noye was asked whether he wanted to see Detective Chief Superintendent Brian Boyce.

According to the officers he replied: 'I'll leave that to you.'

Detectives had an equally frustrating interview with Brenda Noye, who was also at Dartford police station and was proving to be a tough customer.

'I can't help you,' she immediately told the detectives as they walked into the interview room.

'Can't or won't?' asked one.

'Look, I can't help you,' she repeated.

Once again, at the end of the interview, she refused to check or sign the notes that were taken. The Noyes certainly had their own way of dealing with the police.

The police had been genuinely shocked by the killing of John Fordham, and resolved to work even harder to start bringing in suspects linked to the Brink's-Mat gold bullion operation.

Garth Chappell found fifty police officers on the doorstep of his country house near Bristol. Nearby, Terence Patch was arrested at his luxurious bungalow. Scadlynn Ltd was raided, and invoice books, papers, telephone books, bank paying-books, petty cash accounts and even a picture of an island scene were removed from the offices for further examination. Among the paperwork were telephone numbers that proved a link with Reader and Noye. The safes were also inspected, and silver trophies and gold watches removed.

Evidence of the Brink's-Mat gold ingots and a non-stop smelting operation were soon uncovered at various locations in the West Country. At one smelting works the police had the following classic conversation with one of the suspects:

'I understand you have been smelting this morning. Is that right?' one detective asked a man just arrested.

'Yes.'

'What were you smelting?'

'I don't wish to say.'

'Why not?'

'I don't want to.'

Minutes later police uncovered two gold bars, still warm, on a sofa in the house next to the smelter. A shotgun and a rifle were taken from the same house. In a lorry parked outside they found another shotgun as well as a crucible with two large ingot moulds still hot enough to have caused condensation to form over the windows. But the most significant evidence was paperwork, which proved the handlers were also making vast sums of money by avoiding payments of VAT on the gold.

An initial check of Scadlynn's records in the national VAT computer at Southend revealed a surprising picture. Since the summer of 1984 the company's fortunes had undergone a remarkable turnaround. Millions of pounds' worth of gold had been going from Scadlynn to an assay office in Sheffield, where its purity was officially calculated, then on to gold dealers on the open market. Suspect Terence Patch claimed this was scrap gold made up from jewellery that Scadlynn had bought, but the amounts were too large for that to be a credible explanation.

Furthermore, the gold had been moved in highly suspicious circumstances in a series of undercover early morning pick-ups. The ingots were so badly smelted that the assay office could not determine their true gold content without re-smelting them. They later compared the bars sent by Scadlynn to a badly mixed cake in which all the currants (the gold) ended up on one side, and few appeared anywhere else in the mix.

The suspicions of the customs officers increased after apparently routine visits to Scadlynn to inspect their VAT accounts following the arrests revealed the names of dealers to whom they were selling on the gold. Garth Chappell even admitted to one VAT inspector: 'I'm a dealer. I don't understand books. Books are all Chinese to me.' Two days later the customs officer returned to tell him he owed nearly £80,000 in outstanding VAT payments. More checks showed that Scadlynn were paying virtually the same as they were selling the gold for. It didn't make sense unless their paperwork was false. They were undoubtedly avoiding vast VAT payments.

In London, police carried out similar raids on various properties belonging to individuals linked to Reader and Noye.

On the Tuesday following PC John Fordham's killing, Kenneth Noye spent much of the day alone in his cell at Dartford police station before investigator Brian Boyce appeared in his cell carrying three knives and asked him if he recognized them.

'No reply unless my solicitor is present,' was Noye's only response.

Two and a half hours later, Noye's brief Ray Burrough saw his client. Burrough immediately told Boyce: 'My client does not wish to say anything at this stage.'

Noye was then asked if he would provide blood, saliva and hair samples for forensic analysis.

Burrough immediately interrupted.

'Permission is not given and will not be given until we have taken counsel's opinion on it.'

Not long after this, detectives visited Brian Reader in his cell. He allegedly admitted to the officers: 'I am sorry about what happened.'

After about twenty minutes of detailed questioning, during which Reader conceded little, he was asked: 'How long have you known Noye?' Reader did not reply, and the interview was brought to an end.

Later, Reader was visited twice by Brian Boyce. On the first occasion he was told that he would be charged with murder and was shown the same three knives as Noye had been. He said he did not recognize them but did however agree to provide hair, saliva and blood samples for forensic examination.

On the second visit by Boyce, Reader was seen with a solicitor present and asked if he was prepared to answer any questions. Reader's reply surprised no one: 'I don't wish to say anything.'

Meanwhile Noye's wife Brenda was moved to Gravesend police station, where she was seen by a Detective Sergeant O'Rourke. It was to prove a more productive interview than the earlier ones.

O'Rourke went in with a sympathetic attitude.

'I appreciate that these are not the surroundings that you are used to, but we have to get to the bottom of this. A policeman has been murdered. A quantity of gold has been recovered from your house. After speaking to you yesterday, I think you want to tell us but you are frightened of something or someone.'

Playing on Brenda Noye's fears did not seem to make much impression.

'I'm not frightened of anyone,' she said. 'I didn't see anything. I was out after. It had all happened by then.'

'All what?' asked Rourke.

Brenda Noye's defence was weakening.

'Whatever happened to him. I didn't take any part. The dogs were making a lot of noise, so Kenny went to see. He was out for a few minutes and the dogs were still barking, so Brian went out and a bit later Kenny came running in and got his shotgun. I knew then that something was wrong.

I went down the drive and could see Ken and Brian standing over something. I got closer and could see it was a man. He didn't move.'

A few more questions followed, then O'Rourke said: 'Let's talk about the gold. You did know they were shifting gold, didn't you?'

'Of course I did. You said yesterday, I am his wife.'

'Did you know it was stolen?'

'Obviously it must be.'

'Did you know from where?'

'No.'

O'Rourke then enlightened Brenda Noye by telling her about the Brink's-Mat raid.

She denied knowing anything more about it, but then Rourke asked Brenda Noye: 'When do you think it started?'

Her reply surprised him.

'Some time before Christmas.'

'How long?'

'I don't know.'

'Every day?'

'I don't know. I told you. I wasn't there all the time.'

'How much was your husband getting?'

'I don't know,' replied Brenda Noye. She added: 'I have already said more than I should have done. I'm not answering any more of your questions.

The interview was at an end. Once again, according to O'Rourke, Brenda Noye was offered a chance to sign the notes of the interview, but once again she refused. Brenda Noye later denied ever making any of the comments attributed to her by the police.

After her visit from O'Rourke, Brenda Noye was moved back to Dartford police station, where she was interviewed by senior officer Brian Boyce, to whom she refused to talk.

Early on that same Tuesday evening, Kenneth and Brenda Noye and Brian Reader were all officially charged with murder.

FOURTEEN

The following day Noye was moved to Bromley police station, where he was interviewed by detectives Suckling and Charman.

By this stage, questions about the gold were the only ones the police could actually put to Noye. He had been charged with Fordham's murder, which meant that it was not permitted to interrogate him again about the killing.

There was a brief silence between the policemen and their prisoner. Noye scratched his chin, considering his next move.

'Tell me, what happens when you go out of here?'

'What do you mean?'

'Do you write all this down?'

'Yes, we make notes on what's been said.'

'I can't say anything then, can I?'

'Why?'

The reply Noye gave showed just how familiar he was with the Brink's-Mat story.

'That Black's a dead man, isn't he?' said Noye, referring to Tony Black, whose evidence had brought Robinson and McAvoy 25-year prison sentences. 'You lot wrote down what he had to say. Now everybody knows what he's done.

He's a dead man when he comes out. You don't think I'm going to get myself killed because you've told people I've helped you.'

Charman interrupted Noye.

'Are you saying you've got things you can tell us about the gold if we don't write down what we say here?'

'The thing is,' continued Noye, 'what good is it going to do for me? I'm going away for a long time for what I've done. I don't see you can help me if I tell you anything. They won't cut my sentence. It won't make any difference at all.'

Charman sensed that his prisoner was edging towards some kind of a deal.

'The things that have happened to you over the past few days cannot be altered in any way, and it would be wrong if we suggested they could. We've arrested you with what I'm pretty sure is some of the Brink's-Mat gold. Our interest is to recover what's left of the £26m worth which was stolen. You can help us. I'm convinced.'

Noye was scathing. 'I can help to get myself killed as well. You know what these situations involve. I'm a businessman. If I thought there was any way I could put things in my favour, I'd tell you as much as I know. But this is a pretty one-sided sort of deal, from what I can see.'

Noye was then told about the surveillance operation on Hollywood Cottage, including the day Reader left Noye's house with that heavy briefcase and went to central London.

'That was gold from the Brink's-Mat robbery, wasn't it?' pressed Charman.

'Like you said, there's other people involved. I can't take

the blame for what they do,' said Noye.

When Suckling tried to suggest that Noye was one of the actual robbers on the raid, he looked stunned: 'It doesn't start with me, no. I've never done a robbery in my life.'

Noye was then asked how he paid for Hollywood Cottage. He claimed it had been with money from an insurance claim on a boat and other money he had earned.

Asked how long he'd been helping to dispose of the gold bullion, he ingenuously replied, 'How long have you been watching me?'

'Since 8 January,' replied Suckling. 'But we know it goes back beyond that.'

'How?' asked Noye.

It seemed a brilliant ploy – the prisoner was interrogating his guards.

Suckling went on: 'Because of what people down in Bristol and Hatton Garden have said.' Suckling then mentioned a fence who'd handled much of the gold.

'I don't know him. You haven't seen him with me, have you?' challenged Noye.

Charman answered, 'We'll accept that. Will you accept that not everybody is capable of disposing of or dealing in gold?'

'Yes, I'll accept that,' replied Noye.

'Will you accept that you have been to Jersey with others in a private plane and that you bought gold there?' continued the detective, incorrectly (Noye had taken a chartered flight for the trip).

Noye smiled.

'Yes. So what?'

Suckling then told him they believed the gold was bought to provide legitimate paperwork to cover the moving of stolen gold. He was also told that he had been watched at the Beaverwood Club handing gold over to Reader.

'Perhaps that was the gold I bought in Jersey?' he ventured.

'It wasn't,' replied Suckling. 'We know that gold is still in vaults in Jersey.'

Charman tried to drive home just how much the Flying Squad already knew about the gold run, saying: 'From what we've seen, the activity round you tends to indicate that you are the trusted middleman who has got the contacts and the money to get what's necessary done.'

'I know what you want from me, but any business I do with you will get me done in,' was the dramatic reply.

'Aren't you exaggerating a bit?' asked Suckling.

'I know enough about the people involved to know that if I say what I know, and anything happens after that, they'll know it can only have come from me. If I do anything to get you back that gold which they think belongs to them, then that's me done.'

'Well two of them can't bother you, surely; they are locked up for twenty-five years,' said Charman.

Noye then began to voice suspicions about how the police had got on to him. He named a man who, detectives believed, had taken part in the original raid but whose involvement they had been unable to prove.

'He probably gave you the name because you gave him

some help. He's made sure his share is all right. The only sort of deal I'll do is like my business – if it's all in writing and signed by the people concerned.'

With that Noye fell silent for a few moments, then told the detectives that he wanted to speak to lead officer Brian Boyce.

'We will speak to Mr Boyce when we leave you,' promised Suckling. 'What can you tell us about Tony Black?' he added, picking up on Noye's remark at the start of the interview.

'I can tell you he's as good as dead,' said Kenneth Noye. 'I know all about false identities and all that, and I know that won't help him at all. They'll find him and they'll have him.'

'Who's going to have him, then?' asked Suckling.

'There's enough money from this to get anyone to do it. They don't need to get their hands dirty.'

'Do you know if anyone has been hired or propositioned to do it?'

'No, but they'll get that sorted out. It's easy enough.'

Noye was then asked about instructions for the furnace, which were found in the apple store and – once again – about where he got his money from.

'I'm a businessman. I told you what I am,' he insisted.

Noye's attempt to sound respectable annoyed Detective Charman intensely.

'What you are, Mr Noye, is a man well acquainted with villains, armed robbers and the sort of men who come into large amounts of money, who will come to you to launder their cash. You're trusted to keep your mouth shut, and you share in the profits of crime by percentages, without having to put yourself up front.'

'I put myself up front the other night, didn't I?' Noye bitterly responded. Charman continued: 'It always goes wrong for these people at one time or another. Why protect them? I suspect that if they were in your position, they wouldn't hesitate to put your name forward. In fact, there's something to bear in mind for the future with this inquiry. A lot of people have been arrested.'

The appeal failed. 'Then they will have to watch themselves like Black, won't they?' said Noye coolly.

As the interview drew to a close, Noye inquired again about Fordham's family, asking how they were.

'I think you can guess that as well as we can,' said Suckling.

'If that hadn't happened, I think we could be talking now,' said Noye.

'What do you mean? What could we be talking about?' asked Suckling.

'All I'd have to worry about would be the gold, and I think perhaps I might have got a deal and you might have got what you wanted.'

Three hours later Kenneth Noye was interviewed in his cell by Brian Boyce, following his earlier request. Boyce entered the cell with his deputy, DCI Ken John. Noye immediately made a point of shaking Boyce's hand using one of the secret grips by which Freemasons the world over recognize each other.

Noye smiled. He believed that if Boyce was a Mason

then he might appreciate the gesture. Boyce was far from impressed, and noted the incident as yet another example of Noye trying to manipulate police officers, whatever their rank.

Boyce explained that he wanted to ask questions about the gold found outside Hollywood Cottage. Boyce made a point of warning Noye in the usual manner that anything he said could be used as evidence later.

Noye then turned to the police chief.

'Mr Boyce, can I speak to you alone?'

'Yes, if you prefer,' responded the senior detective. DCI John immediately left the cell.

Noye continued: 'I want to speak to you off the record. I won't if you write anything down. Have you got a tape recorder going?'

Boyce replied that he had not. He even opened his brief case and emptied out his pockets to put the prisoner's mind at rest.

'I won't write anything down,' promised Boyce.

Noye began by asking Boyce if he considered him to be a cold-blooded killer.

Boyce said he didn't know, but there seemed to be nothing in his record to indicate that he was. Noye then asked Boyce what he thought would happen to him. Boyce said it was up to the court.

'Yes, but what you say can make or break me,' replied Noye.

Boyce emphasized that all he could do was present the evidence. The rest was up to the court to decide. Noye then began to say that he was a very rich man and that he wanted to give some money to John Fordham's wife and family. Boyce said he understood.

Next Noye turned to matters closer to home. If he went to prison for a long time, his life and that of his family would be destroyed.

Noye asked Boyce whether he had any family, and was told he had. Then Noye inquired when the detective was due to retire.

'I conclude some thirty years' service in four years,' replied Boyce.

'I'll make sure you have a good retirement,' said Noye quietly but firmly. 'I'll ensure you have plenty of money when you leave the police. I'll put one million in a bank anywhere in the world that you tell me. No one will be able to trace it. I just want you to ensure I do not go to prison.'

Boyce's face showed no emotion – or surprise.

'You're wasting your time talking to me this way.'

Boyce went on to say the only kind of help he wanted was for Noye to reveal the whereabouts of the Brink's-Mat bullion. Boyce re-emphasized his point. He told Noye he had better weigh up whether or not he was going to tell him where the bullion was.

Noye replied that he would think about it but that Boyce should remember his offer.

'I am a man of my word,' said Noye.

He repeated his offer to compensate Fordham's widow and children and told Boyce to think about his £1m offer. Boyce said there was no question of accepting, and repeated what he had said earlier.

At the end of the conversation Noye made a point of

mentioning that there had been no written record of their interview. He didn't look happy when Boyce informed him that the contents of the conversation would be written down immediately after Boyce left the cell.

Noye recovered his composure before Boyce left and told him: 'You are on your own.'

Then he offered the detective a bribe yet again.

Months later Boyce was accused in court of offering to get Noye a reduced sentence. He denied it categorically and related how the bribe offer was made.

'I couldn't be mistaken about being offered a million pounds,' said Boyce.

The day after he had brazenly tried to bribe the lead detective on the Brink's-Mat inquiry, Kenneth Noye was interviewed again by detectives Suckling and Charman, who wanted the combination for the safe found buried in the floor of one of the rooms at Hollywood Cottage.

Initially Noye refused to reveal it, saying he feared the police could use it to plant evidence. He wanted to talk to his solicitor before deciding what to do. All it contained, he insisted, was a diamond, some other jewellery and some cash. Once told, however, that unless the combination was forthcoming the safe would be forced, Noye revealed the figure sequence.

Noye was then informed that the prefix of a bundle of notes found near his sister's house in nearby West Kingsdown corresponded to that on £50 notes found at Reader's house and on people involved with the gold runs down to Bristol.

Suckling gently turned the screw further. 'You must admit that the series of £50 notes, like our observations of you and the others, seem to link all of the people concerned in the disposal of the gold.'

Later that same morning, Brian Reader and Kenneth Noye were both charged with conspiracy to handle stolen bullion.

Noye's only response was: 'No reply until I see my solicitor.'

Over in Bexleyheath, Kenneth Noye's parents Jim and Edith were moving out after almost forty years living in their bungalow in Jenton Avenue. They told neighbours that their beloved son Kenneth had built them a house at the end of a cul-de-sac in West Kingsdown, next to where his sister Hilary lived. Mr and Mrs Noye admitted that it didn't matter whether or not they sold their bungalow because their son had already paid for their new property.

Just before they moved out, Mr and Mrs Noye allowed the police to thoroughly search the house, garage and gardens. Officers even dug up Mr Noye Senior's vegetable patch in the search for some of the missing Brink's-Mat gold. The only thing of interest the detectives did come across were hundreds of new telephones stored in the garage. Neither Mr Noye – a former telephone engineer – nor his wife could explain where they came from.

The murder charge against Brenda Noye was eventually dismissed at a committal hearing at Lambeth magistrates' court in south London two months after her initial arrest because of insufficient evidence against her. However she was rearrested as she left court and charged with conspiracy to handle stolen bullion.

FIFTEEN

Around this time another of the suspected Brink's-Mat robbers – George 'Georgie Boy' Francis – found himself at the centre of some extensive police attention when officers swooped on his pub and adjoining property in Kent. Wily Francis protested that he had nothing to hide, and they went away empty-handed.

But villains linked to the Brink's-Mat job started hearing some typical underworld rumours about George Francis and how he might have done a deal with the police in exchange for being allowed to keep his liberty. When certain criminals – both inside and outside prison – heard the gossip they decided something had to be done.

In May 1985 – with Kenneth Noye in custody awaiting trial for the murder of DC John Fordham, and McAvoy and Robinson long since incarcerated – Georgie Boy was holding court as usual behind the bar of his pub, the Henry VIII, near Hever Castle in Kent.

A hooded gunman, dressed entirely in black, burst in and shot Francis at point-blank range before escaping on a motorbike. Francis survived after an operation to remove a 9 mm bullet from his shoulder but the message had been sent loud and clear to all those connected with Brink's-Mat who had not yet been sent to prison. *Keep your trap shut.*

After the killing of a policeman, now one of the suspected robbers had been gunned down. The curse of Brink's-Mat had well and truly kicked in.

Soon after John Fordham's death, his C11 partner Neil Murphy suffered a minor nervous breakdown and was caught trying to leave a shop near his home without paying for some cassette tapes. Newspapers at the time referred to the incident as the 'onion-field syndrome', named after a book by the former Los Angeles detective Joseph Wambaugh about a policeman who began stealing when tormented by guilt following the murder of his partner. It was a true story, and in the case of that officer a psychiatrist wrote that his behaviour 'reflects his need to manipulate the environment to agree with his obsession that he is an unworthy person, to punish himself and to relieve the anxiety of unconscious guilt, and to unconsciously avoid his police colleagues who he felt looked critically at him . . .'

The incident involving Neil Murphy was far less serious, but there were some clear similarities. The store did not prosecute, and Murphy was allowed to retain his job with C11 after having psychiatric counselling. He explained that no dishonesty had been involved – his mind had simply been miles away.

Meanwhile another sinister group of characters was starting to take an unhealthy interest in the Brink's-Mat gold.

They had played no part in the planning, the robbery itself or even the initial aftermath but now they were circling like hungry wolves around a lump of dead meat, each wanting a chunk of the Crime of the Century.

The police were desperately trying to avoid any more bloodshed but there was an overriding feeling that Fordham's death and the shooting were just the tip of the iceberg. Detectives attempted to keep tabs on what was happening but all that did was encourage some rogue officers to nurture their favourite villains. What John Symonds, a corrupt London cop, said in a taped conversation with a London gangster a few years earlier summed it up perfectly: 'Always let me know straight away if you need anythin' because I know people everywhere. I'm in a little firm in a firm. If you're nicked anywhere in London I can get on the blower to someone in my firm who will know someone somewhere who will get somethin' done.'

The discovery of the gold at Noye's house had enabled the Metropolitan Police to formally take over the DC Fordham murder investigation from Kent because it clearly linked the case to the missing Brink's-Mat bullion. The decision was reached after a top-level meeting at Scotland Yard between Brian Worth, the Yard's Deputy Assistant Commissioner in charge of serious crime operations, Anthony Coe, Kent Police's Assistant Chief Constable in charge of operations, and Detective Chief Superintendent Duncan Gibbins, head of Kent CID.

The operation was placed in the hands of Commander Philip Corbett from C11. Running such an operation was usually outside the department's remit, but the fact that it was one of their officers who'd been killed superseded normal procedures. Corbett had also received the relevant training in running an inter-force inquiry and, after all, the investigation into Noye had been initiated largely by intelligence provided by C11. It made little odds, however, as C11 allowed the on-the-ground investigation to continue to be handled by Brian Boyce and his officers in C8.

As far as some coppers were concerned, the Fordham killing galvanized the police efforts to bring the other Brink's-Mat suspects to justice. Corbett recruited master thief-taker Tony Lundy, a straight-talking northerner with an extraordinary record for arresting villains. He had crossed many senior officers and was told in no uncertain terms that he had to work on the Brink's-Mat inquiry or take early retirement. Lundy was given the brief to turn over every single suspect until they had brought the whole team to justice, as well as locating all the gold and prosecuting the killer or killers of John Fordham.

However other detectives, such as DI Tony Brightwell, felt that the Fordham killing in fact diverted the investigation. He later explained: 'The trouble was that John Fordham's death turned around the whole emphasis of the investigation and in some ways it did make it more difficult. The underworld knew we were going to step up our inquiries and they deliberately shrank back into the shadows, knowing full well that because a copper had been killed we would not be holding back.'

Tony Lundy disagrees to this day. He said in an interview in the autumn of 2010: 'Before John Fordham's killing the whole Brink's-Mat inquiry was drifting to such a degree that it looked as if no one else was going to get nicked in connection with the robbery or the handling of the gold.'

Lundy got to work in his own inimitable fashion and soon discovered that the gang's own solicitor, Michael Relton, had became a major conduit through which some of the gold was travelling. He'd joined other gang members in paying large sums of money into newly created bank accounts, purchasing plots of land on the Costa del Sol and investing in properties all over the UK, Europe and even North America. One account, in a bank in Liechtenstein, was in the name of the Moyet Foundation. Suspected Brink's-Mat robber Perry apparently named it in honour of his favourite brand of champagne, Moët & Chandon, but misspelt it. Brian Perry's friend Gordon Parry – who'd been heavily involved in handling some of the gold since the robbery – began taking frequent flights to Zurich. This rash of activity came because the gang had decided they could not wait any longer to start enjoying the proceeds of their crime. It was a huge mistake, which would eventually cost them dearly.

In 1985, acquitted Brink's-Mat suspect Tony White bought a £146,000 house in Beckenham, Kent – in cash. It seemed to be his way of winding up the 'opposition', who consisted of the police and insurance investigators. Insurance agent Bob McCunn was infuriated but also quite relieved. The gang were finally starting to show their true colours by being greedy and flash, and that gave him more opportunities to exert immense pressure on some of them to return the gold.

Then Tony White – the so-called King of Catford – surprised his friends and his enemies by agreeing to talk to the Brink's-Mat loss adjusters. Clearly White still feared arrest and a subsequent long sentence, so he hoped to reduce it by cooperating and assisting in the recovery of some of the proceeds of the robbery.

Tony Lundy and his crack team of detectives followed this up by putting even more pressure on solicitor suspect Michael Relton. As a result, Relton provided the police and law firm Shaw & Croft, who were working on behalf of the insurers, Lloyds, with detailed information about bank accounts and property and even produced letters of authority to overseas banks so that evidence could be collected directly. After receiving a number of death threats, Relton got cold feet, but by then Shaw & Croft already had enough detail – and the crucial letters of authority – to begin freezing various bank accounts and assets both in the UK and abroad. Tenacious insurance investigator Bob McCunn even discovered that a couple of the robbers had apparently bought an oil well in Kansas.

As Tony Lundy later explained: 'For once we had the support of every single officer from all sides of the police because one of our own had been killed in the line of duty. There was a healthy obsession inside the force to bring the perpetrators to justice, whatever the cost.'

By this time, police believed that at least half the gold had been smelted and sold back to legitimate dealers, including Johnson Matthey, to whom, ironically, it belonged in the first place. Much of it even ended up as expensive jewellery. Meanwhile the remaining gold, worth at least £10m, was, they believed, buried and undiscovered. The proceeds of the robbery had already gone up in value tenfold, thanks to property investments, bank interest and the ever-rising price of gold.

At one stage detective Tony Lundy managed to persuade McAvoy and Robinson – both then serving their sentences at Long Lartin prison in Leicestershire – to meet him. Lundy believed that because of an appeal the two men had pending against their long sentences, they might agree to hand back some of the gold in return for a shorter term inside. At first McAvoy and Robinson made it crystal clear that they wouldn't consider any sort of deal that might involve grassing up any of their fellow gang members. Lundy had a sneaking admiration for both men, although he later concluded: 'McAvoy was the real boss. He was the one calling the shots. Robinson was quieter and less aggressive and less controlling. But I respected their attitude and because of that they started to seriously consider doing some kind of deal.'

That's when McAvoy astounded Lundy by openly boasting he had control of half the gold. 'That half doesn't go anywhere until I say so,' said McAvoy. Lundy knew only too well that that meant he might be able to get McAvoy's half back if he could persuade both men to cooperate.

Today, Lundy insists that McAvoy and Robinson were on the verge of agreeing a deal when his bosses decided to deal directly with both men. 'The deal immediately collapsed because other officers above me wanted a piece of the glory,' added Lundy. 'It was typical of the way things were back in those days.'

Lundy was considered a loose cannon who needed to be 'pulled in' now and again but he remains convinced to this day that if he had been allowed to slowly work away at McAvoy and Robinson, then that remaining gold might well have been returned.

Instead Lundy and other detectives were sent off travelling the world to try and unravel what many believed was one of the most sophisticated money-laundering operations ever seen. They eventually traced the proceeds of the robbery to the Isle of Man, the Channel Islands, the British Virgin Islands, the Bahamas, Spain and Florida. The inquiry also exposed close links between British, Italian, French, Spanish and American criminals, including the Mafia on the east coast of the United States.

Brian Perry's mate Gordon Parry and crooked Brink's-Mat solicitor Relton were eventually linked to the deposit of at least £7.6m around the world. Many large sums were transferred offshore, via a Bank of Ireland account in south London. At least 170 accounts were opened on the Isle of Man alone. It was a huge, complex, carefully organized laundering operation, which required tenacity and skill to pick apart. Relton would later be convicted for his role in handling the gold and given a twelve-year sentence. In a separate trial, Parry was found guilty on ten counts of handling stolen goods.

Much of the Brink's-Mat money travelled through a series of international accounts before ending up in Switzerland and Liechtenstein. Increasing amounts continued to be invested in property in the London Docklands redevelopment boom of the mid-1980s. A portion was even used to buy a former section of Cheltenham Ladies' College, which was then converted into flats that eventually sold for a total of £1.6m, providing the robbers with a forty per cent profit.

Investigators including detective Tony Lundy and insurance agent Bob McCunn found one investment, bought for £1.6m, that was later sold for £8m. Another building, bought for £2.7m, was sold for £4.25m. A third deal saw them net £1.75m for a property bought for £750,000.

Lundy started looking especially closely at Brink's-Mat handler Gordon Parry, who'd been 'recruited' by his mate, the suspected robber Brian Perry. It turned out Perry's son lived with Parry's daughter. Lundy knew that these sorts of personal connections could provide a useful way into the investigation. As the investigation progressed, it soon became clear what a significant figure Brian Perry was in the gang. Perry was renowned in London's criminal fraternity as a 'good operator'. He had links with all sorts of other notorious faces including the notorious Arifs, a south London Turkish-Cypriot family involved in serious crimes including drug smuggling and armed robbery.

Perhaps unsurprisingly, Brian Perry had made several attempts to provide an alibi for his old friend Mickey McAvoy, but his efforts had failed. The police professed themselves to be bemused by his attempts to back his friend's story up when his wife had already provided an alibi. Some in the underworld suspected Perry wasn't so disappointed at the outcome as it left him in charge of a big percentage of the original Brink's-Mat gold. Perry claimed to be the one entrusted with looking after McAvoy and Robinson's interests after they were jailed. When McAvoy had seriously considered trying to reduce his sentence by offering to help police recover the gold, he negotiated with them through Perry. But, like all proper villains, Brian Perry looked after his own interests before all else. Above the desk in the office of his south London minicab office was a sign which said: 'Remember the Golden Rule. Whoever has the gold makes the rules.'

McAvoy began to suspect Perry was plundering his share of the gold when Perry purchased an expensive family house in Biggin Hill, Kent. By all accounts, the incarcerated McAvoy was outraged. One detective close to him later explained: 'Mickey went ballistic when he heard about Perry's new gaff. It was a real slap in the face for him. After all he was doing a twenty-five-year stretch, while others were out and about enjoying a champagne lifestyle thanks to the job he masterminded.' According to a Channel 4 programme on Brink's Mat, McAvoy eventually got so angry he sent a letter from prison threatening to kill Perry if he failed to cough up McAvoy's share.

It seems that Brian Perry thought himself invincible. He even jokingly referred to the fact that if his mate Gordon Parry were to die he'd get his £3m share of the proceeds. Rumours started to circulate in south-east London that Perry was feeding information to the police in exchange for being left alone.

Detectives believed that Gordon Parry was the weak link in the Brink's-Mat chain so they decided to move in and put him under some pressure. But when police stopped his car in south London, Parry escaped arrest by driving off with a detective clinging to his car until he was thrown off.

After this Parry went on the run, but not before telling a number of associates that he believed he'd been stitched up by his 'friend' Perry. Parry headed out to what he thought would be the safer havens of the Costa del Sol. But the extradition rules between the two countries were about to change, which would mean his days were numbered, and he was eventually arrested and placed in a Malaga police station to await a flight back to the UK.

Back in England, yet more Brink's-Mat-fuelled rumours starting sweeping south-east London. This time it was being said that Parry had grassed up Perry to two London detectives who'd flown over to interview him before he returned to the UK. In fact, the opposite was more likely to be true. Brian Perry was going out of his way to 'smear' his one-time best friend Parry.

One detective later explained that Parry had not grassed anyone up at all: 'In fact, he was incredibly careful about not naming anyone else he was involved with.'

But Brian Perry was determined to make an example of Parry, so he commissioned a hit squad to fly to Spain and kill Parry while he awaited extradition from the Costa del Crime. Word of the plan reached detectives before the killers even arrived on Spanish soil, and Scotland Yard persuaded the Spanish police to move Parry to a secret location. He was saved from almost certain death, and the threat eventually subsided.

Another recipient of police attention was suspected Brink's-Mat robber John 'Little Legs' Lloyd's partner Jean Savage who was arrested after it was discovered that she'd deposited £2.5m at the Bank of Ireland, Croydon, where Kenneth Noye had an account under a false name. Before his arrest for the Fordham killing, Noye and Savage had been seen making deposits at the bank on alternate days. The money Savage deposited was transferred to Dublin, where it was earning £45,000 in interest per month. Savage had previously left the money untouched for months, but then panicked when Parry was arrested in Spain and tried to move it. By sticking her head above the parapet, Savage unintentionally let word of her actions filter through to the south-east London underworld and eventually the robbery investigation team heard about her plans and moved in.

Another notorious character, called Patrick Clark, was soon linked to the robbery through his friendship with Jean Savage. Some officers even suspected Clark might have been one of the actual robbers who took part in the Brink's-Mat raid. Clark deposited £3.2m into an account at the Bank of Ireland's Finchley branch and more than £1m at its branch in Ilford, Essex. Clark later went to America to meet up with Little Legs Lloyd, but was arrested on his return.

Further afield, more and more Brink's-Mat money was being poured into property developments on the Costa del Sol where at least three of the robbery 'team' also purchased homes and put cash into constructing apartment blocks.

Some experts in that part of Spain believe that crime helped create much of the property boom of the late 1980s and '90s that swept through southern Spain's coastal areas, and Brink's-Mat money would have been central to this.

The influence of the Crime of the Century seemed to know no boundaries.

The failure to prosecute certain suspects clearly linked to the Brink's-Mat case seemed to embolden the remaining gang members to go on to bigger and more sophisticated business deals. They'd long since linked up with crooked lawyers and property developers, as well as working in alliance with gun-runners and drug traffickers in Spain and the US. Investments in ventures such as the London Docklands developments of the mid-1980s continued to yield extraordinary dividends.

The Brink's-Mat company, meanwhile, no longer existed as a single entity and its Heathrow vault was decommissioned. Guard Scouse moved on too. His appetite for that kind of work had unsurprisingly diminished after his experiences during the robbery.

Kenneth Noye and Brian Reader's trial for the murder of DC John Fordham took place at the Old Bailey in November 1985. At the request of the defence, proceedings relating to the handling of the gold and VAT fraud were deferred to a later date.

The drama was played out in front of a jury of seven men and five women, packed press benches and a public gallery filled with well-known faces from the criminal underworld. Security was so tight that each time Noye or Reader arrived or left in a prison van, streets around the court were closed off and armed police posted at various vantage points.

Surprisingly for a major Old Bailey murder trial, there were no challenges when the jury was selected. Under English law a defendant had the right, generally exercised through the defence counsel, to reject three jurors and demand replacements without giving any reason. Over the years many defence lawyers had challenged anyone who looked remotely middle-class, the belief being that the more affluent and 'respectable' a juror looks, the more likely he or she is to accept the word of the police against a defendant.

Kenneth Noye used his wealth to secure the services of John Mathew QC. Mathew was a wily, highly respected legal eagle whose professional skills had already got Tony White a pass out of jail. Mathew insisted that neither Noye nor Reader had anything to fear from a middle-class jury because they had nothing to hide. Mathew went on to challenge virtually every police statement in his bid to prove Noye's innocence.

On day one of the trial – immediately after the jury had been sworn in – the court was cleared while the judge, Mr Justice Caulfield, outlined to the jurors the protection they were to receive, including a round-the-clock police guard and the interception of all telephone calls to their homes.

Police fears were fuelled on that first day when Reader's old friend John Goodwin turned up in the public gallery at the Old Bailey. Just a few years earlier he'd been sentenced to seven years for nobbling the jury in a burglary trial in which he and Reader were co-defendants.

Scotland Yard officers visited the jury at the end of each day's hearing to make sure there had been no approaches. One of Noye's relatives was alleged to have approached a juror in the south London suburb of Bromley while she was out shopping. The woman was immediately given two police guards. Seventy-two police officers were assigned to jury protection duty during the Noye and Reader trial. It was a huge show of force, and seemed deliberately intended to tell the criminals that they should not even attempt to influence the jury.

The start of the trial brought an immediate objection from the defence to the use of photographs of the house and grounds of Hollywood Cottage, which were to be distributed to the jury. The photographs, Noye's QC Mathew pointed out, had been taken in daylight and could give a misleading impression as Noye's alleged murder of Fordham had occurred at night.

The judge agreed, and asked if the defence wanted the jury to see the property for themselves in conditions similar to those of the night in question. That offer was readily accepted. The court was adjourned and later that evening it reconvened in one of the most bizarre settings in British legal history.

At 5.50 p.m., in darkness and during a heavy rainstorm, three limousines ferried the jury to the gates of Hollywood Cottage. The jurors pulled their coats over their faces to hide their identities from the waiting television crews and press photographers. Ten minutes later, with blue lights flashing, two police cars arrived. Behind them was a green prison van containing Noye with a police back-up Range Rover following. Brian Reader had decided against attending, which was his legal right.

On the tarmac apron outside the gates – just yards from where Fordham had been found dying by his colleagues – the Old Bailey clerk convened the court. The official shorthand writer beside him was sheltering under an umbrella, while he painstakingly recorded everything that was said. Then there was the judge, complete with bowler hat.

Noye had an escort of four policemen and four prison officers, one of whom he was handcuffed to. The jury and a clutch of legal representatives were shown the grounds. Following at a discreet distance were more than thirty journalists, straining to hear every word.

Up at the house Brenda Noye and her two young sons were grouped together at a lighted window waving forlornly to Noye, hemmed in on both sides by his burly escorts. Moments later, Brenda Noye handed out a coat and a pair of Wellington boots for Noye to wear. They were thoroughly checked under torchlight by two police officers before he was allowed to put them on. The expression on Noye's face was a combination of aggressive confidence mixed with injured innocence. It was the way he looked for much of the trial.

In the days of legal arguments that followed, Noye's decision to splash out on Mathew – one of the best defence counsels in the land – proved to be money well spent.

Mathew admitted that Noye had indeed carried out the

stabbing – but insisted it was justified defence after Fordham had struck Noye in the face when he was discovered.

In that admission, much stress was laid on the way Fordham looked that dark night. Dressed in camouflage clothing and a balaclava, he would, said Mathew, 'have struck terror in the bravest of us'.

Mathew told the court that Noye's reaction had been: 'Shocked terror. He froze, terrified with fear. Then he was hit in the face, in the left eye – he didn't know with what, but he sprang to life, thinking in a flash that he had been struck with some kind of weapon and assumed that the other man was armed. He presumed he had seconds to live; he thought his end had come, and in a blind panic "stabbed and stabbed".'

Brian Reader's counsel also insisted that there was no case to answer. Reader exercised his right not to give evidence at all during the trial. And just in case they thought this indicated he had something to hide, the judge reminded the jury that it was only since 1898 that a person charged with any offence – including murder – had the right under English law to give evidence.

Reader could only be found guilty of murder if, first, Noye was proved to have murdered and if Reader was proved to have given assistance or participated in an assault with the intention of killing Fordham or causing him serious injury. Thus in his case there was no pressure for a manslaughter option.

The court heard that Brian Reader had been seen to make a kicking motion by Fordham's colleague, Neil Murphy, but he did not see where the kick landed, and his claim was made in a statement five months after Fordham's death. Noye's counsel was remarkably open about the criminal activities in which Noye and Reader had been engaged on the night of Fordham's killing. They were illegally dealing in gold, he admitted. But they claimed it was gold that had nothing to do with the Brink's-Mat case.

The bullion found at Hollywood Cottage was the subject of proceedings to be dealt with separately, so in the interests of justice, the full details of the involvement of Noye and Reader with the Brink's-Mat bullion were omitted.

The prosecution in the murder case could only mention it when explaining why the two defendants were under surveillance. With Brink's-Mat, it was alleged, the stakes were so high that Noye and Reader had no compunction about murdering anyone who jeopardized their activities. The prosecution said that Noye had millions of pounds in various bank accounts and referred to an account in Brenda Noye's name at an Irish bank that contained £1.5m.

'I have access to various bank accounts, but the money is not mine,' Noye told the court.

By admitting to both the killing and the fact that he was engaged in a wholesale gold-smuggling operation, Noye was hardly presenting himself as a respectable figure to the jury at Old Bailey. But after those revelations, virtually every part of the police evidence – including the interviews with the two defendants and Brenda Noye – would be vigorously challenged as Noye's QC took the initiative.

*

Five months after their initial arrest and following twelve hours and thirty-seven minutes of jury deliberation, not guilty verdicts were returned against both Noye and Reader. The jury accepted that the killing had been self-defence. Kenneth Noye smiled, looked at his wife, then turned to the jury and said: 'Thank you very much. God bless you. Thank you for proving my innocence because that is what I am, not guilty.' Beside him Reader turned to the jury and said: 'Thank you for proving my innocence.'

The impression was slightly spoiled a few moments later when Noye turned to the back of the court – by then packed with Flying Squad officers – and sneered and mouthed obscenities.

The judge refused Noye's application that his defence costs should be paid out of public funds – Reader was on legal aid – but to Noye it was still money well spent. Anne Fordham, the 38-year-old widow of the dead policeman, left the court – where she had sat every day listening to evidence – in tears. A reporter asked Mrs Fordham about the sympathy extended by Brenda Noye.

'Not accepted,' she whispered.

Many of the trials connected to the Brink's-Mat robbery seemed to end in surprising acquittals. As a result, there have always been whispers in the underworld about how wisely money had been invested. However there is no evidence to suggest that anything other than the true course of justice was followed during these trials.

SIXTEEN

So it was that a supremely confident Kenneth Noye strolled back into the dock at the Old Bailey's Number 12 court in May 1986 – five months after his acquittal for DC Fordham's murder. Alongside him in the witness box were his fellow conspirators – Reader, Chappell, Patch, the A-Team's Tommy Adams, Lawson and an elderly fence called Matteo Constantinou.

They'd all spent the intervening time in prison cells, after being arrested during the lead up to the trial, but nothing had dampened their spirits following what Noye saw as a superb victory over his great enemies, the cozzers, in the Fordham murder trial. The defendants and their small army of fourteen defence barristers were supremely optimistic before the trial, which was expected to last two to three months. All the defendants denied handling the bullion, as they did a second charge, which all except Lawson faced – conspiracy to evade VAT.

As far as the first, more serious offence, was concerned, Noye was the principal defendant, as he had been during that earlier murder trial. The gold distribution chain had started with him. If the jury couldn't agree that he was guilty of conspiring to handle stolen gold bullion, then they certainly couldn't convict any of the others.

Judge Richard Lowry QC seemed an ideal choice to preside the case; his entry in *Who's Who* listed 'fossiling' (searching for gold in old, disused seams) as one of his hobbies.

Noye believed there was a crucial flaw in the prosecution case – there was no tangible evidence that the gold he'd been handling came originally from the Brink's-Mat haul. But, following the death of John Fordham, the police had made some very thorough inquiries into Noye's 'business dealings'. They knew that, after the Brink's-Mat robbery, Noye had deposited large amounts of money abroad, sometimes using a false name. They also had a record of all the replies he allegedly made while being interrogated by the police, together with Brian Reader's damning admission – shortly before he was charged – that the gold he was handling came from the Brink's-Mat haul.

Probably the most significant piece of evidence against Noye was some jottings in one of his diaries, which showed the daily gold price fixes at the time of the Heathrow robbery. Why would he have made those if he was not involved in handling the gold?

What Noye and the others did not realize was that a young barrister was sitting at the back of the court carefully noting down every single reference to where the gold might have ended up after the heist. He was employed by the Brink's-Mat insurers, who remained determined to recover as much of the gold as possible. Armed with that evidence they sent a team of private investigators to study the homes and offices of all the Brink's-Mat suspects.

They targeted many other people, even those who'd not been prosecuted by police. It didn't matter to the insurers whether they'd been charged or not – if they'd used some of the money raised from that gold to improve their lifestyles then that made them legitimate targets. Files were opened on each and every person as well as the many companies linked to the Brink's-Mat case. Documents were carefully assembled.

Kenneth Noye and the others had made the mistake of thinking that it would only be the police who'd pursue them.

'They didn't know where we were coming from. They thought perhaps we had some sort of moral vendetta against them while in fact we just wanted to recover the stolen property,' insurance lawyer Bob McCunn later explained.

During the trial itself, Noye talked about the gold smuggling operation but refused to name any of the individuals involved and claimed that no records were ever kept of the various transactions. Noye was unable to explain why the date of the Brink's-Mat raid had an asterisk placed against it in his wife's 1983 diary, with a doodle drawn alongside.

An examination of Brenda Noye's 1984 diary showed a similar asterisk every twenty-five to twenty-eight days. Noye's defence counsel John Mathew helpfully explained to the court: 'It is clear what those asterisks relate to.'

In his summing up to the court, Mathew admitted to the jury that Kenneth Noye was 'a wheeler-dealer; he may have evaded his tax responsibility; and he may have had trouble over the years (but not for some years) with the law, but at least one can say he has never been an idle layabout.

'As he has said, "I don't do any transaction without a deal on the side." Not paying your taxes and smuggling, in this day and age, you may think possibly unhappily, are looked upon by many as being in a totally different bracket to the offences of theft and handling stolen property.'

Two and a half months after the trial began, the court rose and the jury of eight men and four women retired to consider its verdicts. The jurors were informed that – under the supervision of court bailiffs – they would be looked after at an £80-a-night London hotel. No discussion of the case would be allowed outside the jury room.

The loss adjusters handling the Brink's-Mat insurance claim for Lloyds were so concerned that the defendants might be acquitted that they launched a civil action against them the following morning. In a High Court action, a judge agreed that the assets of all seven accused should be frozen pending an outcome of the civil hearings.

And in the middle of all this, rumours began spreading about the jury in the criminal trial. The stories were damaging and highly offensive, and none of them have ever been proven to be true. It wasn't until the following Wednesday that the jury finally returned with their verdicts.

Noye, Reader and Chappell were found guilty both of the conspiracy to handle stolen bullion charge and the VAT charge.

By the time the last defendant Constantinou's conviction for evading VAT was announced, the judge had to shout to make himself heard. Patch, Adams and Lawson were all acquitted.

(Tommy Adams's equally notorious brother Patsy proved that London's premier crime family the A-Team really did have Teflon skin when he was acquitted of importing three tons of cannabis shortly after Tommy's court appearance.)

'I hope you all die of cancer,' screamed Noye at the jury as the verdicts against him sank in.

Noye's wife Brenda then shouted across the court from the public gallery: 'Never has such an injustice been done. There is no fuckin' justice in this trial.'

Pointing to the jury, Brian Reader exploded.

'You have made one terrible mistake. You have got to live with that for the rest of your life.'

Reader's twenty-year-old son Paul scuffled with police officers as he shouted: 'You have been fuckin' fixed up!' He was arrested for contempt of court and later bound over for the sum of £100 to keep the peace for twelve months. Defence counsel Mathew was infuriated by the Noyes' outburst and told Kenneth Noye his comments from the dock would not help when it came to sentencing.

Down in the cells beneath the Old Bailey, customs officers immediately slapped a £1m writ on Noye for the VAT they said he'd evaded. A six-page High Court writ was also served on him from the Inland Revenue, claiming nearly £1m in back tax.

The following day, in a bid to make amends, Noye, casually dressed in pale-blue sweater and open-necked shirt, apologized to the judge before sentencing was announced. His outburst, he said, had been made 'in the heat of the moment'. Then he stood resignedly as Judge Lowry jailed him for thirteen years for plotting to handle the gold and fined him £250,000. Noye was also fined a similar amount for evading VAT, plus an extra year's imprisonment, and ordered to pay £200,000 towards the cost of the case, which was estimated to be £2m. Noye then received another two years' imprisonment for failing to pay the two fines. He couldn't pay – his assets had been frozen.

Judge Lowry said the fines could be considered 'paltry' compared with the sums of money involved in handling the gold. Chappell was jailed for a total of ten years for both offences, fined £200,000 and ordered to pay £75,000 towards the cost of the prosecution, while Reader, described by Judge Lowry as Noye's 'vigorous right-hand man', was jailed for a total of nine years. Constantinou was given a year, suspended for two years, on the VAT fraud.

A day later it was announced that Kenneth and Brenda Noye plus two others would face trial over the Meissen china found in one of the secret compartments at Holly-wood Cottage and at one of the houses in Hever Avenue, West Kingsdown. As Noye's assets were frozen, he applied for and was granted legal aid. Later Noye also received a four-year concurrent sentence for receiving the stolen property. No evidence was offered in the case against Brenda Noye and she was discharged. A charge of conspiracy to handle stolen bullion that had been hanging over her was also dropped. One of the other defendants pleaded guilty to assisting in the retention of stolen property and was fined £500 and ordered to pay £150 costs.

Noye's sister Hilary Wilder and her husband Richard, a legal executive, both of whom also lived in Hever Avenue, West Kingsdown, faced trial for receiving £50,000 from the proceeds of the Brink's-Mat gold, which had been discovered by their neighbour in a package by a garden fence. Both were later cleared, although the money was eventually reclaimed by the Brink's-Mat insurers.

In London's underworld, reaction to the sentencing varied enormously. Krays associate Freddie Foreman said: 'As far as the police were concerned this was the first opportunity they had to convict Noye, so they made sure he got the maximum sentence. They couldn't have given him a day more.'

Many criminal faces were infuriated that the death of Fordham had undoubtedly sparked an even more energetic probe into the dealings of every single person who was even vaguely linked with the Brink's-Mat bullion. 'There was no reason for Noye to kill that copper. He could have just let his dogs sort him out. It was such a stupid thing to do and it caused a lot of us problems we could have done without,' commented one Brink's-Mat team member.

Unsurprisingly, undercover police officer John Childs – first on the scene following Fordham's death – was shocked by the outcome of both Noye trials. 'We all thought the trial was just an open and shut case and that Noye was guilty of John's murder. We were all devastated when he was acquitted. The second trial seemed less important because Noye had been acquitted of the murder and that was totally, in my view, a miscarriage of justice.'

DC Fordham's partner Neil Murphy was convinced that Kenneth Noye was far from innocent in the John Fordham case. 'He was playing the very sincere, quiet family man you know, who just happened to go out into his garden, saw someone dressed like we were who jumped on him.

'So he says: "Okay, I don't know what made me do it, but I picked up this knife and okay I stabbed him ten times, and okay I don't know what made me do it, but I thought he was attacking me." I won't accept that that's what happened – ever.'

Both cops and robbers were well aware that ever since the heist, enormous sums of Brink's-Mat money had been deposited in banks across the world and that no matter what was going on in court, the infrastructure continued to exist. Just after the end of the second Noye trial, a married couple from Britain were stopped by German border guards at the Swiss frontier, and £500,000 in new £50 notes was found in their car. It was part of a consignment of £710,000 that they apparently planned to deposit in a bank in Switzerland.

Multiple companies now existed – in Panama, the Cayman Islands, Spain and London – that had been set up to purchase property with Brink's-Mat proceeds. Money was often transferred from bank to bank until it arrived back in London to fund new 'business' enterprises.

By the end of 1986 police and insurance investigators had concluded that between six and seven million pounds continued to float around in myriad bank accounts and a trust fund in Liechtenstein. That figure was growing constantly, thanks to more and more lucrative property deals in markets such as London's booming Docklands area and the Costa del Sol.

However not all the deals were profitable. Ironically, some of the Brink's-Mat gang were taken for a ride – by other criminals. Four of the gang had invested $100,000 each in some oil fields in Texas. It wasn't until Brink's-Mat insurance investigators visited the area that they found out the oil wells had been dry for more than ten years. The villains had been well and truly fleeced.

In other deals financed by the Brink's-Mat gold bullion, large areas of prime land were purchased in Sussex for more than a quarter of a million pounds. But the land had restricted planning permissions attached to it and no houses could be built on it. It was worthless. There was also $1m paid out for some land in Florida, which was even more useless because it was in a swamp.

Some relationships with criminals in the States proved more positive. Elsewhere in Florida tenacious detectives investigating the robbery and its aftermath came across clear evidence linking some of the gang with the Mob. One man they had been watching for months was seen in London in the company of a 27-year-old criminal called Scott 'Iceman' Errico. Errico was the chief enforcer for a Miami-based drug gang known as the Thompson

Organization. He turned out to be a hit man, and police in the US had linked him to the murders of at least three men.

The connection to Errico convinced detectives that they were now dealing with international organized crime. Scotland Yard officers were assigned to visit Florida many times over the following few years to try and trace the gold and establish the strength of those UK criminal links to the Mafia. At the time of his meeting in London, Scott Errico was on the run after being arrested for murder, kidnapping and drug smuggling.

Two years later, detectives monitoring Errico's Brink's-Mat contact identified him during a full surveillance operation when he visited London again. Determined not to allow Errico out of the country, police stopped him at Heathrow as he was about to board a plane to Spain. When he was searched, three switch-blade knives were found in his jacket pocket. In his suitcase was £15,000 and two false passports. Detectives also found £1.3m in an Isle of Man bank account under one of Errico's aliases.

Errico tried to fight his extradition back to the US because he knew he could face the death penalty there. He was eventually extradited amid rumours that he had offered one million dollars cash to anyone who could spring him before he arrived back in his home country.

Over on Spain's Costa Blanca, well away from the Costa del Sol, a friendly Brit called John Fleming was living the high life with drugs and women, thanks to rather a lot of money that seemed to have mysteriously fallen into his hands not long after the Brink's-Mat robbery. Some even wondered if he had been one of the actual blaggers. Naturally Fleming denied it to all and sundry, but detectives decided to put him under surveillance in Spain. Fleming was arrested by Spanish police and told he would be extradited back to the UK on charges of handling some of the Brink's-Mat proceeds. But after being given bail, Fleming flew to Costa Rica with no intention of ever returning to Europe.

Fleming was eventually thrown out of Costa Rica and extradited to Miami. On the plane he sat next to a Scotland Yard detective who later reported Fleming as saying: 'The world and his fucking wife knows I had something to do with it, but you don't have fucking nothing. If you want me you will have to drag me back in fucking chains.'

It would take another eight long months before Fleming was finally sent back to Britain.

In the summer of 1986, a memorial stone was unveiled to John Fordham in West Kingsdown. Lord Denning, former Master of the Rolls, paid tribute to Fordham and said he'd made the ultimate sacrifice in the line of duty. Prime Minister Margaret Thatcher sent a wreath with the message: 'In honour of John Fordham for his devotion and service.'

SEVENTEEN

Shortly after the imprisonment of Noye and his Brink's-Mat associates, a serving detective and an ex-cop with links to the south-east London underworld both died in suspicious circumstances.

Detective Constable Alan 'Taffy' Holmes was a member of the Serious Crime Squad and had been one of the investigators probing the affairs of Kenneth Noye. But in July 1987, Holmes shot himself dead in the garden of his Croydon home. He had apparently 'cracked' after being questioned for hours by officers from Scotland Yard's Complaints Investigation Bureau about his association with Noye and another serving officer, Commander Ray Adams.

Then, in the autumn of 1987, ex-private investigator Daniel Morgan was found with an axe embedded in his skull in a south London car park. Detectives involved in the inquiry initially believed Mr Morgan had been killed because he was about to expose police corruption. But it was also known that he had encountered Kenneth Noye and a number of other members of the Brink's-Mat team. This was hardly surprising: he was from the same manor as the robbers, and had grown up at a time when police and villains often worked together on strangely intimate terms.

Two other former detectives were later acquitted of all illicit activities in connection to Morgan's murder. They were known to be close to known Noye criminal associate Kevin Cressey, who later helped bring another crooked policeman to justice.

In fact Noye was at the centre of many of the rumours about police corruption that were flying about at the time. One detective visited him at Albany prison on the Isle of Wight to try and persuade him to help with their investigations into an allegedly corrupt senior Scotland Yard officer. With a half-a-million-pound house on the outskirts of London and a villa abroad, the detective under suspicion was allegedly well known to Noye. He'd also come under the press spotlight for his wealth, and within two months of his latest appointment he'd been the subject of a full-scale inquiry by the Yard's Complaints Investigations Bureau.

The investigation – under the supervision of the independent Police Complaints Authority – was prompted when a detective constable arrested a drug dealer in southeast London who made allegations against various officers. The investigation centred on the senior officer's relationships with his informants – one of whom was allegedly Noye.

Kenneth Noye refused to help the internal investigation, although he used the visit by the Scotland Yard detective as an excuse to complain about the conditions at Albany prison. Noye was a shrewd operator, and there was no way he'd help the 'opposition' unless there was something in it for him.

On the streets of south-east London and in police stations across the capital and Kent, many were watching with nervous interest as murder, double-dealing and betrayal began to engulf many of those associated with the Brink's-Mat robbery. In reality the 'curse' represented an internecine struggle over who was owed what. But the stakes were so high that death and destruction seemed to walk hand in hand.

Meanwhile tenacious Brink's-Mat police investigator Tony Lundy was delving ever deeper into the myriad financial deals connected to the robbery. He even came across evidence that the gold had indirectly helped finance a group of Boston criminals with close connections to the IRA. 'Brink's-Mat reached far and wide. It overlapped borders and criminal classes and it pulled into its web all sorts of villains, including terrorists and American Mafioso members,' Lundy explained many years later. The involvement of the IRA was a classic example of the way that Brink's-Mat reached across borders. Another Irish connection came in the form of a shadowy villain called George 'The Penguin' Mitchell who was also in direct contact with the Brink's-Mat gang.

The 51-year-old Dublin-born armed robber-turned-cannabis-and-Ecstasy dealer Mitchell, who was reportedly worth upwards of £10m, was on the run from the Gardaí, the British police and the IRA at the time. They were all keen to speak to him if he returned from Amsterdam, where he ran his hash business (in which some members of the Brink's-Mat gang had 'invested').

In the late spring of 1987, Kenneth Noye's associate John Palmer was cleared of handling gold stolen in the Brink's-Mat robbery. Palmer had spent eight months in custody awaiting trial. In a dramatic sequence of events leading to his arrest he had abandoned his home on the holiday island of Tenerife and tried to enter Brazil before flying back to London to turn himself in to the police. Following his acquittal, Palmer flew straight back to Tenerife, where his booming timeshare business was earning him in excess of £3m a year.

Just before Palmer's trial, legendary face John Fleming was finally extradited back to Britain from Florida. But Fleming eventually ended up spending just two minutes in the dock after a magistrate threw out the charges of handling cash allegedly from the gold bullion robbery. Fleming, forty-eight, smiled broadly after the case against him collapsed.

Even Fleming's solicitor, the ever-present Henry Milner, was surprised by the decision. He said afterwards: 'It was a very slim case but we didn't really expect a magistrate to have the guts to throw it out at that stage after all the publicity there had been about Fleming.'

Outside the court, Fleming was asked by journalists how he came by such immense wealth. He told reporters: 'Where the money came from is a private matter. They have put enormous pressure on me to reveal the source but I have not told them and will not tell you now.'

In an interview with this author in 1995, John Fleming revealed that he had played a big role in the Brink's-Mat robbery but he refused to be more specific. 'It was a dream job. Lots of people made at least a million quid each out of that blagging, so it deserves to be in the history books.'

Fleming revealed that his life had been threatened on 'at least three occasions' because of his links to the robbery. He also claimed that one of those whom he feared the most was a serving police officer. 'That bastard knows that I know where the bodies are buried and he's still after me to this day. I have to watch my back wherever I go.'

The hunt for the gold continued. In a back street in Rother-hithe on a quiet, cold November morning, detectives from the Brink's-Mat task force spotted a man long connected by police to the gold bullion. The man had actually been missing from his £1million Kent home for more than a year.

Police pulled the man's car over and one officer tried to grab at the keys in the ignition through the open driver's window. But the officer wasn't fast enough and instead the car, with the man driving and his son sitting along-side him, shot off while the officer lay on the bonnet before being thrown off into the gutter. Eventually, after a chase, the fugitive's son was arrested but no trace was ever found of the wanted man.

In another twist to the tale, Mad Mickey McAvoy married his second wife Kathy inside Leicester's Gartree prison. His first marriage to Jacqueline had broken up when she discovered his affair with Kathy following the Brink's-Mat robbery. One of his old south-east London associates explained: 'Mickey was always very realistic about his sentence. He knew it was going to be a long haul but he kept close tabs on what was happening outside. But what really kept him going was the knowledge that he'd get out one day and there would literally be a pot of gold waiting for him. Marrying Kathy was his way of telling everyone on the outside that he was preparing for that life in every sense of the word.'

But both McAvoy and Robinson were increasingly irritated by reports from the outside of other gangsters reaping vast financial benefits from what they perceived to be *their* Brink's-Mat gold. The involvement of the Adams family was particularly galling to them because they had apparently played no direct part in the robbery, yet they appeared to be handling much of the gold since Noye's 'departure' from the scene.

'And they were from across the river,' explained McAvoy's old associate. 'That was really getting to Mickey. He considered himself to be the boss of the whole job and there were the Adams lot living it up, all thanks to him.' Head of the A-Team Terry Adams lived in luxury in a nice pad in Mill Hill equipped with a £12,000 security system, including spike-topped electric gates and video intercoms. Terry Adams paid £222,000 to renovate the five-bedroom, four-bathroom house

His sitting-room walls were decorated with a gold disc that is rumoured to have been given to him by a pop star, as well as a signed Arsenal shirt. To top it all he even had a portrait of Al Pacino in *The Godfather* above his mantelpiece. Terry's displays of wealth didn't stop at his house; his lavish spending also took in a villa and a yacht in Cyprus, as well as paying for his daughter to be educated at the Sylvia Young Theatre School in London's Marylebone and buying her a £45,000 Mercedes sports car as a birthday present.

Terry's mansion was regularly used for 'business meetings' by the family. The A-Team were so brazen about their activities that they were openly knocking people off who got in their way. It was reckoned by some that at least two murders had been commissioned from behind the high walls of Terry's flashy pad. Ironically, despite all its levels of security, when it was bugged by the Metropolitan Police and MI5 the house played a major role in bringing about his downfall.

McAvoy knew only too well that Terry Adams and his brothers Tommy and Patrick were involved in drug trafficking, extortion, hijackings and security fraud, making them a prime target for the cozzers. A *Daily Mail* article about Terry Adam emphasized his larger-than-life characteristics.

He was noted for his flamboyant taste in clothes, for his cleverness, and above all for his explosive temper and his delight in cruelty. He like to wear dark velvet suits, as well as bespoke ruffed shirts like those worn by Errol Flynn, his childhood hero. One observer said he looked more like 'a cross between Liberace and Peter Stringfellow'.

But Adams was anything but a soft touch. The article went on to describe a scene that took place at his nightclub, Beluga in North Finchley, not far from his home, that was remarkable in its violence.

In the words of a witness to the events, after one of his henchmen spoke out of turn, 'Terry put down his knife and fork slowly. Then he whacked the guy full in the face. We heard his nose crack. There was blood all over him. Then Terry picked up his knife and fork and carried on eating. We all did the same. So did the guy with the smashed nose.'

Bullets flew when one rival crime family, the Reillys, tried to take things over. Their threat to the Adamses' power didn't last long. Later, one of the A-Team's henchmen, Gilbert Wynter, was tried for the murder of a former high-jump champion. It was alleged in court that he'd not only turned to drug dealing, but was also thought by Terry Adams to be trying to cheat Adams out of money that the crime boss thought was rightfully his. The chief prosecution witness at the henchman's trial would not testify, and though Wynter was able to walk free, his liberty was short-lived, as he was soon to disappear into a concrete tomb under what eventually became the Millennium Dome. Another man feared to been murdered by the family was a drug dealer known as 'Manchester John' who borrowed £100,000 and could not repay it on time. He was beaten up and made to sign over the deeds of his flat. When its value was found to be less than the debt, Patsy, together with Wynter, is believed to have killed and buried him. As with the previous murder case involving Wynter, these allegations were all made in open court.

On another occasion back in London, police raided Patsy Adams's house in the north London suburbs and found a gun and a complete set of bullet-proof body armour. He wriggled out of that one by claiming it all belonged to his wife. One of the brothers was alleged to have been involved in a legendary incident while out at his villa near Marbella on the Costa del Sol. Rumour has it that he cut the ear off the son of another famous British gangster during a fight in a restaurant over some missing drug money.

So fearsome was the Adamses' reputation by the late 1980s that they'd even begun franchising out their name to other criminals, who wanted to profit from the power it lent them.

When detectives bugged Terry Adams's conversations they revealed him revelling in memories of old beatings and even looking to arrange fresh assaults. 'When I hit someone with something I do them damage,' he told a friend in one recording. 'And I went to the geezer and I went crack. On my baby's life, Dan, his knee cap come right out there . . . all white, Dan, all bone and . . .'

Even more sinisterly, at one point in the recordings Terry Adams was captured saying of a woman who'd crossed him: 'She's gotta be done. She's gotta have acid flung in her face.'

At one time Tommy Adams ran a jewellery shop in Hatton Garden that the family used as a base. Saul Nahome, one of the Garden's jewellery dealers, was recruited to become a highly trusted financial adviser to the family. Nahome was shot dead by a motorcyclist in a north London street, and his death is believed to have been linked to the 'distribution' and laundering of the Brink's-Mat gold.

In 1989 Terry Gooderham, a club accountant, and his

girlfriend were killed and dumped in Epping Forest, Essex. Mr Gooderham allegedly crossed the A-Team over money, and like so many others before him, he paid for it with his life. There was talk afterwards about some Brink's-Mat cash that had 'gone missing'.

Armed with lots of Brink's-Mat cash, Patsy Adams had steered the A-Team towards the drugs explosion of the mid- to late eighties. Throughout this period the A-Team were collecting friendly, greedy coppers like kids collect Dinky toys. As their powerbase grew, the brothers realized they could use drugs as currency to bring pressure and influence to bear on judges and politicians. Meanwhile their ownership of clubs had spread even further through the lucrative West End to as far west as Fulham, on the other side of London from their home manor.

One club owner in west London later told this author: 'The Adamses sent a couple of their fellas down to see me because they knew I was up to my eyes in debt and they wanted the club. I didn't argue with them. They chucked me a few grand and I was out the door in minutes. I didn't want no aggro.'

But not even Terry Adams could have foreseen the ripple effect of the Brink's-Mat robbery. He'd been happy to handle the gold and start turning it into cash on behalf of a few friendly faces across the river. His own empire was booming, and he owned businesses and clubs right across London by this time, so it was only natural to start dealing with people from south-east London.

But what Terry Adams didn't realize was that in doing so he was putting his own security and that of his beloved family directly under the police microscope. It effectively alerted detectives to a wide range of other illegal activities involving the A-Team. As with so many other Brink's-Mat 'spin-offs', it would eventually lead detectives to solve more crimes than they could ever have imagined.

Meanwhile, John 'Little Legs' Lloyd continued to enjoy the high life on his toes, even though Brink's-Mat detectives had little doubt he was one of the original robbers. Shortly after his friend Kenneth Noye had been nicked for the killing of John Fordham, Little Legs sensibly made sure that word got out that he was still a long way from home.

The police presumed he'd gone to America. In fact Little Legs was still continually popping back and forth to his old east London and Kent haunts, completely unbothered by the worldwide manhunt in his name. At one stage, Lloyd owned a car-hire business in Kent. He was a regular visitor to the infamous Peacock gym in Canning Town, as well as often dropping into his beloved Lovatt pub in the East End for a swift pint.

He even boasted to one associate that he preferred flying back to London on British Airways "cause they've got a better safety record than all the other airlines.' It was while he was on the run in the US that Little Legs famously had his shorts specially tailored so they flattered his short, stubby legs. He also splashed out a few thousand dollars on some surgery to correct his disfigured toes.

A Miami court ordered Lloyd in his absence to pay $400m to Brink's-Mat insurers but he never coughed up a penny. Little Legs later described the court's decision as 'a fuckin joke'.

Back in London, a warrant along with a £10,000 reward still existed for Lloyd's arrest in connection with Brink's-Mat.

Little Legs knew he was one of the lucky ones because McAvoy and Robinson and many of the other 'associates' were now under lock and key. He also understood perfectly well that they were going to get more and more angry as they sat festering and wondering about what was happening to their share of the gold.

EIGHTEEN

Make no mistake about it, none of the Brink's-Mat 'team' wanted to be in jail. Prison was there to take away their liberty, to lock them up and keep them from their beloved families, away from society. But they all knew they had to behave, because the first man out of the gate was the cleverest man. They left the trouble-making to other, lesser mortals.

All around them in prison were drug addicts and social misfits. McAvoy, Robinson and all the others were professional criminals who saw it as part of their job to withstand life behind bars and bide their time. They watched as inmates injected themselves with filthy needles. They heard the gossip about who were the 'girl-boys' and who'd just give blow jobs. But none of that mattered to these hard-nosed characters, because they all had 'businesses' to run. They considered themselves above the riff-raff, and let everyone know it.

As one former south-east London detective pointed out: 'Like other parts of life there's a pecking order in prisons, and the more successful the criminal is the higher up the pecking order he will be. He'll have an easier life because he'll have gofers running around doing his chores for him.'

Certainly, prison life was never that hard for the Brink's-Mat 'team'. Their reputation as hard men went before them, and many of their fellow inmates were convinced that Kenneth Noye, for example, had been 'fitted up' over the Brink's-Mat handling charges because DC John Fordham had been killed in his garden. As one prison officer at Albany prison on the Isle of Wight explained: 'From the day the Brink's-Mat boys arrived to the day they left, no one laid a finger on them or even said a bad word to their faces. Those guys were revered, almost hero-worshipped for the crime they had committed.'

The Brink's-Mat prisoners were consulted by inmates and staff alike on numerous internal prison matters and the 'house' rules – such as phone calls and special privileges. But there were some screws who would occasionally (and rather stupidly) try and pull rank on them. They objected to their power and influence inside prison.

Before the arrival of all those jailed in connection with the Brink's-Mat robbery, vast dossiers on each of them were forwarded to the relevant prison governors, revealing their every known habit. All were Category A prisoners, which meant they were considered dangerous and likely to try and escape. They had to be accompanied at all times by a prison officer. Even at night the attention was unyielding – guards were ordered to make sure the Brink's-Mat members were checked on every fifteen minutes.

The Brink's-Mat inmates themselves knew they had put two fingers up to lawful society by stealing so much gold and then refusing to hand it over after their arrests. But all of them were determined to just get on and serve their time with the minimum of fuss.

Inside prison, McAvoy and Robinson – crawling painfully slowly towards freedom after their extremely lengthy sentences – continued to bide their time in the knowledge that when they did finally get released they would be able to lay claim to a pot of gold, which would set them and their families up for the rest of their lives. McAvoy and Robinson made a point of remembering all the names of the useful screws, some of whom made it clear that in exchange for a backhander they'd ensure that the two got pretty much whatever they wanted. Money spoke louder than words – even in prison.

But McAvoy, Robinson and the others who'd been jailed knew that if they blatantly bribed prison officers it would cause no end of problems – after all there were numerous closed-circuit TV cameras to record the prisoners' movements. They were all very careful to pick their moments.

Certain detectives have tried to imply that some of the 'BM boys' offered Scotland Yard information on their fellow Brink's-Mat criminals in exchange for a reduced sentence.

But the Brink's-Mat inmates knew perfectly well that this was nothing more than a clumsy attempt by the police to split the robbers into warring factors. They all insist to this day that they would never have grassed each other up.

However Mickey McAvoy was known as 'Mad' for a reason. Much more than Robinson, he had a habit of allowing things to eat away at him. He even wrote to some of his Brink's-Mat 'mates' still on the outside, letting it be clearly known that he was 'thinking' about them.

In one bitter letter McAvoy wrote to acquitted robber Tony White from his cell: 'I won't have anyone else keeping my share for their own needs. He will sign his own death warrant to go through with it. If he believes we are away too long to worry about it, well, it will be done for me. I have no intention of being fucked for my money.'

In April 1990, the tentacles of Brink's-Mat reached once more across Europe and into the Costa del Crime. Two of the gold handlers who'd never been caught by the police had a score to settle over some missing cash from a massive cocaine deal. They in turn were under enormous pressure because a bunch of other Brink's-Mat gang members had allowed their cash to be used as an 'investment' in the drugs. As one of their associates later explained: 'And when that went pear-shaped there was hell to pay.'

The finger of suspicion was pointing right at one of south London's most legendary faces – former Great Train Robber Charlie Wilson. He'd been living in Spain for a few years running a highly lucrative drugs importation gang with close connections to the Colombian cartels, including the most famous drug baron in the world, Carlos Escobar, and the so-called 'Professor' – the cocaine kingpin of Amsterdam, who was the filter for virtually all drugs coming in and out of Europe.

Unsurprisingly, the Brink's-Mat investment in one of Wilson's 'shipments' had been made on the basis that he was a professional who would never fuck them over. Unfortunately, somewhere along the line this message was not passed on to whomever it really should have concerned.

The shipment, and thus £3m of the Brink's-Mat investors' money, went missing

Many believe that Charlie Wilson knew his time was up unless he either found the missing shipment or paid back all the cash. He did neither, and in April 1990, a young British hood knocked on the front door of Wilson's hacienda just north of Marbella. Moments later the man pulled out a gun and shot both Wilson and his pet husky dog before coolly riding off down the hill on a yellow bicycle.

Wilson, fifty-eight, was found by his wife Patricia, fifty-five, choking to death by the side of his swimming pool, the body of his pet dog at his side. He died in an ambulance on the way to a Marbella hospital.

The £500,000 villa, with its mock castle turrets, was cheekily named Chequers, and had clearly been built with security in mind. All the windows were permanently barred and a 6ft stone wall surrounded the property. Charlie Wilson had been sentenced to thirty years' imprisonment for armed robbery and conspiracy to rob after the £2.5m train robbery in 1963. Like all the other Great Train Robbers, the former south London bookmaker never revealed his true role in the planning of the raid. But underworld legend had dubbed him the 'treasurer'.

Fellow Great Train Robber Ronnie Biggs, still on the run after escaping from prison in 1965, heard about Wilson from his hideaway in Rio de Janeiro. Biggs, sixty, told reporters: 'Charlie was full of fun and had a wild sense of humour. He was very easy to get along with. This is a sad, tragic loss.'

It was a murder that shocked the underworld. Even Charlie Wilson's old enemy, the police, were appalled by an act of such cold-blooded violence on a revered villain. But what no one realized at the time was that the curse of Brink's-Mat had once again claimed another victim.

It later emerged that Wilson had been murdered in Spain by a hit squad believed to include one of south-east London's most feared young gangsters, Danny Roff, who had close connections to a number of members of the Brink's-Mat gang. Roff was allegedly one of the gangsters owed money by Wilson. Both men had met and socialized with most of the Brink's-Mat gang down the years.

Another villain with Brink's-Mat links was Nick Whiting, an old school friend and close associate of Kenneth Noye. Whiting had been questioned by police over allegations that he was involved in laundering some of the proceeds of the robbery. The word went out that Whiting had 'opened up' to his interrogators. A former saloon car racing champion, 43-year-old Whiting lived in palatial splendour at Ightham, Kent, and had built up a fortune of more than a million pounds, apparently from a garage business in nearby Wrotham.

In June 1990, just a few weeks after Charlie Wilson's cold-blooded murder in Spain, Whiting was abducted from his garage by an armed gang who also stole five top-of-the-range cars. The cars were all quickly recovered from nearby locations but there was no sign of Whiting. Then a few days later surveyors carrying out preliminary investigations for a new theme park at Rainham Marshes, in Essex, stumbled across Whiting's body hidden in undergrowth.

The father of three had been stabbed nine times and then shot twice with a 9mm pistol, a so-called 'hit-man special'. The two men eventually charged with his killing were later acquitted.

A matter of weeks after Nick Whiting's murder, 27-year-old Stephen Dalligan – brother-in-law of acquitted Brink's-Mat defendant Tony White – was gunned down in the Old Kent Road, in the heart of south-east London. Dalligan survived but refused to talk to police about his criminal associates or any of the circumstances behind the shooting. Detectives investigating knew only too well that yet again all roads led to Brink's-Mat. Being involved with the robbery was extremely dangerous, and it seemed that other villains were sending out a clear message to their 'associates'.

Back in prison, Brink's-Mat insurance investigators visited the incarcerated prisoners connected to the robbery on at least half a dozen occasions. However, many of the gang members were worried that their conversations were being monitored, and in the end most insisted that the investigators had to deal directly with relatives or their legal representatives.

The pressure was being piled on those associated with the Brink's-Mat robbery because investigators feared the gold would soon completely disappear. They already had proof that millions of Brink's-Mat pounds had been spent on huge shipments of drugs from Morocco and South America.

In Albany prison on the Isle of Wight, Kenneth Noye

had other priorities as he ticked off the days of his incarceration. He wanted to be transferred out of the jail's tense, top-security atmosphere to somewhere nearer to home. Noye made numerous requests to the prison authorities and eventually ended up at the relatively relaxed Swaleside prison on the Isle of Sheppey in Kent. Noye received a hero's welcome in Swaleside, where he encountered numerous familiar faces from the Old Kent Road pubs and clubs he'd frequented throughout his adult life.

Within weeks of arriving at Swaleside, fitness fanatic Noye was given the best job inside the jail – gym orderly. This gave him access to a phone for incoming and outgoing calls. Soon he was running his criminal 'empire' from the end of that phone.

Younger, extremely fit inmates – many of whom Noye met through his new job – looked to Noye for advice and guidance. They respected him, and he rewarded their loyalty inside prison with promises to 'invest' in their criminal activities once they got out.

When one prison officer celebrated his birthday, Noye bought him a £600 watch-bracelet. Noye and the officer even declared the gift to the governor. 'There was nothing the authorities could do about it because it was all done out in the open,' explained another officer.

Noye had a vast supply of phone cards so that he could use the main prison phone whenever required, although he preferred the privacy of the outside line at the gym. He even got his favourite cigars brought in for him by friendly screws. Besides his own TV in the cell, Noye also kept a desktop computer and stereo, and Brenda brought her husband a brand-new duvet for his bed.

In addition, Noye got his wife to bring in various items of sports equipment including boxing gloves, weightlifting belts, three tracksuits, badminton racquets and shuttlecocks. He donated it all to the prison gym – on condition he had first refusal to use any of it himself. And – proving his undoubted influence and power inside Swaleside – Noye even paid out of his own pocket for a funfair to be set up in the grounds one Saturday for inmates and their families during a special open day.

Noye insisted on paying for every single ride so that none of the prisoners or staff families had to spend a penny of their own money. The whole event cost him many thousands of pounds. 'A lot of us were surprised that Noye was allowed to pay for it but there was nothing in the rules against it,' one prison staff member later explained.

While he was in jail, Kenneth Noye sold Hollywood Cottage for more than £1m and encouraged wife Brenda to purchase a £300,000 detached house in nearby Sevenoaks. It wasn't nearly as isolated as their previous home, and Noye had made a fat profit of more than half a million pounds through the sale. Even from inside prison, the Brink's-Mat team knew how to make a tidy sum out of their various 'investments'.

Naturally, Kenneth Noye told anyone who would listen in prison that he was only defending himself when he killed John Fordham. 'He jumped on me first, I swear it,' Noye insisted. 'I had no choice.'

Inside Swaleside prison, Noye eventually joined forces

with Pat Tate, one of the jail's most feared inmates. Tate was already well known to many criminals after staging a daring escape from a magistrates' court in December 1988. The heavily tattooed, 18-stone Tate had been charged with armed robbery after a knife gang held up a Happy Eater restaurant in Laindon, Essex, and stole £800. Outside the court he leapt on a 1,000 cc motorbike driven by a pal and escaped. Two policemen and a WPC – who tried to stop him fleeing – were injured in the process.

Tate became Kenneth Noye's personal body builder and minder. Amongst the bench presses and dumb-bells, Tate convinced Noye that there was a fortune to be made out of a new designer drug called Ecstasy. As Brink's-Mat investigation chief Brian Boyce later pointed out: 'As the drugs explosion came about I think everyone turned to drugs and it was drugs that became the highway and conduit for all other criminal activities.'

Out on the mean streets of south-east London, many blaggers were fast concluding that the lucrative days of armed robberies were numbered. Security vans were monitored with radar by the police, and it was virtually impossible to rob a bank in broad daylight. As a result, drugs were emerging as the main criminal currency that could be turned into huge fortunes by London's underworld.

Noye's south-east London associate and robber-turned-drug dealer Gordon McFaul explained: 'It was gettin' hard work goin' robbin'. Villains stopped wantin' to go robbin'. They became more interested in drugs, like. Many of these villains had hit their forties and fifties, and drugs provided the perfect retirement pension and it was a lot safer than "going across the pavement" [robbing]. Puff [cannabis] and coke were the favourites. You'd bung a few people at customs here and you'd get the stuff through the ports easy. Drugs were wiping out the armed robbery trade. It was as simple as that.'

Drugs were undoubtedly easy money compared to robbing, and there was usually even a middleman to take a fall if the law caught up with anyone. Before meeting Pat Tate, Noye had been reluctant to get involved in the drug trade because it was unknown territory to him. But he knew that other Brink's-Mat gang members were already heavily involved, so if they wanted to replace all those millions that were starting to be frozen by the Brink's-Mat insurance agents then drugs really were the only answer.

NINETEEN

Ecstasy was just starting to take off in Britain in the late 1980s. Unlike heroin and cocaine, 'E' could be sold to teenagers as user-friendly – it was initially claimed to be far less lethal than its Class A equivalents. An amphetamine, it propelled the release of a chemical – serotonin – which gave an immediate rush to the brain. However it wasn't long before its known side effects, including panic attacks, kidney, liver and heart problems, became evident.

Nevertheless Noye and other members of the Brink's-Mat team could smell a real earner with 'E'. It had the potential to give them a return of ten times on the gold bullion money they'd invest in it. Inside Swaleside prison in Kent, Pat Tate and Kenneth Noye soon spread the word. From the late 1980s to early '90s, Brink's-Mat cash would deluge Britain with Ecstasy.

'Ecstasy provided the gang and their fences with a perfect investment opportunity,' explained one of the detectives involved in the Brink's-Mat inquiry. 'There is absolutely no doubt that the flood of Ecstasy into Britain started largely because of the Brink's-Mat cash that was floating around at the time.'

Certain members of the Brink's-Mat team had already invested money in cocaine, but they'd soon follow Noye's example and move onto 'E' because it was even more profitable and far less risky. Drugs had fast become the backbone of all business opportunities inside and outside prison. All it needed was a few phone calls and the money would come pouring in.

Brink's-Mat investigators even encouraged the prison authorities to allow Noye and other Brink's-Mat inmates a free rein because they were convinced they might lead them to others involved in the Brink's-Mat job, as well as to the remaining gold. The Brink's-Mat inmates knew that being in prison had its advantages because it meant they were all one step removed from the purchase of the drugs. In other words, it was actually more convenient for them to control the drug deals from inside prison because they had the ultimate alibi if anyone tried to finger them.

But the Brink's-Mat gang members knew that being behind bars wouldn't stop the insurers chasing after what legitimately belonged to them. Many of the Brink's-Mat criminals' bank accounts had been frozen but most of the gold was still missing. Significantly, the villains now acknowledged that the Brink's-Mat insurance investigators were working under their own steam, not in the pockets of the police, so some of the robbers had decided to negotiate with them in order to get them off their backs. Brink's-Mat wanted its money back – nothing more, nothing less.

Insurance agents had already spent many months following the wives, families and associates of the gang. They'd checked out everything – from the money spent on weekly shopping for the family to the types of cars they bought, to the cost of the luxury holidays the wives regularly took while their husbands were in prison.

In the middle of 1988, lawyers representing the Brink's-Mat gang met insurance investigators once again and tried to work out a deal that would suit both sides. But it would take time because none of the villains wanted to be completely cleaned out of cash. They also expected to stay in control of the situation, even from inside prison. McAvoy was particularly obsessed with 'holding the reins'. As one of his oldest friends explained: 'Mickey trusted no one, and the only way he could deal with people was to be in complete control of the situation, or at least as far as he was concerned.'

The Brink's-Mat insurance representatives were relieved to find that dealing with the men's lawyers and account-ants was much easier (and safer) than talking to some of the alleged robbers still at liberty. Many of those who hadn't been convicted were negotiating on behalf of the incar-cerated members of the Brink's Mat 'team'. As one of the investigators pointed out: 'With some of these characters you had to watch your back constantly to see who was sitting nearby. Guns were often shown tactfully, just to remind us who we were dealing with.'

But McAvoy, Robinson and Noye would never show such disrespect to the insurance agents. As far as they were concerned, dealing with the Brink's-Mat investigators was just another aspect of their job. They'd got involved in a risky venture, so they needed to find a way out of this latest spot of bother.

*

Naturally those Brink's-Mat gang members who were in prison also continued to receive numerous visits from police detectives still trying to persuade them to reveal who else was involved in the robbery, the subsequent laundering operation and the location of the remainder of the gold. All of the men showed complete and utter contempt towards the police. They said they weren't interested in deals anymore. On one occasion Kenneth Noye lost his temper with two detectives, thumped his hand on the table in front of him and warned them to 'Fuck off out of my life!'

As one of the detectives later recalled: 'That was when we saw Noye's true colours. He didn't like us putting him under pressure. He was not a pleasant man. He had a temper that was terrifying.'

On 14 November 1992, all the incarcerated Brink's-Mat gang members watched themselves portrayed on television from their prison cells. The story of the raid had been made into a prime-time TV film called *Fool's Gold* starring Sean Bean as Mickey McAvoy. Unsurprisingly, the Brink's-Mat gang members were irritated that the new round of Brink's-Mat publicity – fuelled by the film – inevitably sparked further police activity at a time when insurance investigators were still pushing hard to recover all the stolen gold.

While in prison, at least two of the gang were told that they'd been barred from membership of the Freemasons. It annoyed them enormously as they had been busily planning all sorts of new ventures linked to their Masonic contacts for when they were released. They still needed that impressive Masons' network to ensure that their criminal careers could continue unhindered.

But one setback wasn't going to stop them from keeping a lot of fingers in a lot of pies.

Having reaped enormous profits from the Ecstasy and cocaine deals, certain members of the Brink's-Mat gang decided to go it alone and cut out the tedious middlemen who seemed to accompany every big drug deal and always took a chunk of the profit. The Brink's-Mat gang members knew that the risks would be higher than before but they believed that by building an independent empire to handle all the deals their profits would soar.

Their contacts inside the Kent Constabulary and Met Police remained invaluable. While still in prison, Kenneth Noye began to get reports from the National Criminal Intelligence Service (NCIS) through one of his police contacts. He discovered that his own movements and phone calls were being monitored and that officers from the south-east regional crime squad had joined forces with the American Drug Enforcement Administration (DEA) to target Noye and other members of the Brink's-Mat gang, who'd recently started setting up drug deals through Noye's old contacts in the Miami Mafia. Noye was told by his inside source that US drug enforcement agents had monitored prison phone calls he'd made to an intermediary to Florida, and had almost enough evidence to implicate him in a huge drug deal. Noye immediately pulled out of the deal and the NCIS realized they had been compromised.

A six-month ongoing investigation into Kenneth Noye had to be abandoned at a cost of tens of thousands of pounds.

Elsewhere, the curse of Brink's-Mat continued on its murderous path. One of the gang's London-based money launderers, Donald Urquhart, was shot dead by a hired assassin in a London street in January 1993. It later transpired that the gun used in the killing was supplied by another Brink's-Mat associate, policeman-turned-underworld-gundealer Sydney Wink.

Police later revealed that a hit man had stalked Urquhart, fifty-five, for up to three months before shooting him in front of his girlfriend as they left their local pub in Marylebone High Street in central London. When detectives examined the Urquharts' car, they found it was equipped with three telephones and a fax machine – he had used it as an office for many of his business deals. Urquhart was a former hod-carrier who claimed he'd built up his fortune during the property boom of the 1970s and '80s. But detectives soon uncovered his various 'interests' in the Cayman Islands and Jersey tax havens.

No one seemed safe – apart, ironically, from those Brink's-Mat gang members still serving lengthy sentences for their role in the Crime of the Century.

TWENTY

It wasn't just drugs that the Brink's-Mat gang were expanding their operations into. Kenneth Noye was released from prison in the summer of 1994, and soon afterwards spent a month on the northern half of the Mediterranean island of Cyprus. Noye intended to invest hundreds of thousands of pounds into a timeshare development that he believed would earn him a fortune, just like his old pal John Palmer. Palmer's Canary Island timeshare empire had made him a legend in the underworld and earned him tens of millions of pounds. His fortunes had taken a slight knock when, in December 1991, having earlier been acquitted of handling Brink's-Mat gold, Palmer was given an eighteen-month suspended sentence for his part in a mortgage fraud. His old friend Garth Chappell, who had been found guilty of involvement in the Brink's-Mat theft, was also convicted on the same charge. Palmer, who had already admitted obtaining nearly £65,000 by deception, was also ordered to pay £13,052 compensation and £5,000 costs.

But this didn't stop him retaining a vice-like grip on his vast domain and travelling everywhere with a shotgun-toting 'associate'. By the mid-1990s Palmer was looked up to by many villains as the perfect example of a 'runaway success'. Kenneth Noye was convinced he could make a similar fortune in northern Cyprus. Three million tourists – mainly from the UK – visited the south of Cyprus every year but only 30,000 came to the north; an explosion of popularity was inevitable. However, even after his release, Noye was very much still a target for the police. All his movements and phone calls on the island were monitored by British secret service agents in collusion with the Metropolitan Police.

If Noye knew he was being watched, he certainly didn't seem to care. In northern Cyprus his entrepreneurial spirit knew few boundaries. Halfway through his stay on the island, Noye found a stretch of isolated coastline just north of the port of Famagusta. It was cheap and seemed the perfect location to build a timeshare empire. Noye's scheme would cater for tourists wanting to reserve for themselves several weeks each year in an island villa. While in northern Cyprus, Noye agreed to invest more than £500,000 in the development and employed his old criminal associate Brian Reader's brother Colin to run it on his behalf. Noye called it the Long Beach Country Club.

The attraction of the timeshare – as Noye had already learned from his old friend Palmer – was that by selling access to the properties in blocks of one week at a time, the amount made from all the weekly bookings added together would be much greater than the actual real-estate value of the property. Noye helped finance the project by selling some of his gold stock and a number of other properties, including a trailer-park business in Florida. He even got one crony to fly some cash out to him in northern Cyprus.

Noye believed that within five years the Long Beach Country Club would be booming. With his £500,000 investment in thirty-two timeshare villas; the sale of the weekly units would bring in more than £100,000 per villa, and his share of the profits would amount to a staggering £17m.

Back in London, another character connected to the Brink's-Mat job was about to fall victim to the curse. Ex-Metropolitan Police officer Sydney Wink was a gunsmith and weapons dealer. His speciality – although this was never proved in a court of law – was renumbering illegal weapons, including those used by members of the Brink's-Mat gang.

Wink was strongly suspected of supplying the guns used in two earlier murders – the 1992 contract killing of Brink's-Mat money launderer Donald Urquhart and the shooting of PC Patrick Dunne by three Yardie gunmen.

A week after this, in August 1994, officers investigating PC Dunne's murder raided Wink's Essex home and discovered his dead body – Wink apparently put a pistol to his own head and pulled the trigger. Many have speculated since that he was 'helped on his way', but there is no evidence to suggest it was anything other than suicide, no doubt sparked by double-dealing criminal activities that had led to the killing of a fellow police officer.

The network of connections between the Brink's-Mat gang and the police grew ever more complex. When certain members of the Brink's-Mat gang got wind that the British intelligence services were keeping an eye on them, they began casting around to try and 'buy' the services of a hard-up British intelligence officer. They believed it was only a matter of time before they found someone they could 'turn'.

Many ex-spies suffered from personal and money problems, making them especially vulnerable to tempting offers from cash-rich criminals. 'The gang actually believed they could buy anyone off if the price was right, and they didn't like the way they were still being watched closely,' one detective later explained.

Eventually Kenneth Noye made contact with a former intelligence officer whose security clearance had been withdrawn but who still had access to certain computers. The agent agreed to keep Noye informed – for a price – because he was bitter about the way the intelligence services had treated him.

But what Noye didn't realize was that the 'agent' had been planted to spy on him. As one Brink's-Mat police insider explained: 'The idea was to monitor Noye's activities. We knew he was well aware of our surveillance so this seemed the best way of keeping an eye on him without him knowing.'

Police had also been tapping phones belonging to Michael Lawson, Noye's criminal associate (and good friend) who'd bought the smelter that was found in Noye's house by the Brink's-Mat investigators following the death of PC John Fordham. Police taps were also put in the offices as well as on the mobile and hotel telephones used by both men.

Surveillance officers were astounded when Noye 'entertained' three prison officers and his best friend from when he was inside Swaleside prison at his new house in Sevenoaks, Kent. This flagrant breach of the rules only came to light because Customs and Excise officers also had Noye under surveillance and traced the prison officers' car registration number to Swaleside prison.

An unexpected development came in 1994 when John 'Little Legs' Lloyd was named on the *America's Most Wanted* TV crime show. A couple of weeks after it was first screened he took the biggest gamble of his life by walking, with his brief, into Rochester Row police station to give himself up. The Crown Prosecution Service eventually ruled that there was insufficient evidence linking him to the Brink's-Mat job. The gamble had paid off. Less than a year later, Lloyd, according to police sources, allegedly donated a five-figure sum to a consortium of insurance companies because he knew that even though there wasn't enough evidence to prosecute him in a court of law, he had been fingered for his role in the Brink's-Mat raid. Lloyd was advised that by making this 'donation' he would at least avoid being hauled into a civil trial.

Another man who, like Noye, had recently been released from Swaleside was his former henchman and fitness trainer Pat Tate. Within weeks, Tate was running Essex's main Ecstasy supply route after getting financial backing from Noye and other Brink's-Mat gang members for his drug business. The gold from the heist was almost single-handedly helping finance the huge influx of the designer drug into the UK, reaping massive ten- and twenty-fold profits for the gang in the process.

In December 1994, a brick was thrown through the toilet window of Tate's house. When he peered outside, a gunman opened fire from close range with a revolver. Tate raised his right arm to shield his face and the bullet hit him in the wrist, travelled up his arm, and smashed bones in his elbow.

Tate later admitted to his mother that his own murderous habits might have provoked the attack. He even hid a gun under the hospital bed where he'd been taken following the shooting. Just a few months earlier Tate had ambushed a 27-year-old drug dealer called Kevin Whitaker, who worked for a rival gang of drug pushers in Romford, Essex. Tate and an associate had paralysed Whitaker by forcing him to snort a substance called ketamine. Vets use it to numb horses before castration, but it is known in the world of narcotics as Special K. One of Tate's associates then snatched a bag containing £60,000 worth of cannabis.

As helpless Whitaker's muscles froze, the laughing gangsters pierced his groin with a syringe and pumped a deadly concoction into his blood. They had injected him in the groin with Ketamine, or Special K, a paralysing drug, often used on horses. Powerless but conscious and pleading for mercy, Whitaker was then injected with lignocaine. He died within minutes and they dumped his body in a ditch near Basildon, in Essex.

Pat Tate was trying to scale the underworld ladder at least two rungs at a time, and he'd arrogantly overlooked the fact that revenge was now in the air. This was also combined with resentment amongst many other Essex criminals that he – Tate – was using the Brink's-Mat proceeds to elevate his own standing, even though he played no part in the so-called Crime of the Century.

As all this was going on, the bid to recover the Brink's-Mat gold and its proceeds continued. The insurers even brought a civil action against the Woolwich Building Society to gain access to all the transactions made by suspected Brink's-Mat robber John 'Little Legs' Lloyd's daughter Jacqueline Seton, who lived in Chislehurst, Kent. She was also named in a writ against six people in a civil action alleging they had 'wrongly interfered' with the gold and demanding full restitution for its value.

In January 1995, the High Court ordered Mickey McAvoy to make a payment of more than £27m to the insurers – in effect making him responsible for the entire raid, although it was acknowledged that he was unlikely to pay the entire sum back to the authorities. In any case he claimed, unsurprisingly, that he didn't even know where the gold was (although everyone in the south-east London underworld knew only too well that he was expecting a windfall when he finally got released from prison).

In June 1995 – with the pressure mounting – Kenneth Noye actually agreed to return nearly £3m of the proceeds from the Brink's-Mat robbery. In a confidential settlement, Noye gave laundered money back to the Brink's-Mat underwriters. It later emerged that investigators had traced the money that was held in bank accounts in Britain and Ireland to him.

Noye also gave up his claim to the eleven bars of Brink's-Mat gold worth £110,000 which were found under the patio of Hollywood Cottage. Noye conceded the deal after underwriters agreed to make no claims against his recently acquired £300,000 mansion in Sevenoaks, which was now in his wife Brenda's name.

According to evidence that would later be given in court, at a pub just off the Old Kent Road – small and dirty enough to keep most ordinary punters out, and therefore chosen for its privacy by a number of south-east London faces – Kenneth Noye and 'Little Legs' Lloyd began planning a vast cash-card-cloning scheme that they believed would net them an even bigger fortune than that yielded by the Brink's-Mat robbery. Lloyd – common-law husband of Brink's-Mat handler Jean 'Lady Goldfinger' Savage – was looking for backers to set up this audacious crime, so it was only natural he would turn to his old Brink's-Mat gang members for an 'investment'.

The hole-in-the-wall job (also known as the ATM scam) had the potential to be the biggest crime ever committed as it involved stealing *one billion pounds* from cashpoint machines. This was a classic instance of one crime being financed by the proceeds from another – in this case, the Brink's-Mat job. Its legacy wasn't just murder and mayhem, it also encouraged criminals to seek out bigger and even more lucrative 'targets'. And there was another even more outlandish reason behind the willingness of certain members of the Brink's-Mat gang to back the hole-in-the-wall job with cash. They believed that this crime would be so big that it would overshadow Brink's-Mat to such an extent that the police would at last ease off on their current investigation.

The gang's plan was to tap into the latest banking technology, which meant they needed to recruit corrupt communications engineers and computer experts in order to make huge numbers of cloned cashpoint cards. These would then be used to empty cash from the bank accounts of thousands of ordinary people. If they pulled it off, it could throw the entire British banking system into chaos.

It emerged in the evidence given in court that computer boffin Martin Grant was recruited from inside Blantyre House open prison in Kent, where Kenneth Noye had been held during the last few months of his sentence. Grant had been jailed for attempting to murder his wife and child, so was as far away from being a professional criminal as you could get. In prison, he had studied for a degree in electronic communications. Grant was allowed out on day-release for work experience at a van-hire business owned by Paul Kidd, another villain involved in the cash-card-cloning scheme.

In the late spring of 1995, a few months after the plan's inception, the hole-in-the-wall criminals and their Brink's-Mat backers enjoyed a champagne dinner at a Kent hotel followed by some late night 'entertainment' in the company of a group of prostitutes who'd been hired for the entire night. Amongst those villains was nervy computer wizard Martin Grant. Unbeknownst to the gang, Grant – who was plainly out of his depth amongst the hard men of south London – was already feeding information about the cash-card scam to police. He'd confessed to a prison chaplain about the planned robbery and later made a statement of over 300 pages to Scotland Yard detectives.

On that evening, when the men were supposed to have sex with the prostitutes, Grant got cold feet. He didn't want to sleep with any hookers, not even the ones specially recruited in London's West End by the Brink's-Mat criminals. Kenneth Noye became particularly infuriated with Grant when he turned down one of the girls. Tensions had been building between the two men for weeks, and Noye had only agreed to keep Grant on the team because his computer knowledge was invaluable.

Eventually Grant forced himself to go through the motions and sleep with one girl to indicate he was still 'on their team' and avoid giving himself away as a grass. It was a disaster, and the other gang members made fun of him because of his failure to perform. They had none of Grant's scruples and swapped hookers amongst themselves as well as taking mountains of cocaine. But Kenneth Noye remained furious with Grant, and he told the other villains he was very suspicious about his behaviour.

Later, Grant provided a fascinating insight into Little Legs Lloyd and his friend Kenneth Noye. 'Noye and Lloyd were just names to me at first. They meant nothing. But people inside prison talked about them as if they were gods.' Grant said he attended one meeting with the gang where Noye and Legs produced prison paperwork on his (Grant's) record and family background, which clearly had been given to Legs by prison staff. Those details included the addresses of Grant's mother and brother.

Then, in a chilling incident, Little Legs drove Grant up to his mother's house in the Midlands, walked him through the front door and introduced himself to Grant's mother, 'just to let me know he knew where she lived,' Grant explained: 'John Lloyd then phoned Kenny Noye to say he had met my mum. I was so scared.'

Grant added: 'Kenny Noye and Lloyd told stories about hijacking vehicles in the early days and what they did to people who crossed them.' Grant said they also made continual references to other criminal associates in Spain and the United States.

After they had eventually arrested the hole-in-the-wall suspects, detectives were so worried that Noye and Lloyd might harm Grant that they put him in a safe house with armed officers twenty-four hours a day, only moving him by helicopter. Grant lives in fear of the two criminals to this day: 'I know they hold a grudge against me and I'm very nervous about it.'

Nevertheless, the information Grant had provided allowed the police to swoop. At Blantyre House prison – where Kenneth Noye had once been an inmate – a warder and inmate were arrested in July 1995. At least six other prisoners were moved from the prison, following a number of nationwide raids by Scotland Yard's cheque and credit card squad.

On 25 July 1995, the mansion in Yalding, Kent, of southeast London legend in his own lifetime Billy Hayward was raided by detectives investigating the same hole-in-the-wall scam. Officers seized more than 70,000 blank cash cards and 28 computer disks. They immediately arrested

Hayward and four other suspected members of the firm.

Detectives decided they didn't have enough evidence to go after the Brink's-Mat backers, including Kenneth Noye, even though they knew the names of the robbery gang members who'd invested money in the scheme through their associate Hayward because they were even named in open court.

Not surprisingly, a murder contract was eventually put out on computer boffin Martin Grant. This was allegedly taken out by the rest of the gang, who rightly presumed he'd grassed them up. As Roy Ramm, one of the senior detectives involved in the case, later explained: 'The ATM scam was a classic example of a group of south London robbers and villains who saw an opportunity to get a great deal of money, but did not have the technical expertise so they worked outside their circle and brought in somebody who eventually destroyed them.'

Over on Spain's Costa del Crime, an artful old face from the 'Good Old Days' of the Krays and the Richardsons was circling the proceeds of the Brink's-Mat robbery, much to the concern of gang members like McAvoy and Robinson. Joe Wilkins was one of a dying breed of London villains who loved playing everyone off against each other. The cops, other mobsters, even poor old Joe Public – they all provided an income to dodgepot Joe Wilkins at one time or another. Joe Wilkins exuberantly performed the roles of sometime fraudster, Soho vice king and friend to many of London and Spain's most notorious British gangsters.

Rumours had flown around that the Houdini-like

Wilkins was given a 'helping hand' to flee prison in the early 1990s, specifically so that he could move to Spain and work as a major informant for the police and security services, who'd long been obsessed with nicking many of the villains who were still living in luxury there. At 6ft 3in tall, Joe Wilkins was a handsome, larger-than-life character who favoured Michael Caine-style horn-rimmed specs, and was married for a time to the glamorous dancer Pearl Read, who later modelled in her bra, at the age of fifty-six, as part of Age Concern's 1998 advertising poster campaign.

In Spain, Wilkins agreed to introduce coppers posing as businessmen to major villains operating there and in Gibraltar. They were lured into 'investing' their dirty money into a laundering scheme that was really a police front. It turned into a five-year operation that snared dozens of criminals 'washing' money from vice, drugs and tobacco-smuggling rackets. However, that sting eventually led to years of legal wrangling and accusations of entrapment against the police. This ended in August 2003, when, after 414 days, the main case was thrown out at Southwark Crown Court in London, with the judge denouncing the sting as 'massively illegal'. But then Joe Wilkins was never one to do things by halves. This south Londoner with more front than Woolworths was even rumoured to have played a role in the 1989 'Death on the Rock affair' in which three IRA members were gunned down by the SAS in cold blood while travelling through Gibraltar.

In the late 1990s, Wilkins was introduced to one of the Brink's-Mat gang who was on holiday in Marbella. Wilkins suggested that he knew a way in which the remaining

Brink's-Mat gold could be turned into hard cash without going through a smelting process. He claimed that certain Colombian cocaine cartels were prepared to be paid in gold for shipments of drugs, which could – in every sense of the phrase – kill a lot of birds with one stone. The Brink's-Mat gang members knew only too well that the police were still hot on their trail, and this seemed a practical and highly lucrative way of converting the gold into pure cash, with the added incentive of huge profits on the actual shipments of cocaine.

But what no one realized at the time was that, in a similar move to his previous double-crossing, Wilkins had been persuaded to make the approach by officers from Scotland Yard and America's DEA, who wanted to try and close down the Colombian cartels as well as track down the remainder of the Brink's-Mat gold.

Then the Curse of Brink's-Mat struck once again with a vengeance. In 2004 Joe Wilkins died suddenly in Estepona at the age of sixty-eight, and to this day no one knows exactly why. His family have always refused to discuss his death, but one detective who dealt with Wilkins on the Costa del Sol admitted: 'Joe pushed his luck. He was playing us all off against each other and one day his time was up. None of us were surprised but it was still very sad because Joe was a one-off – a likeable, almost loveable rogue who could light a room up with his charisma, but the stupid old sod thought he was invincible and that cost him his life.'

No one who played those sorts of games was safe.

TWENTY-ONE

The tenth of November 1995 was a Friday night like any other in Raquel's nightclub in Basildon, Essex, when a youth called Stephen Smith bought four tablets of Ecstasy. But, later that night, one of those pills would kill a school-girl called Leah Betts, sparking a nationwide debate on the dangers of Ecstasy, as well as outrage against the evil drug dealers responsible.

The consignment of Ecstasy from which Leah's fatal pill came – bought through Kenneth Noye's friend and former Swaleside prison henchman, the 18-stone muscleman Pat Tate – had undoubtedly been purchased with proceeds from the Brink's-Mat heist; it could perhaps be argued that this was yet another example of the curse's deadly work.

Nightclub boss Tony Tucker was Tate's right-hand man, along with another steroid freak called Craig Rolfe. Raquel's piano bar had been transformed into the neon-lit Buzz Bar on that particular night, complete with hypnotic dance music to help bring the young crowd in.

Tate – by now nicknamed the Enforcer – and Tony Tucker were themselves living life on the edge. They took constant rounds of drug cocktails of cocaine, ketamine and Ecstasy, which caused them to suffer violent mood swings. On one occasion Tate got into an argument at a Basildon pizza restaurant over the topping he wanted. He punched the manager and then smashed his head down on a plate-glass counter. The manager was too scared to make a statement to police. But none of this seemed to bother the Brink's-Mat gang, who happily bankrolled Tate and Tucker's drug deals.

The Ecstasy tablets supplied by Tate and Tucker in the club that fateful night were called Apples. Four of them were obtained by Stephen Smith, who gave one to his friend Leah Betts for her birthday that night. The young man bought them in good faith, without being told they were double strength. They cost Leah Betts her life.

This was of little concern to the Brink's-Mat gang. Their only priority was the vast profit they were making. Conservative estimates put the value of the Ecstasy business in Britain by the mid-1990s at more than £500m per year.

The Ecstasy trade adhered to the classic economic rule – buy low, sell high. Most of the Ecstasy flooding into Britain could be bought wholesale by the criminals for as little as £1 a tablet. A large proportion came from the Netherlands, where some of the Brink's-Mat gang members still had close contacts through their earlier gold-smelting activities. It was then sold on the street through people like Tucker and Tate for sometimes as much as £20 per tablet, a huge mark-up.

The Brink's-Mat gang knew that the sheer scale of the production of Ecstasy meant that there was a vast supply network in existence, and it was a much easier way of making money than smelting down gold. From manufacture in Europe to use in Britain, the Ecstasy trade chain was complex, with up to fifty pairs of hands often involved. The Brink's-Mat gang cut that down to just five or six and saw their profits leap. Nevertheless, they were still able to keep their distance from the actual deals, so the risk of being caught was substantially reduced.

Most of the Ecstasy came through ports like Dover, in Kent, and Harwich, in Essex, as well as illegal landings on the quieter beaches of England's south coast. Freedom of movement under EU laws meant it was difficult for customs officers to track down the Ecstasy traffickers, who were capable of smuggling thousands of tablets in something as small as a briefcase. From English ports, the Ecstasy was quickly moved to a warehouse in London that the Brink's-Mat backers had rented specifically for its distribution. It was then taken to wholesale suppliers in the main urban centres of Essex, Kent and East Anglia, as well as the more familiar territory of south-east London. 'Enforcer' Pat Tate was in charge of ensuring that tens of thousands of the tablets every weekend got into the hands of small-time dealers, who were essential to the entire process.

Not everyone in the criminal underworld approved of the switch from robbing banks and security vans to dealing in drugs. Former Krays henchman Freddie Foreman explained years later: 'Drugs were becoming like heavy gangsterism. There were too many people involved. It became widespread. There was also a stigma in dealing drugs. Some people would name so-called drug dealers to police just to get them off the streets. All the people I know and associate with are from the old school and they don't want to know about drugs at all.'

But the Brink's-Mat gang didn't care about what other criminals thought.

However there were other problems brewing for the Brink's-Mat gang. The so-called 'King of Catford', Tony White – who'd escaped criminal prosecution even though he'd long been suspected of being one of the Brink's-Mat robbers – was furious with Kenneth Noye for settling insurance claims on the missing gold bullion because it sparked civil proceedings against White by insurance agents. White found it particularly irritating because he'd been tempted to do the same thing himself.

At a High Court civil hearing, judge Mr Justice Rimmer stated that White did 'at least' participate in the planning of the robbery and added: 'Mr White is a dishonest man with an appalling criminal record.'

The judge also pointed out that White's earlier acquittal at the Old Bailey in 1984 only meant that the jury were not satisfied White was guilty according to the standard of proof required. White and his wife, Margaret, were then ordered by the High Court to repay £2,188,600 and £1,084,344 respectively in compensation to the insurers of the gold. It represented the value of the amount of gold that White was alleged to have been given from the original robbery. White furiously blamed Noye for opening up the floodgates by paying up so easily, and the split in the ranks of the Brink's-Mat gang began to widen by the day.

As time went by, even more new 'camps' started to emerge. The actual robbers still saw themselves on a much higher plane than the backers like Noye and other 'associates', who had only been responsible for turning the gold into hard cash. McAvoy and Robinson kept themselves particularly aloof; they believed that by serving their sentences they had the right to expect every penny of their share to be waiting for them when they finally got released. Anything less than that and, as one south-east London criminal later explained, 'There would be hell to pay.'

There was a feeling amongst the actual robbers that people such as Noye, Reader and Perry were 'taking the piss' because, after serving much shorter sentences, they were now once more out and about, benefiting from the proceeds of the raid The publicity that Noye had garnered ever since the stabbing of undercover cop John Fordham in his garden also greatly irritated the actual Brink's-Mat robbers. They blamed Noye for sparking the police's near-obsession with bringing them all to justice, believing that the killing of a copper had galvanized the police at a time when the Kent and Met forces were not exactly getting on like a house on fire.

Meanwhile Brink's-Mat insurers continued to press for the recovery of the rest of the gold from the robbery. The investigators continued to travel as far afield as Scotland, the Isle of Man, Ireland, Denmark, Germany, Spain, Cyprus, Greece, Hong Kong and the Far East. Investigators also traced a huge sum of money in one bank account in the Middle East after months of constant surveillance. Yet the Brink's-Mat gang could still flex their muscles if they felt the need. One nosy insurance agent, who'd been watching a gang member while he was abroad, had heroin planted on him in an attempt to get him arrested when he arrived back in Britain.

The Brink's-Mat gang remained as obsessed as ever with turning the gold into much vaster wealth. And naturally they continued to cultivate links with policemen and politicians in order to make sure they got advance notice of any potential 'problems'. In many ways the Brink's-Mat gang had become its own secret club. In an effort to hold the gang together they even held parties to make sure everyone involved was still 'on board'. In other words, 'join in or get out' seemed to be the overriding message.

Gang members regularly paid for two women to host parties in a rented house in Bexleyheath, on the edge of the south-east London suburbs where so many of the gang hailed from. They always invited other 'important' people who could be of great use to them. Everyone – from bank managers to police officers to solicitors – was asked. These gatherings were held most Fridays through the second half of 1995 and the first few months of 1996.

The hookers were encouraged to sleep with guests so that the robbers would have even more favours to call in if anyone posed a threat to their many illicit operations. Kent police allegedly knew all about the parties but there was little they could do about them since no actual laws were being broken.

But across the Dartford Tunnel in the badlands of Essex, a deadly feud sparked by the Brink's-Mat gold was about to come to a bloody conclusion.

*

On an icy-cold December day in 1995, an anonymous Range Rover was parked in front of a set of padlocked gates that led to a fishing lake close to the 130-acre Whitehouse Farm, near Rettendon, Essex. The two men who rented out the lake – Ken Jiggins and Peter Theobald – drove towards the car on a lonely farm track blanketed with snow. At first they didn't even notice that one of the rear windows of the Range Rover was shattered.

The Range Rover was blocking their route, so they climbed out of their Land Rover and tapped on the other car's window to ask its occupants to move. But there was no response. The two men they saw inside looked so peaceful that Ken Jiggins thought they were asleep. Then Jiggins spotted that the driver was slumped to one side with blood running from his nose and mouth. His eyes were closed. The passenger was sitting bolt upright with blood all over his face and chest.

Jiggins stepped back from the car window with a jolt and, hands shaking, called the police on his mobile phone. Next, Theobald realized that there was a third dead body slumped in the back seat. It was Kenneth Noye's old prison friend, gym fanatic Pat Tate, who'd been blasted twice in the head and once in the chest. Neither of the men could see any footprints leading away from the vehicle in the snow.

Within less than an hour the place was crawling with police as the Range Rover – registration number F424 NPE – was covered with a tarpaulin and loaded onto a police lorry with the bodies of Pat Tate and his criminal associates Tony Tucker and Craig Rolfe still inside.

Forensic experts spent the rest of the day combing the track and surrounding area for any clues. Overhead a helicopter scanned the fields with a heat-seeking camera for any more evidence of what had happened. Police believed Rolfe, Tate and Tucker had been lured to their deaths by the promise of a massive drug deal.

It wasn't until detectives started searching more widely that they uncovered the Ecstasy connection between the Brink's-Mat gang and Pat Tate. Police discovered that Tate, Tucker and Rolfe had been invited to meet in order to inspect a landing site for a light plane just close to where they died. The aircraft was due to bring in hundreds of thousands of pounds' worth of Ecstasy. Their 'host' was another associate of the Brink's-Mat gang, Michael Steele, fifty-five.

Steele had met the other three men at a pub and climbed in the back of their Range Rover alongside Tate, who was so relaxed about the 'meet' that he didn't even bother bringing along a gun. But as the car turned into a quiet lane off the A130, it had to stop at a closed gate where Steele's accomplice, Jack Whomes, was hiding. Steele opened the back door of the Range Rover to get out and open the gate as Whomes rose from the ground and ran towards the car blasting away with a shotgun.

Only Tate had time to put up his hands and hunch down – Tucker and Rolfe were killed instantly. After Whomes reloaded, Steele is believed to have taken the gun from him and then shot each of the men behind their ears 'just to make sure'.

Interviews with the police and criminals have uncovered that Tate wasn't averse to horse-trading with police if he thought it would be to his advantage. As one Essex drug insider later explained: 'Pat Tate thought he was a clever bastard. There were rumours that he'd been feeding Old Bill with info to keep them off his back.'

Was the Brink's-Mat gang's involvement in the Ecstasy trade one of the 'titbits' Tate offered the police?

'If it was then I'd say it was certain he signed his own death warrant,' added the Essex drug insider.

Whatever the truth, it didn't stop more 'business opportunities' continuing to come the way of the Brink's-Mat gang. Many more lowly criminals were seeking them out for financial backing in much the same way movie producers seek money to finance new films. Kenneth Noye and at least two other members of the gang got involved in a plan to import a brand-new designer drug into Britain. They spent months in high-level negotiations to buy vast quantities of the hallucinogen khat from African drug barons. Although legal in its raw form, khat leaves were processed by some dealers into capsules of oil, which did breach British drug laws.

The Brink's-Mat gang were persuaded by a number of criminal associates that it would be possible to make even bigger profits out of khat than from Ecstasy, if the market was saturated immediately. They were seriously considering investing as much as half a million pounds in the drug over the following eighteen months. But they were concerned that no one had tried a similar operation before.

The Brink's-Mat gang eventually decided to sit and wait

to see if khat had the impact on the British drug scene that everyone kept telling them it would before they risked too much cash. In the end it never properly materialized on the open market. The gang's business instincts had saved them from losing a lot of money.

But the police were still pressing hard by constantly watching Brink's-Mat gang members such as Kenneth Noye and Brian Reader. This meant that they were starting to find it harder to run their criminal enterprises. The police were constantly turning up at their homes demanding answers to questions about crimes in which they might or might not have been involved in. Though Noye and Reader kept their cool, their patience was wearing thin, and some of the gang members were beginning to really think about moving abroad.

PART THREE:
ALL THE CARDS COME TUMBLING DOWN

'You cannot expect criminals to phone the police up and offer them information just because they want to be seen as "good citizens". We have to get out there and meet them and convince them that we won't land them in the shit if they help us. It's a very tricky balancing act.'

– Former Scotland Yard Flying Squad commander Ken Drury.

TWENTY-TWO

M25/M20 INTERSECTION, SWANLEY, KENT, 1.15 P.M., 19 MAY, 1996

Brink's-Mat gold bullion handler Kenneth Noye had a lot on his mind, loads of things to do and lots of people to see when a small red Bedford Rascal van swerved in front of him as he headed at speed down the motorway slip road. He angrily flashed the full beams of his Land Rover Discovery at the van and blasted his horn as the vehicle slowed down for the first set of traffic lights on the busy intersection, near Swanley, in Kent, right in the heart of what police often refer to as 'shotgun territory'.

As the lights turned green, Noye – shaking with rage – swung his L-registered Discovery across the two-lane roundabout to pursue the van. He was infuriated and had decided to teach the driver a lesson.

Electrician Stephen Cameron, twenty-one, and his pretty blonde fiancée Danielle Cable, nineteen, had set off in the Bedford minivan minutes earlier from their nearby homes to get some bagels for a late Sunday breakfast. Danielle had no idea that her driving had just sparked a tirade of abuse from the motorist in the Land Rover Discovery.

Just then Noye cut them up again and Danielle was forced to brake hard to avoid a collision.

'That was stupid,' said Stephen Cameron, who was sitting next to his fiancée in the van. He looked across at the driver of the Discovery and shook his head.

The two vehicles moved on to the next set of traffic lights just a couple of hundred feet further along the busy roundabout. This time the Land Rover pulled up sharply in front of them. Noye got out. He was wearing jeans and a T-shirt and a short jacket with a zip.

Witnesses later said he seemed to be looking for something in the pocket of that jacket. Cameron, well over six foot in height, stepped out of the van as Noye, now fifty, approached. Cameron towered over the older man as they came face to face. Noye and Cameron exchanged a few words before Noye punched Cameron hard in the face. As he recovered his balance, Cameron noticed something glinting in the other man's hand.

He immediately tried to kick whatever it was out of his grasp.

'Get in the van. Get in the van,' Danielle Cable shouted at her fiancé.

As the two men struggled together, Noye twice plunged a knife into Cameron's heart and liver. In the middle of all this, Danielle Cable frantically tried to stop someone from the stream of passing traffic.

'Help. Please help us!' she screamed.

Cameron – despite his injuries – was still trying to kick the knife out of Noye's hand. That's when Danielle saw the four-inch blade glinting in the sunlight.

Not one of the many passing motorists even attempted to stop to help. Danielle ran to Cameron as he began staggering towards her, clutching his chest. It was only then she noticed the blood all over him.

Cameron told her: 'He's stabbed me, Dan, get his number plate.'

Danielle looked across at the driver of the Land Rover. Kenneth Noye was walking back to his car still carrying the knife in his hand. Another motorist later said he saw Noye smiling.

'Help. Somebody please help us!' screamed Danielle Cable as she once more looked at her fiancé, covered in his own blood.

He collapsed in her arms.

Nearby, the Discovery's tyres screeched as Noye drove off at high speed. Minutes later an ambulance arrived but it was already too late. Cameron never recovered consciousness, and was pronounced dead at a nearby hospital at 2.10 p.m.

Kenneth Noye had a bloodied nose and swollen eyes. He shot back onto the M25, swerving to avoid at least two other motorists. He needed time to think about what to do. After driving around for more than half an hour, he realized he had to break cover and use his mobile phone. He immediately made a flurry of frantic calls in an effort to rally his associates so he could hatch an escape plan. He knew there was no point in waiting around for the police to come calling.

Noye spoke to family and friends a total of seventeen times in the nine hours following the killing of Stephen Cameron that tragic Sunday lunchtime. At 2.04 p.m. Noye rang wife Brenda back at their house in Sevenoaks – just forty-nine minutes after the fatal stabbing. The call lasted just eighteen seconds after Noye decided it was too risky to speak in any detail on the phone.

Over the next hours a series of short and increasingly frantic calls were exchanged by Noye and his friends, family and contacts. At 10.42 p.m. he spoke to the pilot of the helicopter he intended to use to escape the country. After that Noye's mobile went silent for the following two days until his son Kevin made a brief call to it. It was never used again.

Within twenty-four hours of Noye's attack on Cameron, he flew in a 'close business associate's' private helicopter from a field in Bristol to a golf course in Caen, in Normandy, France. From there he took a private jet, laid on by John Palmer, to Madrid in Spain.

Noye knew that the moment the police worked out he was responsible for the road-rage death of Stephen Cameron he'd become the most wanted man in Britain. Having been Public Enemy Number One in the aftermath of John Fordham's killing, this was something he was used to, but, until they made the connection between the two deaths, Noye had to use every available moment to ensure that he put as many miles as possible between himself and his police pursuers.

*

Just as Noye's helicopter rose above the countryside outside Bristol, his Land Rover Discovery, which still contained the knife he'd used to kill Stephen Cameron, was being driven in a bizarre three-car convoy to Dartford, Kent. The last car had a very distinctive number plate and was owned by one of Noye's closest friends. The middle vehicle, Noye's Land Rover Discovery, turned into a scrapyard and minutes later was crushed into a compressed box of jagged steel.

Kenneth Noye's cronies were already playing a significant part in helping the notorious criminal to cover his tracks.

TWENTY-THREE

The murder of hard-working electrical engineer Stephen Cameron shocked the nation. Headlines the following day included POLICE HUNT FOR ROAD RAGE KILLER and HORROR OF MOTORWAY ROAD RAGE MURDER. Across the country there was stunned disbelief that one motorist could take the life of another just because of a row over their driving. Within the Brink's-Mat gang, word of Noye's involvement was already spreading, and they experienced outrage of a different kind – many of them believed that Noye's reckless act had once again focused even more attention on their own activities. As one gang member later told me: 'Noye was at it all over again. He was a fuckin' liability.'

The only clue to the identity of the Land Rover Discovery driver at this stage was a description given by heartbroken fiancée Danielle Cable. She told police that he was about 5ft 10in, slim with brown collar-length hair. He was also clean-shaven, wearing jeans and a dark bomber jacket. Other witnesses who had been crossing the section of the motorway which ran over the scene of the murder provided police with the opening part of the Discovery's registration number, and officers were hoping that video cameras by the motorway might yield some clues. However the footage was no help in identifying the killer. Next the police announced that they were planning to check a thousand drivers of L-registered Land Rover Discovery vehicles.

When an e-fit image of the murder was published in newspapers, it prompted various names to be put forward by members of the public as possible suspects. But it didn't provide any firm leads. Police were being very careful not to reveal the identity of Cameron's fiancée, Danielle Cable, as she was the only real witness to the entire incident. There were genuine fears that the killer might come after her if he knew where to find her.

Not surprisingly, Cameron's family and friends were having great difficulty coming to terms with what had happened. At an emotional press conference given three days after the killing, Cameron's brother Michael said: 'He was the kindest and most affectionate person. We are absolutely crushed and I don't have the words to express it. The family is so close and there is so much love generated that we are going to get through this.'

It was not until they started studying the computer image of the road-rage killer more closely that detectives on the case began to make a possible connection to Kenneth Noye.

Not only was there an uncanny likeness, but Noye's house was reasonably close to the scene of the murder. The team set about making discreet inquiries and established that Noye had been regularly seen driving a Land

Rover Discovery. Perhaps significantly, they discovered Noye had left the country the day after the road-rage killing. The connection was becoming more credible.

More than a week after the killing of Stephen Cameron, police raided Kenneth Noye's Sevenoaks home, looking for evidence that might link him to the crime. They took away papers, clothes and a Range Rover, as well as closely quizzing Brenda.

What they didn't realize was that Noye was actually being shadowed at the time of the killing by undercover detectives investigating his Brink's-Mat criminal activities. However they had not followed him on the day of the murder of Stephen Cameron. The surveillance team monitored his departure from Britain the day after the murder without realizing the significance of his flight abroad.

As one detective later admitted: 'It was just one of those things. No one realized he was someone who was wanted for questioning about the road-rage killing because the police had not identified him by that early stage.'

Behind the scenes, detectives tried everything to find Kenneth Noye before news of his link to the killing became public. This was not revealed to other police forces immediately because detectives feared that Noye might find out that he had become a suspect. 'Noye was lucky. His own continued relationship with some policemen had left many officers deeply untrusting of their colleagues, and that helped him slip through the net,' explained one Kent detective.

On 9 June 1996, Kenneth Noye was publicly named as a suspect in the road-rage death of Stephen Cameron in a huge front-page splash story in the *News of the World*. It was a blow for police who'd hoped they could keep his alleged involvement under wraps until they located him.

COP KILLER NOYE TO BE QUIZZED OVER ROAD RAGE MURDER screamed the headline in Britain's most popular Sunday tabloid.

Just days before the road-rage killing, Kenneth Noye had met with a car dealer he knew called John Marshall, who supplied him with stolen vehicle licence plates, including those used on the Land Rover Discovery linked to the death of Stephen Cameron. Following the murder, tattooed Marshall, thirty-four, vanished into thin air after leaving his £250,0000 home in Little Burstead, Essex, to 'meet business contacts'.

The next day he was found shot in the head and chest in his black Range Rover in Sydenham, south London. Marshall had also been a close friend of executed Pat Tate and his brother Russell. It emerged that Marshall had actually worked as a courier for some of the Brink's-Mat-financed Ecstasy runs to and from Holland, but the identity of the murderers remains a mystery to this day. South London villains and many police officers were starting to wonder if the killings would ever stop. The aftermath of the Brink's-Mat robbery had sparked a huge wave of violence and retribution.

On 11 June 1996, Kent police asked Interpol to issue a worldwide alert on Kenneth Noye, stating that he was wanted urgently for questioning in relation to the murder on the M25 of Stephen Cameron. Every one of the 176 countries who were members of Interpol was sent a 'blue warrant' and requested to alert the Kent police murder incident room at Dartford, if Noye was seen.

Detectives then announced that another character, called Anthony Francis, was wanted for questioning in connection with the road-rage attack. In reality the name was simply a pseudonym regularly used by Kenneth Noye and a number of his other Brink's-Mat associates. 'Anthony Francis' was the registered owner of the Land Rover Discovery L794 JTF which was traced to the house in Brigden Road, Bexleyheath where Noye had paid for those hostess parties earlier that year and during part of 1995.

Both the women who rented the house in Bexleyheath moved out shortly after the road-rage attack. Police eventually interviewed both of them. They also dug up part of the back garden just in case any of the missing Brink's-Mat bullion was anywhere to be found. Nothing was located.

Kent police were informed by the Scotland Yard surveillance team shadowing Noye that he had travelled to northern Cyprus in late May where he had slipped into the familiar surroundings of the port of Kyrenia. Turkish-Cypriot police even had a record of Noye arriving by ship.

But he vanished before the police could link him to the road-rage attack. No one knew where he was now. Worse still, there was no extradition treaty between northern Cyprus and the UK, which was disastrous news for the road-rage police investigation team. Even if Noye was caught, it wouldn't be easy getting him back to stand trial. While he was in northern Cyprus, Noye visited his recently purchased timeshare development, which was still under construction by local builders. The development should have been the perfect refuge – except that too many people knew of his connection with it. Development manager Colin Reader – brother of Brink's-Mat co-defendant Brian – was less than helpful when this author approached him on the island a few months after the killing.

'Fuck off' were the only words he'd utter in response to questions about Noye. It was then made very clear that it would be advisable to leave the development immediately or face physical intimidation.

In Swanley, Kent, the family and friends of Stephen Cameron attended his funeral service. It was a measure of the sense of shock within the community and across the country that so many people turned up for it. Crowds stood outside the church listening on loudspeakers. After the service at St Mary the Virgin church, Detective Superintendent Nick Biddiss – the detective leading the hunt for Cameron's killer – said he believed that 'associates' of the criminal community could have information about the killer and his vehicle. Inevitably the trail would lead Biddiss to the doorstep of yet more Brink's-Mat gang members as part of that process.

At 2.30 p.m. on Wednesday, 13 June 1996, thirty armed French police officers – tipped off by Kent police – swooped on a private plane as it landed at Le Bourget airport outside

Paris. Four squad cars swept across the runway as gendarmes surrounded the Learjet 55, which had stopped at Paris for refuelling en route to Tenerife.

The previous day the Learjet – registration number N104BS – had flown from Bristol to St Petersburg. The plane and some of its baggage were searched, and five men were held for questioning and then allowed to leave two hours later. In the month since the road-rage killing of Stephen Cameron, that same jet had made a series of flights, some of which detectives believed involved Kenneth Noye.

On 28 June 1996, Noye allegedly flew back into Britain and lunched at the China Gardens restaurant in West Kingsdown with some other members of the Brink's-Mat gang. It was as if they were taunting the police, who, the villains believed, had set up Noye because they were still bitter about how he'd been acquitted for the murder of John Fordham.

Come and get us if you can, seemed to be the message.

The police were more and more reliant on their intelligence networks as they sought to track Noye and other Brink's-Mat gang members, who were now creating all sorts of smokescreens to confuse their pursuers. Occasionally scraps of genuine information came to the police from their underworld contacts, many of whom would have preferred to see Noye no longer at liberty since the stir he'd caused was alerting the police to their own illicit activities.

Rumours were also circulating that Stephen Cameron

knew his killer. This was completely untrue, but the lack of hard facts in the case had the knock-on effect of encouraging wild rumours to spread. Equally, in a case that might eventually hang on the question of identity, Noye could argue that the public juxtaposition of his face with the identikit image compiled with Danielle Cable's help damaged his chances of a fair hearing.

At the end of June, Kent detectives revealed that they wanted to speak to a close friend of Noye's called Gerry Copeland. Copeland drove a dark blue Mitsubishi Shogun similar in appearance to the Land Rover Discovery identified by Cameron's fiancée Danielle as the vehicle used by the killer. At this stage the police had still not established that the killer had definitely driven a Discovery, despite being certain of Noye's link to the killing.

There were a number of other Noye 'sightings' in southeast England at the time, suggesting that he was either taunting the police by popping in and out of Britain as he pleased despite being a wanted man, or he was spreading rumours of his presence just to test out the response time of the police and waste their resources.

Underworld sources suggested to police that Noye was renting a villa in Portugal, near Lisbon. They also insisted that he was continually flying in and out of Elstree airfield, just north of London. It was even claimed that he'd popped into a house in Essex for a relative's birthday celebrations.

Over in Sevenoaks, Kent, Noye's wife Brenda was still fielding virtually non-stop inquiries from journalists. She'd never forgiven the media for the way they'd treated her husband following the killing of John Fordham. In an interview with this author in July 1996, she claimed that her husband was being persecuted over the road-rage killing.

Brenda Noye said: 'Don't talk to me about him wanting to come back to help police. He would be an idiot to come back. What they would do is stick him in a Category A prison for two years, pick the jury and get the guilty verdict they want. I have no idea where he is and I don't want to know. As far as I am concerned, he is better off out of it.'

Ironing clothes in the kitchen of the house in Sevenoaks, she added: 'I live in fear of my life. I moved here after the Brink's-Mat case because I feared for the safety of my family. Now I am living in fear again because of all this publicity. Nobody had ever heard of my husband before that bloody Brink's-Mat case.' She also said in reference to the death of John Fordham: 'Okay, he was a gold smuggler, but he was put in a position where he had to defend himself.'

By September 1996, the Kent police's frustration was mounting because Kenneth Noye really did seem to have disappeared into thin air. All the surveillance reports, alleged sightings and underworld rumours had come to nothing.

The *Daily Mirror* put up a £10,000 reward for the arrest and conviction of the 'road-rage killer'. Kent detectives issued an internal wanted poster in the *Police Gazette* in the same week as the *Mirror* reward. It included two photographs of Noye and warned that he was 'violent, carries knives'. The special notice was sent to police forces throughout Britain.

On 26 September 1996, the Brink's-Mat curse claimed yet another victim – Kent 'businessman' Keith Hedley was woken on his 45ft motor yacht *Karenyann* in Corfu by the sound of men apparently trying to steal his dinghy. According to friends who were guests on board, Hedley ran through the boat to collect a shotgun, which he always kept loaded, and fired two shots into the sky to scare the thieves.

The raiders returned fire with three shots, two of which hit Hedley in the shoulder and stomach, fatally wounding him. Police blamed the attack on a group of Albanian pirates. Initially, the incident was brushed off as a tragic example of international piracy, but back in the south London underworld there were rumours that Hedley had crossed the Brink's-Mat gang after some gold he was supposed to be looking after had gone missing.

Hedley had been on his yacht with a woman called Valerie Pallett, who was unknown to his family – including wife Sylvia – back in the UK. All three of fifty-seven-year-old Hedley's guests – the others were an old school friend called Patrick Hills and his wife Jane – were interviewed after the attack. Hedley, a father of two who lived in Borough Green, Kent, and ran three building firms, had been on the island for six days. Hedley's brother David, sixty, from Folkestone, later said Keith visited the island two or three times a year – often with sons Gary, twenty-nine, and Ian, twenty-five. Of Miss Pallett, his brother said: 'I have never heard of her.'

Hedley's sprawling farmhouse was located very near to the Noye family home in Sevenoaks, and had even been searched by police during the Brink's-Mat inquiry. Hedley was never charged, despite the discovery of a sawn-off shotgun on his property. But that police raid had sparked suspicion in the underworld that he might have fed information to the detectives in exchange for having any potential charges against him dropped. Though they had been close friends during the years when they lived near each other, Keith Hedley and Kenneth Noye had fallen out about some money that Noye reckoned he was owed.

Whatever the truth of the matter, Hedley's death was clearly another example of just how dangerous it was to be associated with the Brink's-Mat robbery.

In November 1996, seven men accused of taking part in the Brink's-Mat-inspired hole-in-the-wall cash-dispenser scam were found guilty. John 'Little Legs' Lloyd – still rumoured to be one of the original Brink's-Mat robbers – was described by the judge as one of the main organizers of this latest crime.

The hole-in-the-wall defendants also included Paul Kidd, thirty-six; Graham Moore, thirty-two; Stephen Seton, sixty-five; Stephen Moore, forty-one; the legendary local villain Billy Hayward; and John Maguire, thirty-six. All but one was from Kent or south-east London. They entered guilty pleas after failing in an attempt to have the proceedings stayed as an abuse of process. Kenneth Noye was named in court as playing a part in organizing the crime, but there had never been enough evidence for police to press for a prosecution. The Brink's-Mat connections were there for everyone to see.

After Little Legs Lloyd copped a five-year stretch for his part in the hole-in-the-wall scam, this author paid his live-in love Jean Savage a visit at their immaculate bungalow in West Kingsdown, Kent, which they'd bought from Noye more than twelve years earlier. Jean proved a charming lady, despite her two Rottweilers and the seven-foot-high brick wall complete with electronically controlled gates that surrounded the property.

Following a ten-minute chat on her intercom system, Savage made it clear she wasn't going to talk any further about Lloyd and his criminal activities. In 1999, Lloyd was released from prison and nothing has been heard from him since. 'But he's around and he's looking for new business opportunities – or so I've heard,' one old south-east London face said at the time.

TWENTY-FOUR

Across the river in north London, a bankrupt property developer and drug dealer called Michael Olymbious had been borrowing a ton of cash from the notorious Adams family. When all Olymbious's businesses had gone belly up a few months earlier, he'd fled to Cyprus to avoid his sinister 'bankers' the A-Team. But, as the old saying goes, you can run but you can't hide.

In 1996, Olymbious slipped back into London to see his family. He agreed to attend a meeting in south London the night before he was due to fly back to Cyprus. As he got out of his car, a lone gunman fired a single bullet, which went right through his head.

One of Olymbious's failed property deals involved the Beluga nightclub on Finchley Road, north London. The Adams family had turned it into the epicentre of their criminal empire. At one time the club had been sponsoring world title fights featuring boxer Chris Eubank and promoted by Barry Hearn, one of Britain's top promoters. When a tabloid newspaper exposed the club's links with the Adams family, Hearn immediately severed his sponsorship links.

The A-Team had carefully nurtured contacts in high places for years. In 1996 one establishment figure came under close scrutiny from detectives and MI5 officers trying to break the family's stranglehold on London's club land. This man owned a private company that supplied the Adams family with an arsenal of weapons, including sub-machine guns, from former Eastern bloc countries. The same 'respectable' individual had, it was claimed, even become a member of the A-Team's inner circle.

In the summer of 1997, the A-Team had the front to put it around that they'd donated thousands of pounds to the Labour Party just before their historic election landslide in May of that year. Tommy Adams told associates he'd made several payments to the party through two henchmen, Michael Papamichael and Edward Wilkinson, both later jailed for other Adams-related offences But since gifts of less than £5,000 do not have to be publicly disclosed by political parties it seems unlikely we'll ever hear the real story behind these allegations.

The A-Team had also invested a lot of their dirty money in the world of horse-racing through their old friend and associate, so-called businessman Brian Wright, who'd long since been fingered to the police as yet another villain linked to the Brink's-Mat laundering operation. Wright – known as 'The Milkman' because he always delivered on time – had been linked to race-fixing at meetings across the country. Organized crime investigators had kept an eye on him for years. Through Wright, the A-Team were reckoned to have forged close connections to specific jockeys and bookmakers involved in race-fixing.

In 1997, yet another Brink's-Mat associate came to a nasty end in a classic underworld hit. 'Scarface' Danny Roff was one of the prime suspects in the 1990 murder of Great Train Robber Charlie Wilson in Spain. Roff's nickname came from a distinctive scar under his right eye and a liking for heavy gold jewellery.

'Scarface' had been involved in helping launder the proceeds of Brink's-Mat, and there was already officially a strong link between the robbery and Wilson's murder. Roff, thirty-six, had been paralysed in the spine after an earlier attempt on his life and was in a wheelchair. As he arrived home in his Mercedes in Wanstead Road, Bromley, Kent, he began struggling to get out of his car.

Just then two masked gunmen ambushed Roff and shot him at least five times in the head and chest. As one old south London face said afterwards: 'Roff was always going to end up dying like that. He had it coming. He thought he was fuckin' invincible.' Another Brink's-Mat source said: 'Roff tried to keep a bit of the Brink's-Mat cash for himself after a drug deal and as a result got forced into carrying out the Charlie Wilson hit on behalf of others. But Charlie's people got him in the end.'

A few weeks later, Kenneth Noye encouraged the word to go out that, like Roff, he'd also been executed in a gangland contract killing. It was an attempt to take the heat off the worldwide hunt for him. But the stories were treated with understandable scepticism by police. There was another rumour that Noye had travelled to Brazil to check out potential 'retirement' properties. Others claimed he intended to get plastic surgery carried out while he was in Rio before returning to Britain to live. But as usual, there was no concrete evidence whatsoever to back up these claims.

Kathy McAvoy – wife of incarcerated Mad Mickey McAvoy – reflected some of the rest of the gang's irritation with Noye when in 1997 she told this author: 'He's a fool and an idiot. Only an idiot would do the things he's done. He was a fool because he allowed himself to be caught in certain situations.' Kathy McAvoy claimed that Noye was not liked by the other members of the Brink's-Mat gang. 'He's been portrayed as a hero but he isn't. He's nothing like that. He was no more than a fence.'

Kathy McAvoy would only agree to meet this author in a crowded shopping mall in Bromley, south London, after certain assurances had been made. She also made a point of hammering home the message that her husband and other robbers had little time for Kenneth Noye. 'He's just a load of trouble. Not even one of us really. A bloke from the suburbs, who acted like he was from south-east London when he wasn't,' added Kathy McAvoy.

'I feel sorry for Brenda [Noye's wife]. He's left her to face all the music and it can't be easy. She's a lovely lady,' she added. Kathy McAvoy confirmed that she had talked to underworld figures about Noye's disappearances and there was a collective feeling that 'we'd like him to just stay away for ever.'

*

The key to Kenneth Noye's survival was that all of his criminal associates, friends and family believed he'd been wrongly accused of the road-rage killing, so they were willing to go to great lengths to help him.

The Krays' legendary associate Freddie Foreman summed up the attitude of many when he said: 'Obviously anything that goes wrong, any major crime that happened recently, Kenny Noye is going to have his name put up front.'

Noye and Tony White's brilliant brief Henry Milner – whose legal skills continued to be used by many of south-east London's best-known criminal faces – handled all inquiries about Noye with great skill. But like everyone else, he said he had no idea where Noye had gone.

By the middle of 1997, Brink's-Mat insurers believed they had recovered virtually the whole of the original value of the stolen gold bullion. But that didn't allow for the fact that the £27m had undoubtedly been turned into hundreds of millions through numerous successful investments by the criminals.

With Kenneth Noye on the run, John 'Little Legs' Lloyd in prison for the hole-in-the-wall scam and McAvoy and Robinson still banged up, it was thought that maybe the Brink's-Mat trail would finally run cold. The police presumed that the gang and its associates would put the brakes on their 'business opportunities' and try to keep a lower profile. But greed always conquers brains in the end.

TWENTY-FIVE

In late 1997, Brink's-Mat cash helped finance an audacious plot to spring a gang of villains from inside a British jail. The extraordinary escape plan involved smuggling in quantities of Semtex explosive, blasting a hole in the jail wall and flying the prisoners to freedom by helicopter. One employee at the top-security Whitemoor prison in Cambridgeshire was arrested after an inmate leaked the escape plans to prison authorities. The key figure in the scheme was one of Kenneth Noye's oldest criminal associates, south Londoner George Caccavale, fifty-six. He was serving eighteen years inside Whitemoor for his part as the leader of a nine-man gang jailed for a total of 167 years at Bristol Crown Court in July 1997 after being convicted of being involved in a £65m drug-smuggling operation.

Certain members of the Brink's-Mat gang decided to help finance the escape bid because Caccavale had been a loyal and trusted associate of theirs. But, as one Brink's-Mat source explained, 'Noye and some of the others needed to get George out to recoup their original investment.' They'd ploughed millions into his operation and needed a return on their money, especially since the costs

associated with their way of life were so high. 'We're talking about paying informants, safe houses, new vehicles,
private planes. None of it comes cheap,' explained one
who should know.

Nevertheless, it's a measure of the power they believed
they held that they would even consider such a daring
plan.

In November 1997, three Brink's-Mat associates travelled
by private jet to the Costa del Sol to meet a gang of well-
known drug dealers and armed robbers who'd agreed to
acquire the Semtex and hire a helicopter for the audacious
escape plan. The gang even had an informant working
inside Whitemoor, who was prepared to smuggle the
Semtex into the prison. The informant had been trapped
into helping the gang because he'd been caught in a
compromising position with a woman planted by the criminals. The same man was also smuggling drugs on behalf
of other prisoners inside Whitemoor.

Following the anonymous tip-off, prison authorities
foiled the escape plan just a week before it was due to be
carried out. They'd become particularly sensitive to such
plots since the 1994 escape of six inmates, including five
IRA terrorists, from the same jail.

The Brink's-Mat gang were furious. Until Caccavale was
out of jail, their investments were effectively lost.

In late 1997, while Kenneth Noye was still on the run, he
bought a £200,000 yacht in Cadiz, Spain, and immediately
sub-leased it out to various hashish gangs to use for drug
smuggling from Morocco. He followed this by investing

half a million pounds in a carefully planned hashish smuggling operation operating through one of the most notorious criminals in Gibraltar – just two hours' drive from his Spanish hideaway south of Cadiz. Noye – using a false British passport – never once even had his picture ID checked by border patrol officers from either Spain or Britain.

'It's the easiest border to walk through in the world. I've never ever seen police check the photo ID on a British passport,' said one regular Gibraltar visitor, Anthony Bowman. 'No wonder Noye got through so easily.'

A Spanish police source in southern Spain revealed that British police in Gibraltar actually monitored a man later identified as Noye meeting local criminals around this time. The source explained: 'This is very embarrassing. But there were so few up-to-date photos of Noye that the police in Gibraltar had no idea that the man they had video footage and photos of was Noye.'

Noye had been meeting an infamous Gibraltarian criminal who was under constant surveillance because he was believed to be the mastermind behind one of the biggest drug-smuggling cartels in the world. At that time, Noye had been using a false passport in the name of another well-known local British criminal, which further confused the situation.

But the Spanish police source added: 'It is highly embarrassing that British police were monitoring the most wanted man in their own country without even realizing it.' However the same source also confirmed that just a couple of months later, Spanish police also had Noye

within their sights when they were monitoring the movements of the local girlfriend he had at the time, Mina Al
Taiba. 'She was under surveillance because she was a known
associate of several criminals on the Costa del Sol,'
explained the source. Like the Gibraltarian police, the
Spaniards failed to recognize Noye, so, although wanted
in his Britain for a crime that had shocked an entire nation,
he remained at liberty.

Just before Christmas 1997, Noye made direct contact
with one of his closest police contacts inside Scotland
Yard. As one highly placed source explained: 'Noye was
taking a hell of a risk but he wanted to sound out the
Yard about what would happen if he decided to walk into
a police station and give himself up.' Noye was told he
would not get any special favours and warned that Kent
detectives believed they had conclusive proof of Noye's
involvement in the road-rage death of Stephen Cameron.
Noye's call to Scotland Yard was from a scrambled phone
line, which prevented the police from tracing the call.
But they believed the clarity of the line meant that Noye
was definitely within a 25-mile radius of London when
he made it.

Many of the Brink's-Mat gang's closest associates in the
drug world were not having it all their own way, either.
So-called heroin king James Hamill was jailed for eighteen
years in February 1998 after being found guilty of running
one of Britain's fastest-growing heroin-supply rings. The
police believe that some of the Brink's-Mat proceeds were
'invested' in Hamill's operation. Hamill, thirty-eight, had

aspirations to become one of Europe's most powerful godfathers and he'd taken a lot of advice from two particular members of the Brinks-Mat gang over the years.

Just two weeks before Hamill was jailed in Aberdeen, one of his closest associates – feared Glasgow gangster Stephen Docherty – plunged to his death from a high-rise block. In the high-risk, high-profit drug empires, life often came cheap.

The Brink's-Mat team had been seriously considering joining forces with Hamill and his Scottish gang to supply virtually every type of recreational drug to 'customers' across Britain and possibly even into Europe. But they pulled out immediately after Hamill's arrest.

Kenneth Noye continued masterminding huge drug deals as he continued to evade justice. By early 1998, he was mostly settled in an isolated location on the Spanish coastline, just south of Cadiz. Noye boasted to associates that he'd decided to concentrate on smuggling hashish because he believed that Spanish police were more concerned about so-called heavier drugs such as cocaine and heroin.

At his house, Kenneth Noye – using at least two aliases – occasionally upset his neighbours. As neighbour Tewe Dungholt explained: 'When I met Noye he almost killed me because he thought I was a burglar after I jumped over his garden wall to talk to his gardener, who also attends to my house. I was just walking across his lawn when I saw this man come out of the back door with something glinting in his hand. I immediately realized it was a knife and stopped in my tracks to explain who I was. He put it down by his side immediately and then spoke to me briefly before suggesting I should leave his property. I would not say he was rude, but he was very menacing and I only ever saw him one other time in the street as he drove past in his Shogun.' Herr Dungholt added: 'I realized he was not a man to cross.'

Noye became increasingly confident that the authorities would never catch up with him. He even flew his own father and one of his blonde mistresses in from south-east London to stay with him during the early part of 1998. Noye was being very careful not to implicate his wife at this time so she was deliberately kept 'off the scene'. Their eventual separation was almost definitely prompted by Noye's desire to help protect Brenda from the fallout caused by the road-rage killing.

But the longer Kenneth Noye was on the lam, the more the feeling grew that maybe some of his criminal enemies – including certain members of the Brink's-Mat gang – had decided that they were fed up with all the unwelcome attention he had caused through his alleged involvement in the road-rage killing.

Notorious Costa del Crime resident Mickey Green, described by Ireland's Criminal Assets Bureau as one of the world's biggest cocaine traffickers, had become so adept at escaping justice since his days as a notorious London armed robber thirty years earlier that he'd been nicknamed The Pimpernel by authorities. It was said that Green had evaded arrest on the Costa del Crime for a couple of years by wearing a disguise and using a false identity. In the nineties he spent much of his time in Spain, having been released on a legal technicality the last time the law had got their hands on him. Green was the classic 'Mister Big' with alleged links to the Mafia and Colombian drug cartels. He was a regular visitor to South America, where he nailed down a number of huge cocaine deals with successors to the most famous drug baron in the world, Pablo Escobar, who'd been killed by drug enforcement agents in 1993. There was even talk that Green had been one of the actual robbers who took part in the original Brink's-Mat raid.

Green was using a lot of cash that had been provided to him by certain members of the Brink's-Mat gang because they knew that vast profits could be made out of cocaine if it was purchased direct from the 'source' in Colombia. Green wasn't in the slightest bit fazed by travelling to places like Medellin, a city that was virtually ruled by the Colombian drug cartels.

When American DEA agents monitoring the big Colombian drug barons reported that a 'limey' criminal had been in a series of meetings with gangsters, they passed on his name and details to their colleagues at Scotland Yard, but there was nothing anyone could do without any more concrete evidence. It was also thought by detectives in London that Green should be allowed to continue setting up cocaine deals in the hope that he would lead them to other even bigger fish.

Green always returned from his trips to Medellin looking as if he didn't have a care in the world. He believed he was untouchable. His palatial hacienda, just east of

Marbella, was worth more than £2m, and he'd got a friend to live in a gatehouse and keep an eye on the property whenever he was on his travels. As one of his Costa del Crime associates explained: 'Mickey was from the old school. He'd done well for himself and kept on his toes for much of the past twenty-five years. Good luck to him!'

Well into his sixties, Green had, over the years, been shadowed by British, Dutch and French authorities, who suspected him of major criminal activities. There had even been a rumour that he kept £1m in French francs hidden in a box buried under a flowerbed at his Marbella villa. Green's personal fortune was estimated to be at least £50m.

Michael John Paul Green was born in 1942 in Wembley to a family that originally came from Ireland. He was said to be your original medallion man, with a taste for birds and booze. He first made his criminal reputation in 1972 when a notorious London supergrass called Bertie Smalls named him as leader of a gang of robbers known as the Wembley Mob – at the time the UK's most successful team of armed blaggers. Green was eventually jailed for eighteen years for his part in the robbery of a bank two years earlier in Ilford that yielded £237,000, although he was suspected of involvement in numerous other crimes.

Green got out on parole after serving seven years of his sentence, and was soon back in the thick of things. He teamed up with old Wembley Mob partner Ronnie Dark, and they developed a lucrative VAT scam on gold krugerrands. They bought the gold coins – which weren't liable for VAT – then melted them down into ingots and sold them back to the bullion house, collecting a hefty wodge of VAT in the process. It was reckoned Green and his pals made £6m in under a year.

Green went on to act as a 'consultant' to the Brink's-Mat gang and helped them set up their own VAT-avoidance scam, which is believed to have added at least £10m to the profits from the gold itself. But then Green was arrested by Spanish police in 1987 after two tons of hash were seized in Barcelona. Green was mysteriously granted bail and fled to Morocco, leaving behind eleven powerboats and yachts that were allegedly used to run drugs from North Africa to Spain.

When Green turned up in Paris, Interpol were alerted. French police swooped on his swish Left Bank apartment where they found gold bullion and cocaine but no Mickey Green. That gold was allegedly part of the Brink's-Mat consignment, and it was suspected that he was using it to buy shipments of cocaine directly from the Colombian cartels. In his absence, Green was later sentenced to seventeen years in jail for possession of drugs and smuggling. Green's next stop was California where he rented Rod Stewart's mansion under an alias. A few months later FBI agents knocked his front door down as he was lounging by the pool and arrested him. Green was put on a flight bound for France and the jail sentence that was waiting for him, but he got off when the plane made a stopover at Ireland's Shannon airport. It's unclear why it took more than an hour for anyone to notice his absence.

Using his Irish passport, he slipped unnoticed past customs men and headed for Dublin where he had many contacts. Green took full advantage of the weak extradition laws that existed between the Irish Republic and France at the time and settled in Dublin.

He even splashed out on a massive half-a-million-pound farmhouse just outside the city. But then Green ran a red light at a busy junction in his Bentley and killed a local taxi driver called Joe White. Green was fined and banned from driving, but there was uproar in the local press because he was not given a custodial sentence, despite the death of an innocent man. Under mounting pressure, Irish police made it clear they were planning to grab Green's assets, including his farmhouse property, so, in typical fashion, the Londoner disappeared. It was later claimed during another criminal's trial in London that Green bribed two witnesses in the death-crash court case to make sure he wasn't sent to jail. During the trial of Green's associate, supergrass Michael Michael, a female drug courier told the court that she and an Irishman were paid to lie about the car smash that killed Joe White. Shortly after leaving Ireland, Green turned up once again in Spain and simply carried on where he had left off, still apparently untouchable on the Costa del Crime.

But characters like Mickey Green really got up Mad Mickey McAvoy's nose. He suspected they were spending his share of the Brink's-Mat gold, even though McAvoy had made it crystal clear over and over again that he was fully expecting to be given all 'his' gold when he was released.

TWENTY-SIX

A beige 3-litre Vectra containing two Kent detectives and a Spanish officer headed off slowly behind Kenneth Noye's Mitsubishi Shogun as it began twisting and turning down the hill from his house into the nearby *pueblo* of Atlanterra, seventy miles south of Cadiz. It was late August 1998. The English police had been provided with the number of a mobile phone that Noye was using and used the British security services to track it down to this area of Spain.

Two other vehicles – a Golf GTI and an Astra – joined the convoy from different positions as Noye hit the straight road out of Atlanterra through Zahara and towards the larger coastal port of Barbate. As usual Noye was driving at very high speed, but the officers were all confident he had no idea he was being shadowed.

Noye drove through the busy centre of Barbate and headed onto a narrow road that ran through a forest towards the coastal hamlet of Los Caños de Meca. Minutes later he picked up his mistress Mina from her rented beach-side house, and the couple headed back towards Barbate at high speed.

Behind them, detectives had decided that because the

road was so quiet and the area so sparsely populated they would use only the Vectra to shadow Noye. The two other cars were driven separately back to Barbate to await instructions. But then, as Noye sped through the isolated forest road from Los Caños to Barbate, disaster struck.

As one officer later explained: 'We lost him at the second curve. He just disappeared. There was a crossroads up ahead and he could have gone in any of three directions.'

Instead of panicking, the detectives remained convinced he'd end up in Barbate, so they slowed down and called to the other two vehicles to keep an eye out for him in the town. For the following tense half-hour none of the investigators caught a glimpse of Noye's now familiar dark blue Shogun with its distinctive Belgian plates. The officers began to wonder if perhaps Noye had been tipped off about their operation. It was 10.30 p.m. on a busy Friday night, and the reality was that Noye could have slipped through their grasp.

As the minutes ticked towards eleven, it was decided that the three cars should float around Barbate in the hope of spotting Noye's Shogun parked up in the busy town. They prayed he had stopped to eat dinner somewhere.

In fact, Noye's love of fresh fish had resulted in him heading for El Campero restaurant, right in the centre of Barbate. It served the most delicious cuttlefish, squid, bream, sole, dogfish, mackerel, sardines, anchovies and fresh tuna. At 11.20 p.m. Noye and his mistress Mina walked hand in hand into the front veranda of the restaurant and were seated at a corner table close to the pavement. Noye always chose such tables because if any 'problems' arose he knew he could slip away quickly.

Just as he was sitting down, the three detectives in the Vectra spotted the Shogun. As they circled the square in front of the restaurant they spotted Noye himself almost immediately.

The officers radioed to the other cars to meet them in a street adjoining the square, where they parked two of the vehicles, the Golf GTI and the Vectra. They agreed that they would have to act like drunks in order to get near enough to the restaurant to make certain that it was indeed Noye.

The detectives bought a few litre bottles of beer from a nearby bar, got back into the Astra and double-parked it virtually in front of the restaurant. Then they began playing The Prodigy's 'Firestarter' at full blast on the car stereo. As one detective later recalled: 'Basically we were singing and shouting and acting like it was a Friday night out for the lads.'

Three of the officers then tumbled out of the car and manoeuvred themselves nearer to Noye's table. They watched as Noye ordered a bottle of white Rioja and a seafood salad.

More officers then linked up from the other cars after being radioed in by the team that had spotted Noye and began weaving their way back up the pavement towards the restaurant. Then four of the 'drunks' surrounded Noye's table. Noye tried to ignore them in the hope they would go away. The last thing he wanted was a bit of aggro with a bunch of drunken British hooligans. One of the officers later explained: 'I then dropped my bottle of beer on the floor and leapt on him. There was a smash of a glass on the table and I floored him.'

The detective got Noye in a painful headlock and fell to the ground with him. Two other detectives each grabbed one of Noye's arms, which they yanked up behind his back while a fourth officer handcuffed him. Eighteen-stone Spanish police chief Miguel Fernandez later claimed he was the one who had to sit on Noye – who was struggling fiercely – in order to get him handcuffed.

In the middle of all this, Noye's mistress Mina coolly got up and disappeared off into the night before the detectives thought to apprehend her. Four policemen literally picked Noye up off the floor and carried him to the back of the Astra. As two officers got in the front of the car, Noye shouted: 'Why am I being detained? I want to see a lawyer and I want to see a doctor.'

Minutes after his arrest, Noye was deposited at Barbate's small, scruffy police station where charges were formally read to him. Noye was then searched. All detectives found were a cheap wristwatch and a wallet carrying 1,400,000 pesetas (more than £6,000) in cash.

'What's the cash for?' detectives naturally inquired.

'Spending money for the weekend,' came Noye's sarcastic reply.

Noye also had in his possession a chequebook with five cheques signed to a man called Kerry Stuart Mayne and a further cheque for £5,000 made out to a furniture company. Another chequebook was registered to Mayne, the fake name used by Noye during his stay in Spain and even at a local bank where he'd set up an account.

It also happened to be the name used by one of Noye's main money men, who paid regular visits to Noye when he was out in Spain to keep him supplied with cash. The police discovered a passport in the name of 'Alan Edward Green' in which were found stamps showing he had visited Jamaica and Tangiers on several occasions. Kent police hoped the fake UK passport would ensure that Noye's extradition could be speeded up because it meant Spanish police would not pursue him under his real name.

By approximately 2 a.m. – just over two hours after his dramatic capture – it was decided Noye should immediately be transferred to a high-security jail near Cadiz, 35 miles north of Barbate. Kent police knew all about Noye's friends and associates and they didn't want to take any risks with their highly prized prisoner.

Back in London, the notorious Adams family's power and influence seemed to be everywhere. At the same time as the net was closing on Kenneth Noye in Spain, an official with the Crown Prosecution Service took a bribe from the brothers and leaked confidential information to them to alert them about police plans to close in on the family. Mark Herbert, a £14,000-a-year administration officer working at the CPS headquarters in London, knew exactly who the Adams family were because his own father was a policeman. He didn't just limit his activities to warning the Adamses when the police noose might be tightening. Herbert also took the names of informants off a CPS computer file with a view to sharing them with his criminal paymasters. As Victor Temple QC later told a court, 'it needed little imagination to anticipate what might happen if the name of informants were to fall into the wrong hands.' Fortunately detectives intercepted the hand-written and potentially lethal document.

A court case in September 1998 (just days after Noye's arrest in Spain) ended for once with a conviction and jail sentence for a member of the Adams family. Tommy Adams was given a seven-and-a-half-year stretch for importing cannabis. In public, the police were delighted to have finally made charges stick on an A-Team member but Tommy – chewing gum and laughing as he was taken down to begin his sentence – saw it in a different light.

The police had confiscated £1m in cash from Adams, but they'd hoped for at least £6m. They were convinced some of that money came directly from the laundering of Brink's-Mat gold.

But what got most of London's big firms talking was the rumour that the rest of the A-Team had 'allowed' that prosecution to go through to teach wild man Tommy, who'd been setting up drug deals without telling the rest of the family, a lesson. 'The brothers went to see Tommy in Belmarsh prison,' one Adams associate later explained. 'They told him they were dumping him because he'd gone behind their backs. He'd been caught freelancing and he was paying for it. They could have gone and bribed the jury – £1m is not a problem . . . or given him the bullet, so he got off pretty lightly.'

In early 1999, the A-Team's 'influence' in criminal courts returned with a vengeance when police went for a prosecution over a notorious torture case. David McKenzie was a wealthy 46-year-old financier with an office in Mayfair, in London's West End. McKenzie laundered drug money for the Adams family, but his investments took a nosedive and he lost close to £2m of the A-Team's dirty money. McKenzie said he'd been summoned to a meeting at Terry Adams's mansion in the north London suburb of Finchley for 'a discussion'. He was later found beaten and cut up so badly that one detective said his body looked like a London Underground map. Patsy Adams's golf partner 'Big' Chris McCormack, forty-four – a close associate of all three brothers – stood trial at the Old Bailey accused of causing McKenzie grievous bodily harm with intent.

By this time Terry was privately acknowledged as 'the chief exec of the Adams family board'. McKenzie's courtroom testimony confirmed Terry's status as the main man. 'Everyone stood up when he walked in,' McKenzie explained. 'He looked like a star . . . he was immaculately dressed, in a long black coat and white frilly shirt. He was totally in command.'

The Old Bailey jury of six men and six women deliberated for a day and were then sent to a hotel for the night – with round-the-clock armed police protection. At lunchtime the next day the enforcer was acquitted of the assault. As Big Chris heard the verdict, he turned to the jury and said 'Thank you', before adding: 'Come and have a drink with me over the pub.'

Despite the acquittal, the case made the A-Team realize that they were pushing their luck, and two of them headed out to supposedly 'retire' on the Costa del Sol. At their peak the A-Team were rated as 'ten times more scary than the Krays'.

For now, however, their alleged connection to the Brink's-Mat robbery was starting to cause them a lot of aggravation they could do without.

In May 1999, after many months of wrangling, Noye – who continued to run his criminal enterprises from inside a Spanish prison cell – was finally brought back to Britain to await trial after many months of legal wrangling. He was given an entire wing of the notorious Belmarsh prison, in south-east London, to himself because of fears he might escape.

In a series of tape-recorded telephone interviews conducted inside Belmarsh, one fellow inmate said: 'Kenny Noye was the king inside here. He knew many of the staff and inmates already from when he previously served time. Some of them even knew him from his days as a petty villain in south-east London and Kent. It was like home from home for him.'

Another source revealed that Noye's 'boys' inside Belmarsh prison boasted about how Noye was so confident he would be acquitted of the murder of Stephen Cameron that he'd authorised his sidekick in Spain to continue paying a builder to finish off the Atlanterra *casa* to Noye's very specific orders.

Shortly after Noye's dramatic arrest in Spain, his wife Brenda sold their house in Sevenoaks to a Japanese businessman for £500,000 and moved to Cornwall. Noye had stepped back from Brenda's life in order to give her a fresh start, and she purchased a secluded £250,000 clifftop house called Redsands, in the small fishing village of Looe. With Noye finally back in Britain, many of the other Brink's-Mat gang members must have hoped that the police inquiries would slow down. They might now be able to sit back for the first time in years and start to plan for their futures with the tens of millions of pounds of money laundered from the missing gold.

Mickey McAvoy and Brian Robinson had been following Kenneth Noye's exploits especially closely from their prison cells. They'd become increasingly enraged by Noye's continual hogging of the newspaper headlines. Not only did it cause them more 'aggro' with the police, but it also rankled them that Noye was now the best-known of all the so-called Brink's-Mat gang – and he hadn't even been directly involved in the robbery itself.

As one old south-east London face explained: 'Mickey and Brian considered Noye to be a walking disaster. He just didn't seem able to keep out of trouble, and that, in turn, caused them a lot more aggravation. They were sick of hearing of Noye and they felt he was the main reason why the police's Brink's-Mat inquiry was still ongoing, fifteen years after they were given hefty prison sentences.'

Both men continued to go out of their way to keep a clean sheet inside Leicester's Long Lartin prison because they were patiently biding their time in the expectation that many millions of pounds awaited them on their release. Even when other inmates at the prison had attempted a mass breakout, the two Brink's-Mat 'kingpins' had kept a low profile. Thirty prisoners had barricaded themselves on a landing after guards foiled their escape bid. As a consequence of this and other security breaches, the prison was upgraded to a maximum-security prison. But staff noted that McAvoy and Robinson had played absolutely no role in the trouble.

All the countless theories, rumours and innuendo about the circumstances behind the so-called road-rage killing of motorist Stephen Cameron were soon to be put to the test as Kenneth Noye walked into the number two court of the Old Bailey on Thursday, 30 March 2000 – nearly four years after that fatal incident on the M25. Gone was the confident swagger that had characterized Noye's last appearance in the very same dock fourteen years earlier. This time Noye was grey-haired and dressed in a grey cardigan. He sat hunched like an old man in the dock surrounded by three prison officers, his eyes constantly panning the jury of eight women and four men.

Before the case could proceed, judge Lord Justice Latham ordered round-the-clock protection for each juror. Noye pleaded not guilty to the murder charge and insisted the killing had been an act of self-defence. But, as prosecuting counsel Julian Bevan QC informed the court, 'Noye was angry about the way that van was being driven. Immediately after the stabbing, Kenneth Noye got back in his vehicle, a Land Rover Discovery, and sped off along the M25 leaving a dying Stephen by the road. The Crown's case is that the stabbing to death was not merely unlawful. It was murder.'

Mr Bevan referred to how the driver of a passing Rolls-Royce had seen Noye smile after he'd stabbed Stephen Cameron to death. When that man later gave evidence many believed he was putting his life on the line by 'coming out' about what he claimed to have seen.

The court also heard how Noye had claimed throughout those earlier extradition proceedings in Spain that he was not the killer. But, Mr Bevan told the court: 'He now admits he was the person who held the knife and stabbed Stephen Cameron.' Noye barely even moved a muscle when the prosecutor pointed to photos of huge splashes of red on Stephen Cameron's van.

On Friday, 7 April 2000, Noye took centre stage in the trial. Looking calm and collected but wiping his nose with a spotless white handkerchief, he strolled confidently to the witness box. Noye's testimony was delivered in an atmosphere of hushed expectation. He spoke in a dull, expressionless monotone. Just a couple of feet away Stephen Cameron's parents never once took their eyes off the man who'd killed their beloved son.

Noye claimed he mistook Stephen Cameron and his girl-friend for a couple he knew, and that was why he'd stopped his car. He also insisted that when he'd apologised to Cameron for the mistake, the younger man had said: 'You will be, you cunt, I'll kill you.'

Noye said that Cameron then kicked him in the waist and he tried to punch him back. He said Cameron also pushed him. Then Cameron punched him on the cheek, Noye told the court, and he fell to the ground, where the younger man began kicking him and saying he was going to kill him. Shortly after that Noye got his knife out.

Noye even carried out his own dramatic re-enactment of the incident in the witness box in front of Stephen Cameron's visibly distraught parents. Noye demonstrated the underarm jabbing motion with which he had killed the unarmed man. He claimed he had pulled his knife out from his trouser pocket and told Cameron: 'Don't come near me, nutcase.'

Noye then told the jury: 'His girlfriend was shouting "Get off", I am saying, "Hold up" and he is saying, "I will kill you." I cannot fight – I'm a fit man but I was exhausted. I thought I can't take much more, nobody is trying to stop the fight, not that they could stop him. Then I thought if he catches me again he will take the knife out of my hand and definitely use it on me so I struck out with the knife. I had my head down. I just went like that [demonstrating with a round-arm jab]. I can't remember exactly how I done it, we were close together and I just struck out. I can only remember striking out once but I accept it was twice. He definitely knew I had the knife.'

Noye told the jury he kept a knife by his side every day because he feared being attacked by criminals in league with the police, or being kidnapped and forced to reveal the whereabouts of the missing Brink's-Mat gold. Noye claimed he was frequently stopped by police following his release from prison in 1994. It was at this point that he smiled for about the only time during the trial as he described how they regularly kept him under surveillance. 'They used to follow me around quite a lot.'

Immediately after claiming he'd killed Stephen Cameron

in self-defence, Noye then shocked the court by revealing to the jury that he had stood trial for the murder of under-cover policeman John Fordham. He said he'd killed Fordham for similar reasons. But Noye denied that by the time of the Cameron killing he knew full well that a thrust from the four-inch blade could easily kill another human being.

He was then asked: 'Are you saying that after that ghastly experience you didn't realize it could kill?'

Noye replied: 'I appreciated it could kill but I didn't know where I had to thrust the blade.'

Noye also admitted using the name of Anthony Francis and using a false address for registering ownership of the Land Rover Discovery. 'I didn't want no one to know where I lived,' he told the jury. 'I didn't want no one to know what cars I owned.'

Noye's composure cracked only once, when prosecutor Mr Bevan probed him on his reasons for stabbing Stephen Cameron.

'You believed he would take the knife off you?' asked Mr Bevan.

'Yes,' replied Noye.

'And slit your throat?' asked Mr Bevan.

Noye was rattled by the melodramatic response and said: 'No, no.'

'Let's just leave it there, shall we?' said Mr Bevan.

Then Noye snapped. 'No. We won't leave it, we will get that sorted out right now.'

The court was then dumbstruck when Noye broke down and was close to tears as he described the moment he learned from his wife that Stephen Cameron had died.

Noye also insisted he had 'never hurt anybody, I have never even hurt an animal'.

But under cross-examination he admitted he had 'deliberately' stabbed Cameron and, explaining why he carried a knife, added: 'I would have preferred a stun gun or a CS gas canister but they would be illegal.'

One witness in court claimed that the victim was a violent man, but then confessed to having become close friends with Noye's son Kevin since the road-rage attack. He even admitted that the Noye family had paid for his stay at a hotel during the trial.

On the afternoon of Tuesday, 11 April, Bevan gave his closing speech to the court, and accused Noye of invention and exaggeration in his version of what had happened during the killing of Stephen Cameron. Judge Lord Justice Latham told the jury that they would retire to decide on one of four verdicts: guilty of murder; not guilty of murder but guilty of manslaughter; not guilty of murder but guilty of manslaughter by reasons of provocation; or not guilty. The judge also reminded the jury that a person was entitled to defend himself and use such force as was reasonable in the circumstances. The person had honestly to believe that he was under attack.

The key point was the moment when the knife was used. The judge said: 'If you are satisfied he was not acting in the honest belief it was necessary, but it was in retaliation or to carry on a fight, the use of the knife was unlawful.'

The judge then pointed out that the jury might conclude

that the use of the knife was instinctive and that Noye did not intend to cause serious injury but risked causing Stephen Cameron some harm. If that were so, they could return a verdict of manslaughter.

The jury were finally sent out on the morning of 13 April. Accompanied by armed police bodyguards, the eight women and four men were sent to a hotel overnight following almost a day of deliberation. The next morning the judge advised the jury that he would accept a majority verdict, and asked them to come back into court at midday for an update on their progress.

When the jury finally reappeared, they had reached a majority verdict of 11 to 1. Guilty of murder. Noye let out a deep gasp and held his head in his hands. Lord Chief Justice Latham told Noye: 'The jury having found you guilty of murder, there is only one sentence I can impose and that is one of life imprisonment.'

Noye looked unsteady on his feet as three burly prison officers led him down the twenty-one steps from the dock of number two court to the cells below. A few minutes later a van, its siren blaring, took him back to Belmarsh prison.

In the hours following the verdict, it emerged that Noye's defence, estimated to have cost between £500,000 and £1m, had been funded by the taxpayer after he had been granted legal aid because on paper he was no longer worth a penny.

McAvoy and Robinson heard the news of Noye's sentencing with relief. 'They wanted Noye out of the way,' said one old associate. 'He had caused enough damage and now it was going to be their turn to enjoy life on the outside after nearly twenty years behind bars.'

As one of McAvoy's oldest associates explained: 'Mickey and Brian had served their time like true professionals. They believed they had earned their freedom and a nice life with the proceeds of the robbery. Noye was inside where he belonged, in their opinion, because he'd gone completely over the top during the previous years and caused a lot of problems for everyone else.'

TWENTY-SEVEN

Just as Noye's trial was wrapping up in the late spring of 2000, Brink's-Mat associate Mickey Green's Irish lawyer was shadowed by UK customs agents to Barcelona where he was engaged in legitimate business. The agents had been investigating Green's links to the Mafia and Colombian drug cartels and a massive worldwide network importing narcotics into Britain. When Green turned up at the Ritz hotel in the city, he was immediately arrested by UK customs and Spanish police and transported to the nation's most secure jail in the capital Madrid.

At first, both Spanish and UK police hailed the arrest as the end of Green's career as a criminal. One Costa del Sol detective even said at the time: 'Green's luck has finally run out. He'll go back to Britain to face the music.' An extradition hearing was set for Green, and it seemed just a formality that he would be heading home to London and a long stretch inside.

Besides being wanted in the UK, Green also still faced a long prison sentence back in France for earlier drug offences. It emerged that Green had invested many millions of pounds in legitimate businesses in Spain, but that much of it had been on behalf of several members of the Brink's-Mat gang. Some of the proceeds of the robbery had also helped finance a number of multi-million-pound drug deals set up by Green on the Costa del Crime.

But Mickey Green wasn't known as The Pimpernel for nothing; a few months after his dramatic arrest in Barcelona, a Spanish court refused to extradite him. The Spanish authorities insisted that UK customs did not have enough concrete evidence to mount a prosecution, so Mickey Green was once again a free man. Rumours of bribes swept the Costa del Crime but a customs source later told this author: 'It's sickening to admit, but smuggling charges against Green were dropped after we decided that the evidence from a former associate of Green's called Michael Michael was not strong enough to bring a prosecution back in Britain.' It was Michael's arrest by customs officers back in 1998 that had convinced them to go after Green because Michael had named Green as a Mister Big of the drug world.

At Michael Michael's eventual trial at the Old Bailey in 2001, prosecutor Nicholas Loraine-Smith named Mickey Green as a major drug baron. He said of Green: 'He was and continues to be involved in importing large amounts of drugs into this country.' It was said after Michael's trial that Green had recruited Michael to head the British end of his huge cocaine and cannabis smuggling racket and that they both made millions in the process.

Following his arrest and the subsequent court case, Michael Michael had good reason to fear the wrath of Mickey Green. It was alleged in court that Green had links to the murders of two other criminals with Brink's-Mat connections. One was The A-Team's hit man Gilbert Wynter, who'd disappeared from his north London home back in 1998. As we've seen, his body is thought to be in the foundations of the Millennium Dome. The other murder victim with links to Green was a finance chief for the A-Team who was shot dead outside his home. Informant Michael Michael told UK customs investigators that both men were killed after double-crossing Green and the A-Team in a half-a-million-pound cannabis deal.

Today Mickey Green is rumoured to spend much of his time in Costa Rica, where he owns yet another luxury home. He's also alleged to have links to property in Thailand. As one of those involved in his Barcelona arrest says: 'Mickey's a survivor and you can be sure he's watching his back very carefully.' It's also believed that while still on the run he double-crossed another couple of the Brink's-Mat gang, so he still knows he has to watch his back.

Back in the outside world for the first time in almost twenty years, Mad Mickey McAvoy was already living up to his fearsome reputation. He'd slipped out of prison virtually unannounced around the time of Noye's sentencing which, ironically, had diverted press attention from his release. For the first few months following the end of his sentence he kept a predictably low profile, knowing full well that the police would be on his tail because they still wanted to find the rest of the Brink's-Mat gold.

Behind the scenes, McAvoy put out messages to 'relevant parties' that he was expecting his share of the gold to be delivered to him at the right moment. The responses he started to get back made it clear that it was not going to be handed to him on a plate. That's when McAvoy decided it was time to flex his muscles. If the gold wasn't going to be brought to him then he'd go looking for it himself, and God help anyone who got in his way.

On Thursday, 5 October 2000, 'Big Al' Decabral heaved his 20-stone frame into the passenger seat of his son's Peugeot with great difficulty. He was more used to driving around in his vintage Jag, once owned by legendary gangster Reggie Kray. As he checked the time on his gold Rolex, a man holding a gun equipped with a silencer pulled alongside him in the car park of a Halfords store in Ashford, Kent. Before Decabral even had a chance to plead for his life, two shots rang out and his huge, blubbery body slumped against the dashboard. Terrified shoppers fled in fear of their lives but they had nothing to worry about. The shooter had carried out his job with cold professionalism and immediately left the scene.

Months earlier, Decabral had dared to give police an eyewitness account of Kenneth Noye's stabbing of motorist Stephen Cameron, and then even appeared at Noye's Old Bailey trial to give evidence. As a result, it seems that Decabral had signed his own death warrant. Yet another killing had left a bloody trail that led directly to the Brink's-Mat gang.

One of the most remarkable aspects of the Decabral killing was that so few people seemed surprised. The Kent criminal fraternity were positively underwhelmed by this cold-blooded killing in their midst. Decabral had been sailing close to the wind for years as a petty villain but when he stepped forward and fingered Noye he was opening up a can of murderous worms and many believed he even knew what was coming.

But then Kent and south-east London still remained virtually a law unto itself. The power and influence of the Brink's-Mat gang and a number of other legendary faces made Kent the perfect gateway to the lucrative drug markets of Europe. One retired bank robber even made a small fortune running an unofficial 'ferry service' from a tiny port near Dover across to Holland where drug barons would then get off for 'company meetings' in Amsterdam before slipping back into the UK unnoticed.

'You could get in and out of Europe without the cozzers knowing anything about your movements,' explained retired cannabis smuggler Gordon Scott. 'The fella who ran it had this tasty motor launch complete with bedrooms, a fully stocked bar and he'd even bring on the dancing girls if you booked well in advance.'

The area of Kent countryside stretching from Kenneth Noye's one-time home town of West Kingsdown past Biggin Hill – and its handy airstrip – and across to Swanley was known to detectives as 'the Bermuda Triangle'. As one senior police officer explained: 'Things that went in there had a habit of never coming out again. And we're talking about everything from people to lorryloads of bootlegged fags and booze, not to mention gold.' The construction of the nearby M25 had meant easy access to the Bermuda Triangle at all times of the day and night.

Detectives fully intended to interview Mad Mickey

McAvoy about the Decabral killing because there was a suspicion that he might have had something interesting to say about it, but in the end there was no evidence to link him to the murder. Perhaps someone deliberately killed Decabral knowing it would look as if it had been 'commissioned' by Noye? It was no secret that McAvoy wanted to make sure that Noye never got released from jail. As one south London underworld source explained: 'Think about it . . . it does make sense . . . It would explain why the execution was carried out in such a public manner. Also, a lot of "chaps" had the incentive to frame Noye.'

A few months after Decabral's murder, detectives searching for Brink's-Mat gold were tipped off about a 'burial site' on the south coast. Officers used hi-tech imaging equipment to search a timber yard at the rear of a builders' merchants in Graystone Lane, off Old London Road, Hastings, in East Sussex. After initially conducting virtually a fingertip search, a pneumatic drill was then used to dig deeper in the covered yard. A Scotland Yard spokeswoman told reporters at the scene: 'This search is based on information we have received following a lengthy inquiry which has lasted many months. I cannot say exactly what we are looking for. A drill has been used to dig into the concrete floor of the yard.'

But nothing was ever found and there was a deep suspicion that the original tip was yet another red herring presented to Brink's-Mat detectives simply to divert them away from the right path. There were many occasions when the police thought they had a breakthrough in their search for the Brink's-Mat gold. One time, detectives went digging

for it on a farm in Sussex following a tip-off from an informant. The cat-and-mouse games were continuing, even
though it was nearly twenty years since the original robbery.

In early 2001, Kenneth Noye lost his appeal against a life
sentence for the Cameron killing. Friends and associates
said that he'd keep appealing on all fronts because he was
determined to get released from prison eventually for what
he saw as a miscarriage of justice. (A later appeal was
granted in the autumn of 2010, but in March 2011 his
sentence was upheld.)

But even as Noye's case returned to court, the killings
continued.

The shooting in broad daylight of 63-year-old Brink's-Mat
robber Brian Perry as he got out of his car in Bermondsey,
south-east London, sent a shiver of fear through the underworld. A masked hit man, dressed in dark clothes, shot Perry
in the head, chest and back. Perry was found lying in a pool
of his own blood after local residents heard the gunshots
just after 1 p.m. The masked assassin was seen escaping in
a dark grey or blue Ford Escort fitted with false number
plates. It sped off towards the Old Kent Road shortly after
the shooting. Perry had been murdered in cold blood, right
in the heart of his 'home territory'. Whoever commissioned
the hit was sending out a very clear message.

Many detectives and gangsters believed that Perry's
death was yet more evidence of the deadly ongoing feud
between members of the Brink's-Mat gang. It also sent out
a terrifying warning to other villains. One source very close
to many of the gang told this author: 'Certain people

wanted their share of the gold and when it wasn't there waiting for them they started getting very upset.'

Detective Superintendent Jon Shatford, the new head of the Flying Squad, led the investigation into Perry's brutal killing. The day after the murder, a Scotland Yard spokesman admitted: 'We believe this may be connected to the Brink's-Mat robbery. And we are still looking for proceeds from that incident.' Detectives investigating the hit on Perry sought out Mad Mickey McAvoy for questioning, although they insisted that did not imply he was responsible for the murder.

Perry had earlier served a nine-year prison sentence for his role in laundering profits from the Brink's-Mat raid. It was strongly rumoured that at the time of his death, Perry knew where at least £10m worth of the gold from the heist remained hidden. One source also claimed that Perry was suspected of secretly aiding the police in their inquiries, and that may have been the last straw as far as his enemies were concerned. 'A lot of people were saying that Perry was "helping" the cozzers,' said one Brink's-Mat associate. 'He signed his own death warrant if that really was the case.'

And so the cycle of death and destruction continued. A few months after Perry's death, two of his oldest associates were murdered separately near the busy Kent ports of Chatham and Rochester. Jon Bristow, thirty-nine, and Ray Chapman, forty-four, had both bought boats shortly before they were killed, and in the south-east London underworld it was said that the men had been 'bigging it up' with wads of cash that they said Perry had given them for 'services rendered'.

Mickey McAvoy insisted to anyone who would listen that he just wanted to lead a quiet life after finally getting out of prison. Naturally other criminals tried to implicate him, but McAvoy insisted those rumours were untrue.

On 16 November 2001, Joseph Pitkin, thirty-one, of Verulam Avenue, and Bilal Akhtar, twenty-two, from Canning Road, in Walthamstow, east London, both pleaded not guilty to the murder of Brian Perry. Prosecutor Richard Whittam said Perry's connection to the £26m robbery 'may or may not' have been a reason for the murder.

Prosecutors alleged Pitkin shot Perry while Akhtar drove the getaway car. Neither man had any known motive to kill Perry. A balaclava found at the scene had mixed DNA, which included both Mr Pitkin's and Mr Akhtar's. But in the end the trial was abandoned and both men acquitted after the prosecution admitted that the only evidence available was circumstantial.

Less lucky was John Palmer, who was in court again, this time on charges of committing what prosecutors described as 'the largest timeshare fraud on record'. It was alleged that he had swindled 20,000 people out of £30m. The legal team representing Palmer at his trial had claimed he'd been 'persecuted' because of his alleged links to the Brink's-Mat robbery. Following his conviction for conspiracy to defraud, his lawyers promised a 'vigorous and full' appeal after Palmer was ordered to pay £33m in cash and assets to the state. Palmer had been sentenced to eight years in jail. He was also ordered to hand over £2.7m in compensation to his victims.

Palmer's legal representative Giovanni di Stefano said

the 52-year-old intended to pay the compensation but would appeal all other charges. Mr di Stefano admitted: 'We as lawyers can never predict outcome but we anticipate and sincerely hope that justice will not only be done but be seen to be done regardless of whether he is John Palmer, John Smith or anyone.' Palmer had denied the fraud allegations against him throughout his trial.

Palmer insisted he'd been specifically targeted by police because of his alleged involvement in the smelting down of the Brink's-Mat gold. Mr Di Stefano added: 'Brink's-Mat will always be with him. I'm sad to say that his acquittal has led to a persecution rather than a prosecution.'

However police claimed that Palmer – who often wore body armour – was connected to the Russian mafia and had led a criminal gang involved in fraud, money laundering, drug trafficking, bribery, possessing firearms, and falsifying passports and credit cards.

To add to Palmer's difficulties, there were strong rumours across the London underworld that he'd fallen out with Kenneth Noye after Palmer had lent him his private jet following the murder of motorist Stephen Cameron on the M25. Noye and Palmer were said by sources in the London underworld to be 'at daggers with each other' and as a result both men were kept in separate prisons 'for their own safety'. Noye was under round-the-clock guard in top-security Whitemoor prison in Cambridgeshire, while Palmer remained at an undisclosed jail.

Hundreds of Palmer's timeshare victims sued him for more than £3m, and in 2005 he was declared bankrupt in the United Kingdom with debts of nearly £4m. Palmer was eventually freed after serving half his sentence. Few had any doubt he would return to crime, not least because his victims and creditors were hounding him for money.

In 2007 he was again arrested on a number of charges including fraud. After being held for two years in a high-security Spanish jail without charge he was released on bail, but was ordered to report to court authorities every two weeks.

One of the most extraordinary aspects of the entire Brink's-Mat saga is that it has never stayed out of the public eye for long, and that is still the case today, nearly twenty years after the first crime was committed. As detective Tony Lundy told this author: 'Brink's-Mat had this extraordinary ripple effect on so many other investigations and crimes and it seemed to gain momentum rather than slow down as the years passed.'

But this notoriety meant that some less important faces with links to the Brink's-Mat robbery found themselves in trouble, even if their profile wasn't as high as that of the core Brink's-Mat 'team'. Take Clifford Norris. A slim, almost fragile man of no more than 5ft 7in, Norris had at one time been involved with a multimillion-pound drug empire, which had been at least partly financed by Brink's-Mat money. At the age of thirty, Norris was a key figure in south-east London's drug trade. He owned an expensive mock-Tudor mansion and drove flashy cars.

Norris later admitted he made mistakes, and the drug empire he was involved in was 'out of control'. When, many years after the robbery, he crossed a couple of the

Brink's-Mat gang over a drug deal, Norris went on the run. In August 1994 police followed his wife to a holiday cottage in East Sussex where Norris was hiding. Officers also stumbled upon – next to a set of golf clubs – a silenced Ingram sub-machine gun. After five years in hiding from both criminals and police, he'd finally been tracked down. Norris was sentenced to nine and a half years for drug and firearms offences. On his release in 2001, rumours gradually surfaced that Clifford Norris had tried to reunite with his former Brink's-Mat 'pals'. But Norris was warned in no uncertain terms to keep away. He eventually ended up living in the single room of a mud-coloured hostel above a DIY shop on a jobseeker's allowance of £56.20 a week. The only way he could guarantee he would stay alive was to walk away from all the stolen riches and return to the real world, which proved a much harsher place.

The police continued to keep a close eye on all the Brink's-Mat gang, especially those who'd been released from prison over the previous couple of years. In 2003, gold handler Michael Lawson – one of Kenneth Noye's best friends – was convicted of running a multimillion-pound drug-smuggling operation, but acquitted after an appeal and retrial. However the authorities accused him of laundering the proceeds of drug smuggling through the buying and selling of houses and land. They had a sneaking suspicion that Lawson was still using proceeds from the original Brink's-Mat robbery for some of his criminal enterprises but no charges were ever brought against him.

TWENTY-EIGHT

On 14 May 2003, Brink's-Mat gang member George Francis, now sixty-three, was gunned down at point-blank range as he sat in his car outside the courier business he ran in south-east London. He should have known better after being injured by another shooter seventeen years earlier, but 'Georgie Boy' reckoned he was untouchable. Murder squad detectives immediately sought out Mickey McAvoy to ask him about Francis' execution.

But there was no evidence linking McAvoy to any of the Brink's-Mat murders since his release from prison. Despite having no obvious job, McAvoy seemed to have a comfortable lifestyle. He often flew to the Costa del Crime, where he had access to a luxury mansion.

Brink's-Mat insurance investigator Bob McCann – who'd spent years tracking the missing gold – later said he believed both Francis and Perry were probably 'quite literally fishing for gold and they got too close'.

One retired Brink's-Mat detective explained soon after the Francis shooting: 'Georgie Boy was another man in the know and he paid for that with his life. One by one those involved are being picked off like targets in a funfair shooting gallery. It's bloody terrifying that this sort of thing still goes on in a so-called civilized society.'

Another source said that Francis was also suspected of secretly helping the police with their ongoing inquiries into Brink's-Mat, and that would almost definitely have had an influence on the decision to take him out. Two ageing hitmen were eventually jailed for life for the murder of Georgie Boy but no one ever found out who commissioned the shooters.

The police continued to face mounting criticism about their sometimes clumsy attempts to find the remaining gold. Brink's-Mat insurance investigator Bob McCann explained: 'It's an open secret Mad Mickey McAvoy went straight under police surveillance in the hope he would lead them to the gold, but so far he's just led them on a merry little dance. These characters are not stupid. They knew they are being watched.'

In the early autumn of 2003, Mad Mickey McAvoy was snapped by a press photographer from the *Sunday Mirror*. The newspaper headlined the article 'BRINK'S-FAT'. McAvoy, now 52, bald and a lot heavier than when he went inside, insisted to a reporter he hadn't received a penny of the profits from Britain's biggest gold bullion robbery, and even made out to the newspaper that he was a reformed character, living the quiet life. Home was actually a half-a-million-pound mansion in Locksbottom in Kent. McAvoy was caught on camera as he swept leaves and cleaned the driveway at his home. McAvoy's appearance in the tabloid also happened to coincide with the twentieth anniversary of the robbery, and a two-part

Channel 4 documentary called *Brink's-Mat – The Greatest Heist*.

McAvoy refused to speak on the programme, but gave the TV company a home video of his 1986 prison wedding to second wife Kathy. One of his oldest associates later explained: 'Mickey knew that footage would do him nothing but good because it shows him as a loving husband rather than a villain.' The makers of the documentary series were even accused by police of 'playing along with McAvoy' by not running up-to-date photos or current footage of him on the programme in exchange for him providing the fifteen-year-old video footage of the jailhouse marriage. This desire to avoid recent photos of him being shown wasn't just vanity on the part of Mickey – who had lost all of his hair at the same time as gaining a great deal of weight. He wanted to be able to remain incognito. 'There are photos floating around of him since he got out of jail, and surely they could have filmed him secretly? McAvoy's been made to look like a man who's been unfairly treated by the police and other criminals who took his share of the Brink's-Mat gold. It's a disgraceful whitewash,' added one detective. The programme also for the first time publicly named Brian Perry as one of the actual robbers who took part in the Brink's-Mat raid.

A former detective who interrogated McAvoy in prison told the documentary makers: 'He was known as The General because of his ability to plan and execute a raid. He said if he came out of prison and there was nothing left for him there would be a gang war and people would get hurt. He is very intelligent and is keeping his head down now because he knows the police are still looking at him. Many people believe he is the one who can lead them to the millions of pounds of still unaccounted-for gold bullion. If that is the case, he is taking his time.'

McAvoy claimed to everyone he encountered at this time that he was perfectly happy keeping a low profile and refused to be drawn on the subject of the gold he might be expecting to get after leaving prison. The Channel 4 documentary claimed hit-man victim Brian Perry had betrayed McAvoy by refusing to help him trade in his share of the fortune for a reduced jail sentence.

Perry was portrayed on the programme by an actor repeating the words he had said in a statement to police: 'Once the cell door is closed, what's he [McAvoy] got to trade?' Former Metropolitan Police commander Roy Ramm, who led the investigation, told the programme: 'The message was that Mickey was out of touch. He's saying to us – whatever Mickey thinks, he's out of it.'

Sources close to McAvoy and the programme makers, Blast! Productions, later revealed that McAvoy had 'strung along' the programme's makers for months by promising them an on-screen interview. 'It's obvious he only wanted to know what we'd found out about him from the police and other criminals,' one TV executive later explained.

One of McAvoy's closest associates later explained: 'Mickey's a very clever operator and he never intended to go on the programme in the first place, he just wanted to know what Channel 4 were up to.' But McAvoy himself then 'went fucking ballistic' about the programme because it clearly stated that McAvoy sent a letter threatening to kill Brink's-Mat villain Brian Perry, later murdered by a hit man. McAvoy continued to deny any link and to keep a long distance from any accusations. The programme also featured a scene showing an actress playing McAvoy's wife at Perry's minicab office in south London. One of McAvoy's associates later revealed: 'Mickey was well upset about that scene with his wife, and he was pissed off with the producers for not agreeing to drop the scene.'

Although there was no direct evidence of McAvoy's involvement in any of the deaths linked to Brink's-Mat, police were planning to visit him once again at his luxurious homes in Spain and Kent to find out if he could provide any fresh leads on the identities of the killers.

Inside top-security Whitemoor prison in Cambridgeshire, Kenneth Noye referred all police inquiries regarding the recent spate of murders to his solicitor. One source close to Noye explained at the time: 'Kenny's not worried. He's inside prison so he couldn't have pulled the trigger. I think he's a bit fed up with always being blamed for other people's deaths. He's more interested in continuing his appeal against his murder conviction.'

While in jail, Kenneth Noye was facing up to his life sentence with that same wheeler-dealer attitude he seemed to use to cope with life on the outside. In April 2005 he flexed his muscles in typically Noye style by heading up a delegation of prisoners who claimed that the flickering shadows of wind turbines overlooking the prison were disturbing sleep for many inmates. The machines were switched off at night as a result.

Three months later, Whitemoor prison was locked down

for two days following an explosion in one of the wings. A full search was carried after the firework-like blast, although it caused no damage to the prison. In the middle of all this, Kenneth Noye remained his normal calm self. He'd spent two thirds of the last twenty years of his life in prison and he knew how to play the system better than anyone else.

There seems little doubt that Brink's-Mat gold helped turn Noye's favourite Mediterranean island haven in northern Cyprus into a smaller but much more dangerous version of the Costa del Crime. Brink's-Mat money had helped set up timeshare resorts, build hotels and enabled a number of gangsters with links to the robbery to buy large detached mansions on the island. On a five-mile stretch of the coast between the port of Kyrenia and the town of Lapta, south-east London faces lived a champagne lifestyle behind the gates of their luxury homes – similar to that once enjoyed by British crooks in southern Spain. Less than a mile from the centre of the northern Cyprus town of Lapta was the secluded £2m villa of Dogan Arif, unofficial leader of the Arif gangland family who terrorized south London with their robbing and drug-trafficking operations in the eighties. They also played a role in handling much of the Brink's-Mat gold. Arif had been jailed for seven years in 1990 for conspiring to supply £8m worth of cannabis.

One of the most notorious regular visitors to northern Cyprus was Brian Wright, the so-called 'Milkman' who'd been hovering on the edge of the Brink's-Mat laundering operation for a number of years. Wright had even used some Brink's-Mat cash to partly finance a gang that flooded Britain with £500m worth of cocaine back in 1999 and 2000. By all accounts, Wright enjoyed a lavish lifestyle in northern Cyprus until the long arm of the law eventually caught up with him. On 15 March 2005 Wright was recognized and arrested by Spanish police. He was extradited to Britain, where he denied the allegations against him. After a two-month trial Wright was convicted of conspiracy to evade prohibition on importing a controlled drug and conspiracy to supply drugs, and on 3 April 2007 Brian Brendan Wright, by now sixty, was sentenced to thirty years in prison.

Three years later, another drug baron, Raymond Spencer, fifty, was deported from northern Cyprus to mainland Turkey, from where he was extradited to the UK and jailed for thirteen years at York Crown Court on a smuggling charge. It was a rare occasion when a British villain actually fell foul of the Turkish and northern Cypriot authorities, and most presumed that Spencer was sent home because he wasn't prepared to 'grease the right palms' and didn't come from the badlands of south-east London, whose gangsters remained largely untouched.

A potentially significant discovery was made in 2005. Inside a London deposit box, Scotland Yard detectives found six suitcases crammed with gold and suspected that it might be connected to the Brink's-Mat robbery. The gold 'grains' were carefully wrapped in plastic and wedged inside travel luggage. They'd been found after police raided the deposit box as part of their ongoing Brink's-Mat investigation. The raid – part of the Met's Operation Rize – was on one of thousands of deposit boxes in London opened over a five-day period. These boxes had been targeted based on intelligence indicating that they contained the proceeds of the illegal activities of crime syndicates, who had used safe deposits to hide their assets for years.

Commander Allan Gibson of Scotland Yard's specialist crime directorate told reporters that his officers had never seen anything like it. The haul was said to be the single largest discovery of untraceable gold ever found in Britain. Provisional estimates suggested that the suitcases' contents could be worth £8m. Alongside the gold, Scotland Yard officers also found £30m in cash, much of it stuffed into plastic supermarket bags, which police believed was also the proceeds of organized crime, although they had no concrete evidence that it was all linked to the Brink's-Mat robbery.

'We have identified six suitcases of gold grains which, if real, could be very, very valuable. It's a phenomenal amount. They were wrapped like a large packet of peas and were so heavy officers couldn't pick them up,' Gibson later explained. Police stressed that the focus of their inquiries was on the people who had rented the safety deposit boxes. They belonged to a firm called Safe Deposit Centres Ltd, two of whose directors had been arrested on suspicion of money-laundering offences and bailed to return to a central London police station in September of that year.

The firm had only been established in 1986 – three years after the Brink's-Mat robbery – raising the possibility that the gold had been kept in temporary storage before being hidden inside the company's vault. The discovery also brought back to the public eye the fact that it was still very unclear how much – if any – of the Brink's-Mat bullion had ever actually been recovered.

The discovery of the gold did nothing to stem the bloody flow of murders linked to Brink's-Mat. When a bodybuilder confessed to being the resident 'dismemberer' for the Adams family in 2008 it became clear that some of the bodies he had disposed of were murdered because of their links to Brink's-Mat.

Stephen Marshall, thirty-eight, had originally been arrested after stabbing a former work colleague to death and cutting his body into pieces. When the body was first discovered it led to the case being known as the 'Jigsaw Murder'. Marshall stunned detectives after his arrest by alleging that he'd hacked up four other bodies while working for Terry Adams. Marshall's claims were of great interest to the Brink's-Mat investigators because there was no doubt that some of the bodies he had handled were connected to the Brink's-Mat heist and its murderous aftermath.

'A-Team' chief Terry Adams had been investigated by police in connection with twenty-five murders as well as having built up an estimated fortune of £200m through his vast racketeering and drug trafficking empire, not to mention the money he made by laundering Brink's-Mat gold. Potential witnesses had been too terrified to testify against Terry Adams but he was eventually jailed in 2007 for seven years for the relatively minor charge of money laundering.

Meanwhile his 'butcher' Stephen Marshall, a former gym owner, continued to 'sing like a canary' as they say in the underworld. The jury at Marshall's eventual trial in 2010 also heard from a woman who backed up Marshall's claims that he had been asked to dispose of the remains of murder victims for the Adams family. 'He would cut up bodies. He said he would put them into black bags and bury them, sometimes in Epping Forest,' added the witness, who was not identified for her own safety. She also mentioned he kept different knives for the jobs, as well as a cleaver, chain-saw and hacksaw.

Marshall had worked as a doorman at clubs, which is where he'd first encountered the A-Team. On four occasions – between 1995 and 1998 – he'd been asked to help dismember the bodies of criminals who'd crossed the crime family. His barrister, Peter Doyle QC, said Marshall, of Bore-hamwood, Hertfordshire, had thought it 'sensible' not to ask questions. Marshall was eventually sentenced to life for the original murder and ordered to serve a minimum of thirty-six years after pleading guilty at St Albans Crown Court.

At last it seemed that people were not so scared of talk-ing about the once feared A-Team. One of the brothers' associates lifted the lid on the family in an article in a tabloid newspaper. He said: 'We were in a club. One of the brothers nodded in a geezer's direction. "That one. He's got to go." Later that night the bloke was taken on a detour on his way home . . . and stabbed to death.'

Many thought that the Adamses' former henchman must have had a deathwish but there was some twisted logic to what he was doing. As one A-Team associate later explained: 'It wasn't a stupid move because the family would be less likely to come after someone who was in the public eye.'

As one senior detective who worked on and off on the Brink's-Mat investigation for more than twenty years commented: 'Nothing really surprises us any more when it comes to Brink's-Mat. These villains were out of control, many of them off their heads on drugs bought with their new-found riches. The trouble was that when that money either ran out, or in the case of some of them, never materialized, there was only one way to respond and that was to kill people to show others that even twenty-five years after the robbery was committed, if they dared to cross the gang they would still pay for it with their life.'

And so it is that the Curse of Brink's-Mat still continues to cast a shadow over the lives of so many people. By the end of 2011 stories relating to the case and its aftermath are still popping up in the media with alarming regularity, even though the crime itself was committed during the Thatcher era. It has persisted through four more prime ministers and still it rolls on, leaving death and destruction in its path, leaving good and bad men haunted by the horror of its power and influence over so many people's lives.

EPILOGUE

The Brink's-Mat villains' epic conversion of gold into hard cash brought more money into this country than any other gang of criminals in history. And when they spent it, they often helped keep legitimate businesses afloat in the poorer areas of south-east London, as well Spain's Costa del Sol.

Even the police themselves admitted that they hadn't really made life *that* difficult for them. Detectives only ever laid their hands on about thirty per cent of the stolen gold at most. The rest of it has gone up more than one hundred fold in value since the heist in 1983.

But Brink's-Mat also marked the end of an era in British crime. Robbery was overtaken by far more lucrative, straightforward enterprises such as drugs, arms dealing and racketeering, even people smuggling. And in the last twenty years there has also been a massive influx of foreign criminals into the UK. These characters don't share the same values as the McAvoys and Robinsons of this world.

Many of south-east London's oldest faces have slipped quietly out of the criminal limelight in recent years with no obvious British successors waiting in the wings. Large sections of south-east London have been gentrified, and in many cases the children of those old-school robbers have ended up in straight jobs, often encouraged by their fathers – most of whom will happily admit that crime really doesn't pay. As legendary Krays associate Freddie Foreman says: 'We want our kids to have honest jobs and happy lives, not going in and out of prison and living in fear of a knock on the door. That's not the life I ever wanted for my kids, and I've gone out of my way to make sure they avoided all my pitfalls.'

Today, the UK remains in the grip of organized crime, mainly fuelled by drugs, which first got a stranglehold, in part, thanks to that massive influx of Brink's-Mat cash. Drugs undoubtedly have sparked the majority of the shootings on our streets today. Young gangsters seem to have adopted a 'shoot now, ask questions later' attitude, which has made Britain's cities a lot more deadly than they were when the Brink's-Mat robbery was committed.

The statistics speak for themselves. At least a hundred London murders were linked to organized crime in 2009. That's not including the gangsters chopped into little pieces by their enemies, who disappear without trace. Hundreds more are seriously hurt in shootings across the capital.

Many villains from the Brink's-Mat era believe things have got completely out of control in recent years. One gang member said: 'It's not like it used to be. A lot of these new foreign gangs are run by ruthless characters who wouldn't hesitate to kill their own mothers if they got in their way.' They feel that the younger gangsters are threatening the peace and stability that used to be provided by those faces back in the sixties

One former detective, who spent five years working on the Brink's-Mat inquiry, is convinced that there is still a large amount of gold from the robbery that remains hidden, and at least two of today's younger London gangs have started 'breaking a few arms' in a bid to locate it. 'It's well known that some of the gold is still out there and I understand a couple of really nasty gangs of younger villains have decided to do everything in their power to find it.'

Brink's-Mat continues to impress the underworld – even amongst the new wave of deadly, cold-blooded gangsters – some of whom were not even alive when the heist was carried out. But what of the future? What will happen to all the old faces And who's trying to muscle into the nation's underworld?

Britain has become a key staging post for numerous foreign criminals ranging from African smugglers of people and drugs to ruthless eastern Europeans who rule the sex trade with a rod of iron. None of them play by the same 'rules' as the old-time Brit gangsters epitomized by the 'professionals' who broke into the Brink's-Mat warehouse almost thirty years ago.

Foreign law-enforcement agencies have warned Britain that the influx of gangsters into this country means that organized crime is likely to escalate further in the new decade. Britain has adopted gang-busting legislation similar to that used in the United States and the Irish Republic to seize assets.

Yet some things never change. Millionaire criminals continue to try and corrupt and compromise detectives, according to those who should know, and it is claimed that police corruption has become even more of a problem now than during the Brink's-Mat era. There remains a hard core of 250 'premier league' criminals at the top of the British underworld, many of whom are constantly tracked by the NCIS. This includes at least three members of the Brink's-Mat gang, still active after all these years.

The cold, harsh reality is that criminals will continue to thrive whatever governments try to do to eliminate them. Today, cybercrime has become the ultimate soft target for the underworld. As one old face explained: 'Going across the pavement was a risky enterprise in the old days. Now you can scam someone out of a fortune on the internet, without even leaving your front room. It's a different world out there.'

Both police and villains believe that there is unlikely ever to be another robbery on the scale of Brink's-Mat. Security systems are far more sophisticated today, and few criminals would see the sense in such a high-risk operation. So we're left with the aftermath of a legendary robbery that continues to reverberate to this day. It would not be in the least bit surprising if more victims fall to the Curse of Brink's-Mat before this book is actually published.

As one detective so rightly commented: 'It's going to go on long after every single bar of gold has either been recovered or turned into cash because there are a lot of people out there who believe the Brink's-Mat robbery owes them a living.'

REAL-LIFE CAST OF CHARACTERS

THE DEAD:

JON BRISTOW – made the mistake of knowing one of the robbers and it cost him his life.

STEPHEN CAMERON – encountered Kenneth Noye on a motorway and it cost him his life.

RAY CHAPMAN – also knew the same blagger and ended up in the same boat as his friend Bristow.

ALAN DECABRAL – dared to give evidence against one Brink's-Mat villain and ended peppered with bullets in shopping mall car park.

JOHN FORDHAM – stabbed to death in the grounds of Kenneth Noye's mansion in Kent during a Flying Squad operation in 1985.

GEORGE FRANCIS – paid the ultimate price after one near-miss.

KEITH HEDLEY – ended up being shot dead by three men as he holidayed on his yacht in Corfu in September 1996.

ALAN 'TAFFY' HOLMES – shot himself in the garden of his home after being questioned by fellow police officers about links to Brink's-Mat.

JOHN MARSHALL – shot dead in his black Range Rover in Sydenham, south London.

DANIEL MORGAN – ex-private eye who ended up with an axe through his head.

SOLLY NAHOME – worked for the Adams family and was gunned down outside his north London home on 27 November 1998.

MICHAEL OLYMBIOUS – crossed the most deadly outfit in town, so it was only a matter of time before they caught up with him.

BRIAN PERRY – shot dead by two gunmen as he got out of his car outside his office in south London in 2001.

DANNY ROFF – mowed down by hired assassins outside his home in Bromley, Kent.

PAT TATE – shot dead with two other men in the infamous 'Range Rover Killings' in Essex.

DONALD URQUART – 'iced' by a hit man on the streets of west London.

NICK WHITING – his mutilated body was found on Rainham Marshes, Essex. He'd been stabbed nine times and then shot twice with a 9 mm pistol.

JOEY WILKINS – died under mysterious circumstances on the Costa del Crime after an apparent robbery.

CHARLIE WILSON – even the most legendary villains were not immune to the curse of Brink's-Mat.

THE CURSE OF BRINK'S-MAT

SIDNEY WINK – put a pistol to his head and pulled the trigger, or so they say.

GILBERT WYNTER – now believed to be part of the supporting foundations of the O2 Dome.

THE LIVING:

TERRY ADAMS is currently in prison after being found guilty of money laundering. Police believe his criminal empire has finally crumbled.

TOMMY ADAMS lives on the Costa del Sol after serving time and has (according to other faces) gone into retirement.

TONY BLACK is believed to have a new identity and lives under the constant shadow of death somewhere in the Home Counties.

STEPHEN DALLIGAN was shot six times in the Old Kent Road but survived.

MICKEY LAWSON still lives in the Kent area where he runs a second-hand car business.

JOHN LLOYD was released from prison after serving a long sentence for the hole-in-the-wall scam and now lives back in Kent.

MICKEY McAVOY was released from prison in 2000 and divides his time between homes in Kent and Spain.

KENNETH NOYE remains in jail for the murder of motorist Stephen Cameron. His most recent appeal was rejected in March 2011.

JOHN PALMER denies all connections with Brink's-Mat and is thought to still have a fortune of approximately £20m.

BRIAN READER has retired to the Kent countryside.

MICHAEL RELTON was released from prison many years ago and is thought to be living in quiet retirement in southern France.

THE CURSE OF BRINK'S-MAT

BRIAN ROBINSON has kept a noticeably low profile since his release from prison and rarely sees any of his old underworld pals.

TONY WHITE is believed to have been recently released from prison and is living back at his villa in Spain.

All the main investigators into the Brink's-Mat robbery have now retired, so rather than risk incurring the curse that has afflicted so many cops and robbers I have chosen not to include them in the list of the 'Living' . . .